Anchoring Change

Anchoring Change

Seventy-Five Years of Grassroots
Interventions That Made
a Difference

Edited by **Vikram Singh Mehta**
Neelima Khetan and **Jayapadma R V**

HarperCollins *Publishers* India

First published in India by HarperCollins *Publishers* 2022
4th Floor, Tower A, Building No. 10, Phase II, DLF Cyber City,
Gurugram, Haryana – 122002
www.harpercollins.co.in

2 4 6 8 10 9 7 5 3 1

Copyright © Vikram Singh Mehta, Neelima Khetan, Jayapadma R V 2022
Copyright for individual chapters vests with the respective authors

P-ISBN: 978-93-5629-187-4
E-ISBN: 978-93-5629-188-1

The views and opinions expressed in this book are the authors' own.
The facts are as reported by them, and the publishers
are not in any way liable for the same.

Vikram Singh Mehta, Neelima Khetan and Jayapadma R V assert the moral right
to be identified as the editors of this work.

All rights reserved. No part of this publication may be reproduced,
stored in a retrieval system, or transmitted, in any form or by any
means, electronic, mechanical, photocopying, recording or otherwise,
without the prior permission of the publishers.

Typeset in Typeset in 11.5/15.2 Linden Hill at
Manipal Technology Ltd, Manipal

Printed and bound at
Thomson Press (India) Ltd

This book is produced from independently certified FSC® paper
to ensure responsible forest management.

For my grandfather Dr Mohan Singh Mehta and my father Jagat Singh Mehta, whose lives made a difference.

—Vikram Singh Mehta

For Ma, Aftaab, Shekhar—'time present and time past, are both perhaps present in time future ...'¹

—Neelima Khetan

For Karuna, to be inspired by communities of hope and catalysts of change ...

—Jayapadma R V

Contents

	List of Abbreviations	xi
1.	Synthesis: Towards a Framework for Grassroots Interventions VIKRAM SINGH MEHTA	1
2.	MYRADA and the Emergence of Self-Help Groups in India ALOYSIUS PRAKASH FERNANDEZ	22
3.	Seva Mandir: Exploring the intersections of *Seva*, *Sadhna* and *Kranti* NEELIMA KHETAN	36
4.	The Jamkhed Model: Sowing the Seeds of Community-based Primary Healthcare APARNA THOMAS, SHOBHA AROLE AND RAVI AROLE	50
5.	Eklavya's Journey of Adaptation and Evolution in Public School Education HRIDAY KANT DEWAN AND TULTUL BISWAS	62
6.	Beyond Cerebral Palsy: The Growth of Spastics Societies and Their Contribution to the Disability Movement RAJUL PADMANABHAN	74
7.	Gram Vikas and the MANTRA for Inclusive Community Development LIBY T. JOHNSON	85

8. Dastkar: A Crafted Route to Development 100
LAILA TYABJI

9. Meals That Educated Generations: Lessons from Tamil Nadu 115
CHANDRA MOHAN B AND A.R. MEYYAMMAI

10. PRADAN and the Idea of a Development Professional 126
NARENDRANATH DAMODARAN AND SMITA MOHANTY

11. Wealth Creation through Community-owned Enterprise: NSPDT's Model of Cooperative Smallholder Poultry 140
ANISH KUMAR

12. Development Support Centre: Mainstreaming the Idea of Water Users' Associations 157
SACHIN OZA AND MOHAN SHARMA

13. ANANDI: The Long Road to Gender Just Development 169
SRILATHA BATLIWALA, SEJAL DAND AND NEETA HARDIKAR

14. SELCO: Building Inclusive, Sustainable and Climate-Resilient Solutions 181
HARISH HANDE AND SURABHI RAJAGOPAL

15. Basix Social Enterprise Group: Innovations in Microfinance to Promote Livelihoods for the Poor 198
VIJAY MAHAJAN

16. Kudumbashree: Where Women Climb the Ladder of Empowerment 214
S.M. VIJAYANAND AND SAJITH SUKUMARAN

17. Goonj: Reviving the Barter Economy and Changing the Lens with Dignity at the Centre 226
ANSHU GUPTA

18. Society for Elimination of Rural Poverty: A Paradigm Shift in How Government Tackles Poverty — 239
    K. RAJU

19. ITC e-Choupal: A Lighthouse for Truly Inclusive Value Chains — 249
    SIVAKUMAR SURAMPUDI

20. the ant: Stepping Away from the Trees to Notice the Forest — 260
    SUNIL KAUL AND JENNIFER LIANG

21. The Brewing of Araku Coffee: Regenerating the Economy and Ecology — 273
    MANOJ KUMAR

22. Seeding and Shaping the Labour Migration Agenda: Aajeevika Bureau's Journey — 286
    RAJIV KHANDELWAL AND DIVYA VARMA

23. Janaagraha: Transforming the Quality of Life in India's Cities — 299
    SRIKANTH VISWANATHAN

24. Mitanin in Chattisgarh: Community Health Work as a Social Movement — 313
    SAMIR GARG

25. JEEViKA: Fostering Pathways for the Transformation of Rural Bihar — 325
    ARVIND KUMAR CHAUDHARY AND MAHUA ROY CHOUDHURY

Acknowledgements — 339

About the Authors — 341

Notes — 351

About the Editors — 361

List of Abbreviations

Abbreviation	Full Form
AAC	Alternative and Augmentative Communication
AADI	Action for Ability Development and Inclusion
ABC	Attitude and Behaviour Change
ADAPT	Able Disabled All People Together
ADS	Area Development Societies
AGLED	Agricultural, Livestock and Enterprise Development
ANANDI	Area Networking and Development Initiatives
ASHA	Accredited Social Health Activist
ASSEFA	Association for Sarva Seva Farms
B-ABLE	BASIX Academy for Building Lifelong Employability Ltd
BBMP	Bruhat Bengaluru Mahanagara Palike
BC	Business Correspondent
BMH	Baareh Mahine Hariyali
BPL	Below Poverty Line
BRI	Bank Rakyat Indonesia
BSFL	Bhartiya Samruddhi Finance Limited
CBO	Community Based Organization
CBR	Community-based Rehabilitation

LIST OF ABBREVIATIONS

CDS	Community Development Societies
CEO	Chief Executive Officer
CFW	Cloth for Work
CGAP	Consultative Group for the Poor
CHW	Community Health worker
CIF	Community Investment Fund
CLF	Cluster Level Federation
CMG	Credit Management Groups
CMLS	Centre for Migration and Labour Studies
COMFED	Bihar State Co-operative Milk Producers' Federation Ltd.
CPL	Community Participation Law
CRHP	Comprehensive Rural Health Project
CRP	Community Resource Persons
CSO	Civil Society Organization
DSC	Development Support Centre
ED	Executive Director
FI	Financial Institution
FPO	Farmer Producer Organization
ICB	Institutional Capacity Building
ICCO	Interchurch Organization for Development Cooperation
ICDS	Integrated Child Development Services Scheme
IDS	Institutional Development Services
IEC	Information Education and Communication
IGS	Indian Grameen Services
IICP	Indian Institute of Cerebral Palsy

LIST OF ABBREVIATIONS

IIM-A	Indian Institute of Management, Ahmedabad
IMR	Infant Mortality Rate
INRM	Integrated Natural Resource Management
IRDAI	Insurance Regulatory and Development Authority of India
IRDP	Integrated Rural Development Program
IRMA	Institute of Rural Management, Anand
Jana USP	Jana Urban Space Foundation
JnNURM	Jawaharlal Nehru National Urban Renewal Mission
KYC	Know Your Customer
LEAP	Livelihood Enhancement Action Plans
MAARS	Metamarket for Advanced Agriculture and Rural Services
MANTRA	Movement and Action Network for Transformation of Rural Areas
MEC	Micro Enterprises Consultant
MECE	Mutually Exclusive Collectively Exhaustive
MFI	Microfinance Institution
MFIN	Microfinance Institutions Network
MGNREGA	Mahatma Gandhi National Rural Employment Guarantee Act
MHT	Mobile Health Team
MOF	Member-oriented Firm
MT	Mitanin Trainer
MU	Management Unit
MYRADA	Mysore Resettlement and Development Agency
NABARD	National Bank for Agriculture and Rural Development

NBFC	Non-banking Financial Company
NCERT	National Council of Educational Research and Training
NCLP	National Child Labour Project
NGO	Non-government Organization
NHG	Neighbourhood Group
NHM	National Health Mission
NMC	Nutritious Meal Centre
NRHM	National Rural Health Mission
NRLM	National Rural Livelihoods Mission
NSPDT	National Smallholder Poultry Development Trust
ORS	Oral Rehydration Solution
PACS	Primary Agricultural Cooperative Societies
PCO	Public Call Office
PDL	Public Disclosure Law
PDS	Public Distribution System
PIM	Participatory Irrigation Management
PNRM	Participatory Natural Resource Management
RBI	Reserve Bank of India
RpD	Return Per Day
RRB	Regional Rural Bank
RSETI	Rural Self-Employment and Training Institute
SAPAP	South Asia Poverty Alleviation Program
SC	Scheduled Caste
SDC	Swiss Agency for Development Cooperation
SDGs	Sustainable Development Goals
SERP	Society for Elimination of Rural Poverty

SEWA	Self Employed Women's Association
SHG	Self-help Group
SHRC	State Health Resource Centre
SIDBI	Small Industries Development Bank of India
SNFL	Sarvodaya Nano Finance Ltd
SSI	Spastics Society of India
ST	Scheduled Tribe
S.U.R.E	Specifications for Urban Road Execution
UNDP	United Nations Development Program
UNICEF	United Nations International Children's Emergency Fund
VHAI	Voluntary Health Association of India
VHW	Village Health Worker
VO	Village Organization
WALMI	Water and Land Management Institute
WDC	Women's Development Corporation
WHO	World Health Organization
WRD	Water Resources Department
WUA	Water Users' Association

1

Synthesis: Towards a Framework for Grassroots Interventions

VIKRAM SINGH MEHTA

1) Introduction

AT THE STROKE OF THE midnight hour on 14 August 1947, India's first Prime Minister, Jawaharlal Nehru, asked whether as India awoke to 'life and freedom' and stepped out from the 'old to the new', we Indians were 'brave enough and wise enough to grasp (the) opportunity and accept the challenge of the future'.[1]

Seventy-five years on, there are many who will argue that we have not redeemed our pledge to keep our 'tryst with destiny', not 'wholly' or in 'full measure' or even 'substantially'. They will accept that while India has, in recent years, impressed with its relatively high economic growth rates, it is still home to the largest number of poor people in the world; it is a society divided by class, caste, religion, language and race; and it has a long way to go to overcome the challenge articulated by Bhimrao Ambedkar, the architect of the Indian Constitution, on 25 November 1949, to the Constituent Assembly: 'Political democracy cannot last unless there lies at the base of it social democracy. What does social democracy mean? It means a way of life which recognizes liberty, equality and fraternity as the principles of life ... in politics, we will have equality and in social and economic life, we will have inequality. We must remove this contradiction at the earliest possible moment.'[2]

There is no gainsaying the strength of this contention. The facts adduced are irrefutable. India cannot claim to have kept its tryst with destiny or that its political democracy is in harmonious alignment with social democracy. The contradiction identified by Ambedkar is nearly as true today as it was then.

But not entirely. A narrowing of the lens brings into focus the achievements of a mix of individuals, corporates, civil society organizations (CSOs) and governments in bridging the gap between political and social democracy. The presumption that there has been little or no progress along this pathway over the past seventy-five years is too severe an indictment.

This book is an endeavour to highlight these achievements and to shift the conversational narrative from what has failed to what has succeeded. The editors have looked at the rich tapestry of successful grassroots interventions over the past more than seven decades and selected twenty-four protagonists to tell their story and respond to the questions: What was the reason for their success? What learnings can be derived from their efforts? And how might these learnings be applied as India embarks on the next seventy-five years of its political and social journey.

It was not easy to identify the authors. Our research had established that twenty-four stories barely covered the richness of the variegated efforts that have been made to shift the needle of social progress. So, we established our own internal criteria for the selection.

First, we wanted the selection to be expansive in time. Here, the driver was to identify interventions across different periods over the past seventy-five years.

Second, we wanted it to be geographically broad-based, straddling the various states of our country.

Third, we wanted to cover multiple domains.

And finally, we defined the exclusions. We decided to exclude 'movements' on the ground that whilst they have played a significant role in fostering social change, they are not formal organizations. We also excluded some well-known and oft written about successful organizations and focused instead on identifying lesser-known interventions that might give the coverage textural diversity and reinforce the message that there is good work being done across the four corners of our country.

We had a lot of discussion on the word 'success'. There was no consensus on what it meant in the context of a grassroots intervention. We decided therefore to peg our search around the word 'significance'. We looked for entities that had made an unquestionably significant impact in their domain and social context.

This synthesis chapter is a distillation of the learnings from these twenty-four contributions. I make no attributions. Distilling from the over 750 institutional years of work represented in these chapters has been a challenge. In fact, at the start of the project, given the diversity of the interventions that we had selected, I was not sure I would find unifying patterns that could be pulled together for this synthesis chapter. But that has not been the case. What is interesting, perhaps even encouraging, is the confirmation that successful development rests on a bedrock of common principles and practices. Thus, if past practice and experience is any guide, our future developmental efforts should also be built on these foundations.

A caveat. We decided against looking for third-party writers but requested the protagonists of each initiative to tell their story in their own words. We decided as editors to let these stories unfold as the authors so wished. We did not straitjacket them except to urge that they not repeat what was perhaps already on their website but address the questions that we had posed. The chapters are not, in consequence, even in style or language. But this unevenness is more than offset, I believe, by the flavour and passion of a first-person account.

2) Grassroot Intervention over Seventy-Five Years

'Development has always involved the interaction of states, markets and society. Whether thought of in terms of actors or institutions, the roles and relationships of the public sector, the private sector and civil society have been central themes in analysis and action around the progressive social, economic and political change that constitutes development in its broadest terms.'[3]

In the seventy-five years since our independence, grassroots interventions have to a greater or lesser extent been driven by the interactions of the triad of the state, the market and the society. The relations between these three entities have evolved over the years and that has influenced the nature, shape and scope of social action. In the next section, I locate the specific interventions detailed in the volume to a particular time period and political economy.

Social Action in the Early Decades after Independence

Post-independence, the state positioned itself as a mixed economy with a socialist bent. The Constitution came into force in 1950 and the Planning Commission received the mandate to prepare the development roadmap for the country. The state was to be the dominant actor in Development. The first five-year plan stated, *'As the social structure becomes more complex, the state is called upon to play an increasing role in providing service for the welfare of the people'*. Resources were accordingly allocated towards poverty alleviation, employment generation and access to health and education. Progress was however slow. The resources were insufficient and the state had limited capacity to implement.

Recognizing these limitations, the first five-year plan created the space for the involvement of civil society initiatives. *'Any plan for social and economic regeneration should take into account the services rendered by these agencies and the state should give them maximum cooperation in strengthening their efforts.'* The Central Social Welfare Board was established in 1953 with the objective to support non-government organizations (NGOs) and the participation of 'the people' in development. This catalyzed the establishment of CSOs. Relations between CSOs and the government was, in the main, smooth, but at times when the government felt the CSOs had strayed into their turf, there was tension.

The book profiles two organizations that commenced operations during this period, albeit not until the 1960s.

MYRADA worked initially with primary agricultural cooperative societies. This experience exposed them to the rigidity of bureaucratic norms and intervention and to the fact that not all members of these societies benefited equally. They therefore turned their focus to decentralized, small groups of predominantly women that had already established self-help norms for savings and credit. They helped these groups sophisticate their practice and structure and connected them to the National Bank for Agriculture and Rural Development (NABARD) which, in turn, leveraged its relations with other banks to get them additional loans. MYRADA can take credit for laying the seeds of the now widespread and popular concept of self-help groups (SHGs).

Seva Mandir started work in the Udaipur district of Rajasthan to mobilize rural communities impacted by drought and resource degradation. Its objective was to nurture and manage 'commons'; build village institutions and improve rural livelihoods. It created the model for the management of natural resources by local communities and pioneered Gram Vikas Kosh (Village Development Fund). It also developed a model for early childhood care provisioning. The Gram Vikas Kosh has been incorporated into several government and non-government initiatives across the country and the model for early childhood care provisioning is often referenced in government plan documents and by other CSOs.

Pushing the Boundaries in the 70s and 80s

The decades of the 70s and 80s were socially restive. The inability of the state to address the widespread problem of poverty had widened the chasm between the 'haves' and 'have-nots'. To bridge this chasm, the government encouraged the CSOs to play a supportive role in development. This led to a deepening of the grassroots efforts. The focus of these efforts was to help the poor mobilize for the protection of their rights and to influence the policies related to social development, programmes and institutions. An increasing number of urban educated young forewent the conventional career path to work with these CSOs.

The book has stories of six CSOs and one government-led intervention that started work during these decades.

Drs Raj and Mabelle Arole, graduates in public health from Johns Hopkins University in the United States, pioneered a comprehensive, community-based primary healthcare programme in the Jamkhed region of Maharashtra in the early 70s. Jamkhed was among the poorest and most drought-prone region of the state. The direct focus of the programme was the improvement of health on a sustainable basis. The underlying hope was that this would foster equity, integration and the empowerment of people. The success of the Jamkhed model catalyzed the creation of the Accredited Social Health Activist (ASHA) workers under the National Rural Health Mission (NRHM).

Eklavya's mission was to change the nature of pedagogy in government schools and the public education system. It sought to achieve this by shifting the teaching method in the sciences (including the social sciences) from conventional rote learning and top-down didacticism to scientific temper and enquiry-based study. Its initial geographic focus was Madhya Pradesh, but the intent was to broaden its coverage. Today, its model is replicated across most of the country.

The Spastics Societies were inspired by the personal experience of individuals affected by children with cerebral palsy requiring special attention. These individuals leveraged their resources and international contacts to develop community-based rehabilitation programme for these children. A key factor for the success of these societies was the support of the state and central government through, in particular, the grant of land and infrastructure to establish offices and care centres. Spastics Societies have been instrumental in bringing the subject of disability rights into the mainstream of public policy discourse.

Gram Vikas in Odisha demonstrated how success in one domain can trigger a broader process of social development. Gram Vikas rallied the local community around the issues of water and sanitation. It encouraged the locals to contemplate community ownership and decentralized management of their rural water and sanitation systems. The model was a success. The spirit of collectivity and confidence it engendered impacted positively on the quality of life and sense of dignity of the local community. The Gram Vikas model has influenced the shaping of Swachh Bharat Mission in 2014 and the Jal Jeevan Mission in 2019.

Dastkar recognized early the potential of crafts as a medium for providing voice, dignity and employment to rural communities. It developed a multi-pronged model around strategic design, production and marketing to connect the crafts communities to the modern market without undermining the power and vitality of their traditional legacies. The success of this holistic model has influenced government policy and shaped the work of other crafts-based organizations.

PRADAN broke new ground by creating structures and incentives for attracting educated urban professionals from across the country into rural development and CSOs. Its founders appreciated the need to 'accumulate' human capital to tackle the challenge of poverty and underdevelopment. Many of the young professionals trained by PRADAN over the years have pioneered innovative and impactful rural livelihood interventions.

The Midday Meal scheme in schools in Tamil Nadu, arguably the best known of government interventions, was among the first to link food and nutrition to education and development. Today, the scheme is among the largest social welfare initiatives of the central government and it has been implemented by almost every state across the country.

Liberalization: The Reforms of the 90s

The economic reforms of 1991 impacted the nature of social action. The reforms were driven by the state of the economy but they also reflected the government's concern about its ability to ensure last-mile delivery of its public welfare programmes. To meet this concern, they called upon CSOs to be their local implementing partner. This call enlarged the CSO community in the country. It also influenced a change in their social profile. An increasing number of CSOs got promoted by people from provincial and middle-class backgrounds. Many of these initiatives were disruptive of conventional wisdom.

Six CSOs and one government-led intervention from that decade are profiled in this book.

The National Smallholder Poultry Development Trust (NSPDT) grew from an initiative in backyard poultry to become the country's largest cooperative smallholder enterprise in poultry. It incorporated basic principles of business management to maximize value and it funded its growth from internal resources rather than grants. Further, it vested ownership of the assets in the hands of individuals and not the community and it moved management control from the promoters to professionals. Finally, it instituted rigourous criteria for the selection of its partners. The NSPDT business model was centered around women as entrepreneurs.

The management of irrigation systems (even medium size ones) was until the 90s the responsibility of the government. The local communities were not involved. The Development Support Centre (DSC) disrupted this pattern. It introduced initiatives in 'Participatory Irrigation Management' in Gujarat and Madhya Pradesh and demonstrated the efficiency of local farmer associations in managing small and medium-scale irrigation projects. These efforts led to significant improvements in the equity of water use.

SELCO stands out for its work on developing location-specific and end-user centric, decentralized energy solutions to meet the demands of households for access to affordable and clean energy. Their success has dispelled three myths. One, the poor cannot afford solar energy systems; two, these systems are difficult to maintain and service in rural communities; and three, there is a trade-off between social enterprise and profitability. SELCO has been able to meet the demands of the poor profitably. The chapter spells out the details of their model.

Area Networking and Development Initiatives (ANANDI) was the brainchild of five young feminists who came together in Gujarat to organize rural women and girls from marginalized communities to challenge established power structures and foster social justice, protection of rights and accountable governance for women. Their grassroots interventions, research and engagement with the state and parastatal organizations has influenced the transformation of gender-specific laws at the state and national levels.

Basix recognized that credit was a necessary but not sufficient condition for improving the livelihood of low-income households. It pioneered a livelihood promotion institution that combined technical and business skills, infrastructure, risk coverage and input-output linkages. It is among the leading micro-finance institutions in the country. Its reputation is built on its work on promoting sustainable livelihoods for the rural poor and women, and for its financial robustness that gives it continual access to mainstream capital and human resources.

Goonj built its model on the idea that there is value to be derived from linking the surplus material generated by the urban affluent with the knowledge and labour of the rural communities. In doing so, they challenged the conventional binaries defining charity and aid-centric development (viz 'benefactor' versus 'beneficiary'; 'giver' versus 'receiver'). They also drew attention to the dysfunctionalities and distortions associated with such binaries. Their work has compelled reflections on the optimal approach to development.

Kudumbashree was established by the government of Kerala in the mid-1990s as the State Poverty Eradication Mission. The mission reached out to poor families through the agency of women to build community-based local capacities, democratize local development and spread gender sensitivity. Kudumbashree has been internationally acclaimed. It is one of the drivers of the National Rural Livelihoods Mission (NRLM) of the Government of India.

Innovations in the New Millennium

The role of corporates in social development was not well defined until 2013 when the government mandated that corporates should allocate a percentage of their profits towards corporate social responsibility. Corporates have since become an important and positive partner in development and increasingly so as investor pressure has compelled the large cap companies to look beyond serving the narrow interests of their shareholders.

Arguably, the most notable of corporate initiatives has been ITC's e-Choupal platform. The platform has created a one-stop integrative 'phygital' connect between small and marginal farmers and the market. This has enabled the farmers to learn contemporary farming techniques, improve crop varieties, diversify cropping patterns, buy high quality inputs, hire equipment and better manage local water, soil and biodiverse resources. Most importantly, perhaps, it has given farmers access to real-time weather information, expert advice and market prices, which has enabled them to take informed decisions on the timing of seeding, irrigation, harvest, sales and pricing.

Another initiative that has also drawn on innovative digital delivery mechanisms is Janaagraha. The target beneficiary in this case has been the urban populace. The objective was to redesign the space of urban governance and delivery mechanisms and to create a more inclusive urban environment. Janaagraha's success has been built on the connect between citizens and government at the neighbourhood level engendered by trust in their model of 'city systems'.

A third 'disruptive' innovative initiative was the work started by Aajeevika Bureau. Their focus was the migrant labour community along the Rajasthan–Gujarat–Maharashtra corridor. Aajeevika Bureau was established in 2004–05 by a group of development professionals to render migration safe and effective. The Covid-19 lockdown in March 2020 highlighted their prescience. The work that they have done has helped civic society and government respond to the demands of labour in both the organized and informal sectors.

the ant is relatively unknown because its work is concentrated in the insurgency-racked regions of Assam. But its success in reinvigorating local crafts-based livelihoods, fostering education and delivering improved health services in the face of hostile geopolitics speaks enormously to the potential of effecting change when bonds get built on the pillars of honesty and tenacity. A key factor of success has been the readiness of the local community to collaborate with the ant to strengthen local delivery mechanisms and governance.

In a somewhat similar context, the Araku Valley Coffee Growers Cooperative was also baptized in a difficult environment—the Naxal-troubled albeit resource-rich regions of Andhra Pradesh. It has been successful not only in rejuvenating organic agricultural practices and protecting the ecology but in generating additional income-generating opportunities by encouraging the production of cash and food crops. It's premium coffee brand has today acquired international recognition.

Three government-led initiatives created during this period have also been profiled.

Society for Elimination of Rural Poverty (SERP) was established by the government of Andhra Pradesh. Its focus was on developing Community Resource Persons and SHGs to enable community-to-community learning and the empowerment of women. SERP is professionally managed, albeit being supported by the political class.

The Mitanin programme in Chhattisgarh was catalyzed by civil society and then adopted and scaled by the state government. The agency for scale-up was the State Healthcare Resource Centre (SHRC). What is noteworthy is the rigour with which SHRC/Mitanin selected and trained the health workers to provide healthcare and ancillary services.

Jeevika was implemented by the government of Bihar to address the challenge of poverty and underdevelopment. It was inspired by the work of Kudumbashree and SERP and its focus has been to create a bespoke, contextualized programme to improve the lot of the poorest of poor women. It is a state-wide movement and it has influenced the contours of the National Rural Livelihood Mission.

	Name	Nature of Entity	Theme	Year	Location
1	MYRADA	Civil Society Organization	Rural livelihoods	1968	Karnataka
2	Seva Mandir	Civil Society Organization	Sustainable Development	1968	Rajasthan
3	Comprehensive Rural Health Project, Jamkhed	Civil Society Organization	Health	1970	Maharashtra
4	Eklavya	Civil Society Organization	Public School Education	1972	Madhya Pradesh
5	Able Disabled All People Together	Civil Society Organization	Differently abled persons	1972	Maharashtra
6	Gram Vikas	Civil Society Organization	Community Development	1979	Odisha
7	Dastkar	Civil Society Organization	Crafts-based livelihoods	1981	Delhi
8	Tamil Nadu Midday Meal Programme	Government Initiative	Food Security and Education	1982	Tamil Nadu
9	PRADAN	Civil Society Organization	Sustainable Development	1983	Delhi
10	National Smallholder Poultry Development Trust	Social Enterprise	Rural Livelihoods	1993	Madhya Pradesh

	Name	Nature of Entity	Theme	Year	Location
11	Development Support Centre	Civil Society Organization	Water Management	1994	Gujarat
12	ANANDI	Civil Society Organization	Gender Equality	1995	Gujarat
13	SELCO	Social Enterprise	Rural Energy Access	1995	Karnataka
14	Basix	Social Enterprise	Rural Livelihoods, Microfinance	1996	Telangana
15	Kudumbashree	Government Initiative	Women Empowerment/ Livelihoods	1997	Kerala
16	Goonj	Civil Society Organization	Clothing Security/ Disaster Response	1999	Delhi
17	ITC e-choupal	Corporate Programme	Agriculture	2000	West Bengal
18	Society for Elimination of Rural Poverty	Government Initiative	Poverty Alleviation/ Women Empowerment	2000	Andhra Pradesh
19	the ant	Civil Society Organization	Community Development, Education, Craft	2000	Assam
20	Araku Valley Project, Naandi Foundation	Social Enterprise	Ecology, Livelihoods	2000	Andhra Pradesh
21	Janaagraha	Civil Society Organization	Urban Governance	2001	Karnataka
22	Aajeevika Bureau	Civil Society Organization	Labour Migration	2004	Rajasthan

	Name	Nature of Entity	Theme	Year	Location
23	SHRC Mitanin Programme	Government Initiative	Health and Food Security	2004	Chattisgarh
24	Jeevika	Government Initiative	Women Empowerment/ Livelihoods	2006	Bihar

3) The Unifying Thread

A read through the twenty-four chapters in this volume throws up a clear message.

There is no single silver-spoon response to the complexity of India's social challenge. There is no one-size-fits-all solution to the myriad of problems that must be addressed. Each issue has to be tackled through tailored, localized responses. There is however a unifying thread that binds these varied interventions. A thread that transcends geography and time, and connects seamlessly because it is woven by the commonality of the objectives of each intervention.

In this section, we have identified the five main strands of the weave of this thread. The strands are not mutually exclusive. They run into each other but for purposes of simplicity, we have segregated them below.

a) Conviction and Belief

All of the authors in this volume were driven by the conviction that they were addressing what they saw as the 'salient problems of our time'. They were of the view that if the poor could be empowered to find their voice, that if they could be provided with appropriate skills and resources, and enabled though supportive institutions to take charge of their own lives, the myriad of the social and economic issues affecting our country could, step by step and incrementally, be sustainably addressed.

The authors recognized that 'the poor' must not be regarded as one homogenous group and that the exercise of helping them cannot be a mechanical one that does not factor in the multilayered and internally contradictory nature of this social and economic category. They recognized that such an exercise must be consultative and participatory and enable the infusion of ideas from outside. Ultimately, however, it must be centered around the poor. They are not passive agents. They must be the driving agents of change. They must have an equal stake in the process and the outcome. The CSOs are important but they should see themselves as facilitators.

The authors were also unified in their conviction that the sine qua non for the success of their initiative was the centrality of 'dignity'. Here the authors are alluding to not just human dignity or the dignity of the community, but the dignity of the intervention itself: the dignity of giving and taking. Many authors credited their success to donors and partners that looked at their financial contribution through the broader lens of subserving public welfare and social good.

What was also striking was the common conviction that only by challenging orthodoxy could the needle of social change be tangibly moved. The protagonists in this volume did not cut their mental cloth to fit the prevailing convention. They did not look for perfect or short-term solutions; in fact, many started work even before they had fully developed their thinking and/or secured the requisite resources. It was this conviction that gave them the fortitude to stay the course; to continue when the odds were stacked against them; to look to breaking new ground. It was the reason their interventions made a difference.

b) Design

As already indicated above, sustainable social improvement is possible only if it is designed around the beneficiary. The external world may provide leadership and resources; it may motivate and influence; and it may help build partnerships and channel technology. But in the absence of the participation, involvement and ownership of the 'people' themselves, sustainable transformation is not possible. The necessary requirement will be missing.

The authors acknowledged the importance of creating an institutional frame that provided, on the one hand, structure and discipline and, on the other, transparency and support. The former would help bring on board the right people; establish clear lines of accountability and fiduciary rigour; and enable research and innovation. The latter would facilitate dialogue and change if and when circumstances required and provide a safe environment for all involved to introspect on the quality, substance and relevance of their role.

A majority of the authors wrote about the significance of alliances and strategic partnerships. Some acknowledged that without the support of such partnerships, they could not have succeeded. The partners helped them secure the required tools or resources; others suggested that it helped them gain access to markets (local and global) and others, that it was an essential prerequisite for securing scale. Aside from these specifics, the unifying principle was the significance of partnerships and alliances in developing a supportive ecosystem for grassroots intervention.

c) Process

Most of the authors emphasized the inseparability of means and ends. The 'how' of an intervention was as important as the 'what' of the outcome. The challenge was to prevent a wedge from being driven into this connect.

All stakeholders involved in grassroots intervention are impacted by the process. To that extent, all involved—the development agent as much as the beneficiary—are as much a part of the problem as they are contributors to the solution. The process as it enfolds can change the contours of the objective and behavioural attitudes and, as that happens, pressure does build up to weaken the umbilical link between means and ends. This is so especially when the emphasis on means has already slowed progress and there is external pressure. The authors suggested that this is a conundrum that tests principles, values and conviction.

d) Leadership

Stability, continuity and tenacity of leadership are key factors of success. The contribution of individuals from outside the organization especially bureaucrats is also crucial. Women leaders are also identified as major contributors to successful transformation, more so in galvanizing their peer-level community than more broadly.

e) Ecosystem

An adverse policy environment or unsupportive bureaucrats and politicians can seriously stall progress. It is important therefore to develop a healthy relation with the government. This can be a frustrating exercise especially when, at times, bureaucrats refuse to contemplate changes in policy despite demonstrable examples of success. CSOs, however, have no alternative but to persist, not just to push their interventions but also to create the enabling policy frameworks for the CSOs of the future.

External relations must also be built with the financial sector, skill development institutes and academia.

The book contains many examples of the positive impact that all such linkages have had on securing intellectual, financial and experiential benefits.

4) Government-led Initiatives

The stories of successful government-led initiatives in this volume highlight the benefits of a partnership between the state and civil society. Several of these stories were initially conceptualized and developed by CSOs but scaled up by government. Others were started by the government and then CSOs were brought in to support the implementation.

A social programme led by or dependent on the government faces unique uncertainties. There is the uncertainty of continuity in the event the intervention is identified with a political party and that party loses power. The authors do however point out that government-led initiatives that have acquired public traction and ground-level acceptability are seldom closed down for politically partisan reasons. This is because it would be too costly politically. The key to success and sustainability for a government-led programme lies, therefore, on the quality and impact of its intervention.

The authors also highlight the significance of leadership and the role of individual bureaucrats. The success of government-led initiatives has often pivoted around the calibre and conviction of identified officials. People who recognized the importance of tenure and continuity and persuaded their line leadership to let them complete their task than shift them in the normal course of bureaucratic transfers.

5) Inner Dilemmas and Cautionary Advice

A fundamental dilemma is when to accept failure. Grassroots intervention will confront disappointments and failure. That is a given. The challenge is to acknowledge it, draw the appropriate lessons and move on.

There is pressure however to sweep the subject under the carpet and to constrict the nature of the conversations around it. This is because of the absence of an environment that enables free and frank exchange. The onus for building such an environment lies on all stakeholders, in particular, the donor and the development agent.

The other problem is the subjective nature of the definition of failure. What constitutes failure? This question can trigger a deep philosophical debate. Thus, for instance, one of our authors has wondered whether the status of the women that gain visibility and confidence through participation in social programmes has improved within their family. Has the fact they have a job and/or are earning a higher income raised their standing with the male members of their family. If not, can one claim the programme is a success? The question has not been answered although the implied counter is that that this would be akin to throwing the baby out with the bathwater. A first step has to be taken before a second larger step can be made.

A second dilemma relates to focus. Should the individual beneficiary be the primary focus of the intervention or should it be the collective enterprise? Our authors (except one who believed it should be the former) are of the view that this is a false binary. The focus should be on maximizing the interests of both. Here too, like with the definition of failure, there are many ways of dissecting the response. Several stories in this volume provide examples of how a balanced response can be delivered.

Finally, there is the dilemma of 'ownership'. It is relatively easy to create a member-owned enterprise. But not so easy to inculcate in the members the concept of ownership. Or to get them to internalize the responsibilities and accountabilities that go with it. Clearly the legalities of incorporation will not, in itself change attitudes. What will change attitudes will be exposure, experience and personal principles.

A read-through reveals nuggets of caution:

The presumption that by addressing one aspect of a social issue or one component of poverty (viz. education, health, job, credit, etc.) will result in an osmotic improvement along other dimensions of sustainable livelihood is wrong. An increase in income will not automatically result in better nutrition or better health. It would be counterproductive, therefore, to look for silver-bullet solutions that can fix everything. As one author put it, 'addressing a problem or crisis in isolation can actually be dangerous'.

Local self-government (panchayats and other local bodies) is the third-tier of representative democracy. Any effort to deepen democratic values and social democracy should therefore prima facie include local self-governments in the solution. The question does arise, however, whether given that the third tier of government is inseparably linked to top down, party based politics, this should be the direction of travel. Instead, should it not be built around institutions based on communities, women self help groups, user associations and youth?

The youth trigger a further note of caution. The widening gap between their aspirations and the capacity of the state to deliver could lead to social disruption and dilute the interest of the young to engage with social change. A hopeful interpretation is that in the absence of conventional career opportunities, idealistic youth might turn to CSOs for fulfillment. The book does suggest that an increasing number of young people from across all social classes are getting involved with grassroots intervention.

Finally, there is the issue of money. Funds are a necessity. But what our authors highlight is the importance of ensuring funds from the right donors at the right time. 'Right' funds empower the CSOs. It gives them the courage to admit to failure. It gives them the means to stay the course. 'Wrong' funds can however create distortions and a shifting of the goalposts. It is not easy to know what is 'right' and what is 'wrong'. Some of the stories in the volume offer guideposts.

6) Framework for Future Development

The twenty-four stories of successful grassroots intervention over the past seventy-five years offer learnings for the creation of a development framework for the next seventy-five years. These learnings are presented below in summary. A reading of the book will reveal their richness.

- Grassroots interventions should engage with the government formally and informally. It would be counterproductive to be perceived to be working against the interests of governmental authorities or political interest groups. This said, there are many examples of grassroots interventions that have succeeded despite lacklustre, if not determinedly negative, government responses.
- The poor and the disadvantaged can change their destiny. They can compete against the privileged and the advantaged. What they need is knowledge, technology and skills. This is where the CSOs can play a major role. They can be the conduit for these resources; they can facilitate the creation of cultures of consultation and collaboration and they can provide bridging solutions for the poor to leverage the power of their collective will.
- Women are more effective than men in effecting change and in striking a balance between the imperatives of change and the compulsions of our legacy. The stories in this volume show that women leaders have successfully overcome traditional hurdles but without dispensing with tradition. A developmental model that does not give women a central role will be sub-optimal.
- The organizational culture (as distinct from structure) of grassroots intervention should be non-hierarchical and distributive. Decision-making should be based on mutual trust and understanding. This does not mean there should be no leader. On the contrary, leadership is of paramount importance. But the leader has to be of a particular type. He has to lead through his values, beliefs and conviction; he must have the hard patience to stay the course and he must have the humility to search for learnings from the poorest.
- Individuals matter. And not just those vested with formal authority. Behind each of these successful interventions in this volume, there are exceptional people who have through sheer dint of intellectual vitality, physical effort and 'urgent patience'[4] moved the social needle. Such individuals will be required in the future. But they can only do so much. Looking forward at and given the mounting challenges across multiple contexts, there is an onus on everyone to get involved.

- The challenge of poverty alleviation is dynamic. To address it, one has to be adaptive and innovative. What was revealing about the stories in this book is the extent to which each of them invested in research and knowledge creation to stay ahead of the curve and to generate innovative solutions. There is a risk that this might create a divide between those who think and those who act and that must be managed. But there is no gainsaying the significance of building solutions on the pillars of detailed empirical research and data.
- Finally, sub-optimal outcomes should not be accepted. The refrain that grassroots transformation is a public welfare initiative and should not therefore be subject to market comparators is a case of false equivalence and results in poor processes, poor infrastructure and poor quality. It is also patronizing. The approach should be to benchmark each and every intervention against the best. That must be the basis of evaluation. Only then can the poor be assured of sustainable and positive change.

7) Conclusion

Dipankar Gupta in his book *From People to Citizen: Democracy's Must Take Road*[5] points out that the Indian Constitution is unique in introducing the word 'Citizen' in its very first paragraph. No other Constitution, according to him, introduces this word so early in the text. The French Constitution does so in Article 1 but not in the first paragraph and all other Constitutions do so at a much later stage. The reason he believes the drafters of our Constitution chaired by Ambedkar did so was because they were alert to the umbilical relationship between citizenship and democracy. The grant of the former was the sine qua non for the attainment of the latter. They saw citizenship to be distinct from the People. 'Citizenship was the conferment of equal rights to everybody in the state', a definition drawn from formulation offered by the social scientist T.H. Marshall in his book *Citizenship and Social Class* which was published in 1950, the year the Indian Constitution was formalized.[6] And unless and until such rights were secured, democracy would be incomplete. Marshall was clear that the conferment of equal rights did not mean that everybody was the same or that everybody would reach the same levels of achievement. What he meant was that everybody must have equal access and it is upon 'that foundation of equality, the structures of inequality may be built'.

As we celebrate seventy-five years of our independence, we know that the aspirations and dreams of those who formulated our Constitution have not been met. Citizenship at least as defined by Marshall and others has not been conferred on the People. Access is not universal. People do not have the basics or the opportunity to 'develop differentially'. And, to that extent, democracy is indeed incomplete.

What this book endeavours is to forewarn against despair. There is an increasing tendency to look at the rear-view mirror and concentrate only on the failures of our polity to deliver the expectations of our founding fathers. And in doing so, inadvertently perhaps, perpetuate the belief that these dreams and aspirations are not attainable.

This is a mistake. For, as is brought out in this book, the journey towards these objectives began decades back and progress has been made. The stories compiled in this volume are markers of hope and future possibilities. They bring out what can be done. They establish that every entity of our society, whether government, business, NGOs or individuals, have, at some time or other during the past seventy-five years and, in some small way, successfully delivered to the people the conditions for citizenship. They confirm that so long as we keep such markers in sight; so long as we draw the appropriate lessons from the past to chalk out the road map for the future and so long as we remain focused on the journey and are not deterred by the distance to cover, there is good reason to believe, to draw from Dipankar Gupta's article in *The Times of India*, that one day we will secure what our Constitution-makers must have had in mind when they introduced the word 'citizen' upfront in the Constitution. 'Now that we have made Indians, let us make them Citizens.'[7]

2

MYRADA and the Emergence of Self-Help Groups in India

ALOYSIUS PRAKASH FERNANDEZ

MYRADA[1] IS A NON-GOVERNMENT ORGANIZATION working in backward and drought-prone areas, with more than a million families in eighteen districts of Karnataka, Andhra Pradesh and Tamil Nadu. Initiated as the Mysore Resettlement and Development Agency (MYRADA) in 1968 to support the resettlement of Tibetan refugees, the organization shifted its focus in 1978 to work with rural communities around the settlements, and subsequently extended to other areas. MYRADA focuses on building appropriate peoples' institutions rather than on the delivery of goods, and is recognized for its pioneering work in micro-finance and other initiatives (dryland agriculture, health and education) for sustainable development of rural communities.

History of a Collaborative Effort

The story of the self-help group (SHG) movement is popularly associated with MYRADA. True, MYRADA has played a role in the emergence of SHGs, but the history of their integration into official development strategy and their spread across the country clearly reveals that the process was the outcome of a collaborative effort by financial institutions—such as the Reserve Bank of India (RBI) and the National Bank for Agriculture and Rural Development (NABARD)—and banks, state institutions such as Women's Development Corporation (WDC), as well as thousands of voluntary organizations.

Groups of the poor, initially called credit management groups (CMGs), comprising only the poor had emerged in MYRADA's projects in 1984–85. But MYRADA did not design the CMG model; it did not set the external criteria for membership (the CMGs self-selected their members), nor lay out the outcomes (agendas were set by the CMGs). The CMGs were the originators and MYRADA helped them along by building on the existing relationships of trust. It listened to the CMGs, stood by them and supported them in operationalizing their model mainly through skills training and Institutional Capacity Building (ICB), which equipped them to take on new challenges.

The emergence and spread of CMGs/SHGs in India, was a slow process; they did not fit into the typical five-year project time span for government or private donors. CMGs were first set up in 1984–85, and were re-named 'self-help groups' by NABARD in 1988. SHGs modelled themselves closely along the lines of the CMGs: starting with regular savings being credited into the group common fund, providing one bulk grant/loan to unregistered CMGs only after adequate institutional capacity building, and internal lending of group savings.

The pilot project linking banks to SHGs, launched by NABARD in 1992, recognized and adopted these features. It was only in 1996 that the SHG model was mainstreamed into banking practice as a transition strategy, that was expected to gradually lead to the full inclusion of poor people into the formal financial system.

Here, we briefly provide a history of the SHG movement, filling the gaps in the years between 1987 and 1996. This is not only a useful record but more importantly, as we discuss later, valuable learning and insights from these years could be relevant in the current context of the process around the three recent agricultural laws, which sought to reform traditional agricultural marketing systems. One reason why the new laws faced opposition was because they were not accompanied by a transition strategy that allowed farmers to take the lead in ensuring that their livelihoods would not be jeopardized.

SHGs as the Institutional Base of a Transition Strategy

RBI, NABARD and MYRADA realized that any attempt to include poor workers from the informal sector directly into the formal financial system would be an impossible task. A transition process was required, preferably through an institution like the CMG/SHG, with which informal workers and poor people were comfortable, and which could help build their self-confidence in relating to a more formal financial system, such as a bank. The SHG–bank linkage programme that accepted the SHG model, gave poor, informal workers their first link to the formal system. This transition strategy was not only geared to help the poor shift to a formal financial system, but it also sought to create a more level playing field by leveraging their own institutions and networks.

The poor are typically deprived of equal opportunities by unequal relations in a society dominated by caste and families with economic and political power in the informal sector; women are additionally stifled by patriarchy. These have been obstacles to their growth. RBI and NABARD promoted SHGs as a financial transition strategy to enable the poor to take the first step to relate with the formal system; this was expected to gradually lead to formal financial inclusion. There were already thousands of branches of public sector banks, regional rural banks and cooperatives providing small loans; these could be co-opted into the SHG programme, so there was no need to start a new bank only for microfinance.

They also realized that the provision of finance was not enough; there were several other hurdles poor people had to navigate to access formal finance. In this process, they were helped by NGOs and state WDCs, organizations that worked on empowering the poor, especially women, and to help them overcome these hurdles. MYRADA's role—in keeping with its mission: 'to build poor people's institutions'—was to enable CMGs/SHGs to develop as institutions confident and capable of enhancing the income sources of their members, and to help them overcome or circumvent hurdles to self-reliance, respect and growth posed by the control of institutions by powerful groups.

How Did the CMGs Emerge? Working within Existing Power Relationships

Although informal groups, based on relations of trust and mutual support (affinity), have always played a role in rural society, with MYRADA's support, they coalesced into CMGs in the context of issues they faced in the

Primary Agricultural Cooperative Societies (PACS). The government had set up the cooperative structure to promote development, and MYRADA had worked with PACS in the early 1980s.

However, interactions with the poorer families within the PACS revealed that these societies tended to strengthen existing inequalities based on caste, tradition and economic status. Rural society in India is structured into layers: landowners and those with social and political power are on top, and the landless and the marginalized groups are at the bottom. In such a highly structured ecosystem, a cooperative structure like the PACS does not benefit all the members. MYRADA discovered that the PACS were dominated by powerful families, who captured the top positions of president, vice president and treasurer, and used the societies to further strengthen their position. For example, they borrowed money from PACS at interest rates of as low as 8 per cent, and loaned it to poorer families at rates of 30 to 40 per cent per year. Borrowers were also compelled to work on the farms of the top PACS officials, and were at their beck and call.

MYRADA encouraged the poorer families to question this situation. They began to meet in small groups with our staff to discuss how to get equal rights. As the groups coalesced, we named them 'credit management groups' with a focus on management. The CMGs did not challenge the PACS directly, realizing that they would fail if they did; besides, they also had to continue to live alongside the powerful groups in the village. They decided to forge an alternative path that they could design and control. These were originally civil society institutions, not the financial intermediaries that they have become today.

By 1986, when there were about 100 CMGs in MYRADA, we decided to approach NABARD for support. This was not only for finance, but also to change policy to allow CMGs to be recognized as a transition strategy by formal financial institutions, and thereby enable their expansion; our letter to NABARD dated 29 August 1986 was a request to support CMGs.

MYRADA supported the CMGs by harnessing the traditional strengths of the rural poor, rather than concentrating only on their needs. These traditional strengths that have helped them survive major crises in the past and support each other daily, were relations of mutual trust and support among small groups which MYRADA called affinity. These relations existed both among men and women, but were expressed differently. Affinity was the binding factor, which shone through in their lives, and enabled people in informal groups to come together in a common activity and support each other through it. This MYRADA discovered while supporting the food-for-work programme during a drought: our work helped us analyse how poor people organized themselves to implement common activities. They chose to work in small self-selected groups, united by relations of affinity. Similarly, the CMG members selected their membership on the basis of internal affinity. MYRADA realized the potential of these informal groups to provide a basis for the emergence of their own institution. All that MYRADA did was to pick up this unique strength of affinity, and support it to develop organizational features through training in ICB; this was required to help CMGs cope with new roles.

There was a traditional habit of savings (especially among women), which they could access easily to meet urgent family needs. Being a member of a CMG protected their savings from unreasonable demands by other family members, as these were deposited in a bank account in the name of the group; these savings built up a common fund in each CMG, from which, after a few months of ICB, loans were extended to members.

The women were determined to make time to privately meet and talk about issues that affected them. This required a place to meet which provided adequate privacy and where all castes of women were comfortable; men who dominated public spaces in villages tried to eavesdrop and often resorted to harassment when warned not to do so. There were many instances in the 1980s of men forcibly interrupting women's CMG meetings, dragging them out, throwing stones on the roof, and even setting fire to the straw stacked on the roof of the meeting place; but the CMGs continued to function.

While MYRADA provided inputs to foster gender balance, such as information on appropriate sanitary practices and the importance of participation in local initiatives and institutions of governance, it was the CMGs/SHGs which put these messages into practice at their own pace. The CMGs often went two steps ahead, then took a step back to avoid tension; but, in the process, they built, managed and sustained their institutions, and were able to create a more equitable environment at home and in society. The CMG agenda was never restricted to financial transactions, as is the practice today in government and microfinance programmes involving SHGs. And it was because of this broad-based agenda that the WDCs in several states decided to incorporate the SHG model in their strategy for women's empowerment.

Proliferation of CMGs and SHGs: The Power of a Collaborative Process

The CMG/SHG movement spread because of a collaborative effort by various institutions. Its history between 1987 and 1996 is not well known, but it was during this period that a base was established, which provided the policy framework for the SHG—bank linkage to take off as a pilot in 1992, and then be mainstreamed in 1996. In 1987, formal financial institutions entered the CMG scenario when NABARD gave a grant of Rs 10 lakh to MYRADA, which it used to train CMGs and match their savings.[2] More significantly, NABARD went further; it took ownership of the CMG programme as it was searching for a new approach to provide credit to poor families, which could be more effective in supporting livelihoods than previous programmes like the Integrated Rural Development Program (IRDP). The features of the CMGs that emerged in MYRADA differed from those of the IRDP. The CMGs started with regular meetings and savings (of an amount decided by each CMG) that were deposited in a common group fund. MYRADA provided the groups with the training required to conduct a meeting, draw up an agenda and maintain records of attendance, decisions and financial transactions. It also provided a bulk grant from its budget to increase the size of the group's common fund. The practice of subsidizing livelihood assets was not part of the model; CMG members could take loans from the common fund for any purpose with the group's approval.

These features of the CMG programme found approval with the NABARD chairman, P. R. Nayak. He was familiar with MYRADA's work, having been the development commissioner in Karnataka, where MYRADA is based. As deputy governor of RBI, Nayak provided an organic link between RBI and NABARD, which helped to mainstream the CMG/SHG concept and enabled a policy shift towards allowing them to be recognized by formal financial institutions. While expressing my gratitude at NABARD's support to the CMG model, I also asked for NABARD's help in formalizing the following CMGs' features:

- Shifting from extending loans to individuals with subsidies, as in the IRDP, to extending one bulk loan without a subsidy to the CMG, and allowing it to decide on the purpose, size and repayment schedule. This was the CMG practice, as it allowed them to accommodate a vast diversity of livelihood activities and the irregular flow in the income stream in the rural sector; the agricultural cycle did not fit into the monthly repayment model.
- Allowing unregistered CMGs to open savings bank accounts; some banks dealing with MYRADA projects had already opened such accounts on the grounds that these were Associations of Persons.
- Allowing banks to lend to unregistered CMGs provided they kept records of meetings, attendance, savings and loans, and had a good repayment record from internal lending. CMGs were reluctant to register themselves, believing it would make them vulnerable to harassment by low-level government officials.
- Providing funds to NGOs for training CMGs in ICB.

The NABARD grant of Rs 10 lakh was used to match the savings in the common fund of each CMG and for ICB training. Nayak suggested that the name be changed from 'credit management group' to 'self-help group'. It was a name that had become common in other countries, though their model was different from the CMG model. It is to the credit of Nayak and his successors like P. Kotaiah and Y.C. Nanda, as well as the senior management of NABARD, that their efforts led to the fruition of our suggestions within nine years. Support from RBI, especially from C. Rangarajan, was also critical to enable the policy decisions that institutionalized the SHG movement in the formal financial system.

Between 1989 and 1996, top officials at NABARD strongly supported banks extending a single bulk loan to a group. Among them was

S.C. Wadhwa, the chief general manager of NABARD in Karnataka, who played a major role. This was a critical feature of the CMG/SHG model, as a bulk loan that allowed SHGs to take decisions on lending to members was a critical feature of the transition strategy. However, it was not easy to change the traditional lending patterns of banks. They felt that for the CMG/SHG to take such decisions, the NGO involved had to train them in ICB. As a result, NABARD allocated ample funds to NGOs for training SHGs.

From 1987 to 1992, MYRADA developed several training modules. These were eventually collated into a training manual titled 'Capacity Building of Self-Help Affinity Groups' and translated into several languages. The modules focus not only on financial management but also on wider objectives of empowerment and institution building. The first bulk loan to a CMG in Karnataka was given on 13 September 1991 by Vysya Bank. It was a loan of Rs 10,000 to the Venkateswara Mahila Sangha of Mudaguli village in Bangarapet Taluk.

At around the same time, similar efforts were underway in Tamil Nadu to incorporate the SHG strategy in a state project managed by the WDC and co-funded by the International Fund for Agricultural Development. NABARD and Tamil Nadu's WDC officials played a significant role here as well. The first bank in the country to adopt the linkage model on project scale was Indian Bank, which advanced a bulk loan to the group and allowed the members to take decisions on lending among themselves. MYRADA had a project in Dharmapuri, Tamil Nadu, where it had fostered SHGs in 200 villages prior to 1990, along with programmes related to education, health, agriculture and training in technical skills. It was asked to play a lead role in training government staff and NGOs in Tamil Nadu to help in the process of forming and building the capacity of SHGs.

This programme gave NABARD important insights into the vast diversity in livelihood choices by SHG members, and on the management of subsidies. It recognized the potential of SHGs to empower poor women in their social and domestic lives by creating greater access to resources. It commissioned a study titled 'Transaction Costs of Lending to the Rural Poor'. The study was published in Brisbane, Australia, by the Foundation for Development Co-operation, an organization that had supported a similar movement in Nepal. In the CMG/SHG model, the transaction costs of banks that gave a bulk loan to SHGs were found to be far lower than those of banks that extended small loans to individuals.

Towards a Credit-Plus Approach to Empowerment: Extended Social Impacts

MYRADA realized the importance of having analytical data on trends in the size and purpose of loans and in repayment performance, especially in discussions with bankers. It collected and analysed data from SHGs in all its projects between 1990 and 1995. The data provided valuable information on the wide variety of loans being handled—many of which banks would not have accepted—and on the varying loan amounts for one particular asset (such as the purchase of a crossbred cow), unlike the uniform loan amount for the same asset in the IRDP. There is a valid concern in IRDP that allowing discretion in loan sizes would open the door to corruption; but the SHGs gave this discretion to people who were aware of the diversity of local situations and had the power to vary allocations accordingly. The SHG members knew each other well; they were the Facebook of the 1980s and 1990s, and hence they could accommodate this diversity. Over a period of fifteen years, NABARD invested time and money at the national, state and district levels to collect feedback, analyse progress, remove hurdles and extend the SHG movement to the most neglected and remote parts of the country and to make it a priority programme among financial institutions. The data analysis also helped MYRADA assess whether additional support services were required to help SHG members enhance the impact of loans and decrease investment risks. The data was shared with NABARD and was found to be useful, especially in discussion with bankers and in policymaking. For example, when the data showed that a large number of loans were used for agriculture on drylands, MYRADA decided to take up watershed management in a major way to reduce the risks in dryland agriculture and enhance productivity. This watershed programme was planned and implemented in a participatory manner, with people (especially SHGs) taking the lead; it was started in Gulbarga in 1986 after the Karnataka government opened up to people's participation in development programmes, as an extension of its focus on

Panchayati Raj. This highlighted the importance of a credit-plus approach for inclusion in sustainable growth, and not merely a focus on finance. The objective of empowerment was also given priority in ICB, backed by pressure from the SHGs. Some important examples from the late 1980s were the decisions to keep the girl child in school till graduation, and to construct and promote the use of toilets. The SHGs decided that loans would not be extended to members who did not comply with these decisions.

Several studies were conducted, some by students of Institute of Rural Management, Anand (IRMA), on the social impact of the programme. A major study by a team from Humboldt-Universitat zu Berlin, published in 1998 after several months of living in MYRADA's Holalkere Project showed inter alia: i) a remarkable shift towards more balanced gender relations domestically and in society; ii) an increase in interventions by SHG members (largely poor and from the lower castes) in public initiatives; and iii) an increase in respect from upper castes for SHG members for their achievements.

This is supported by the fact that SHGs spent most of their meeting time (usually around two hours) discussing non-financial matters. An extract from the minutes of a visit by NABARD officials to CMGs in Kolar on 8 December 1988 reads: 'We proceeded to Chikkakavanchi CMG, which had received NABARD's funds. The Sangha had already collected savings amounting to Rs 120 and Rs 175 towards loan recovery. After financial transactions, they discussed issues related to artificial insemination, milk procurement and fodder availability. After that, they took up village issues related to road repairs. They invited members from Maruthi CMG from the same village. Seeing the jeep [of the visitors], the village leaders also joined the meeting.' Further evidence of the spreading social impacts, such as the decision of SHG members to successfully contest panchayat elections, is available in the 'Rural Management Systems' papers published regularly over the years by MYRADA, available on its website.

Institutionalizing the Linkages with Formal Finance: The Atmanirbhar Effect

The issue of allowing unregistered SHGs to open bank accounts was widely debated by RBI around 1990. In the mid-1980s, MYRADA had persuaded some banks that handled its funds in the rural areas to open accounts in the names of CMGs, on the grounds that they were Associations of Persons. But this had to be brought into policy. On 24 July 1991, on the initiative of C. Rangarajan, RBI issued a circular advising commercial banks to participate in a pilot project to link 500 SHGs to banks; it stated that 'groups could be formal (registered) or informal (unregistered)'. Following this, a format for 'Articles of Agreement between an Unregistered Association of Persons'—in this case, the SHG, which was recognized as 'the borrower'—for use in lending to SHGs was drawn up by Corporation Bank and circulated by NABARD.[3]

Finally, after RBI received the report of the working group that it had set up in November 1994, it issued a circular dated 2 April 1996 that summarized and approved all the innovative policy decisions. The outcome of this major collaborative effort over a long period was remarkable: by 2004, there were 573 banks lending to SHGs through 41,323 branches, and 4,323 NGOs involved in training and mentoring SHGs. By March 2005, banks had provided credit to 16,18,456 SHGs involving about 12 crore poor people, making it the 'largest cooperative microfinance initiative in the world', in the words of C. Rangarajan. It is the largest example of the Atmanirbhar Bharat Abhiyan (Self-reliant India Mission—an initiative of the Government of India).

From Transition to Permanence

By this time the original objective of promoting the SHG movement as a transition strategy had changed. It was now considered a permanent feature of the basket of schemes to eradicate poverty through financial inclusion. Unfortunately, as time passed, the financial aspect took over, while the objective of empowerment was downplayed. This was due to the weakening of the WDCs, as their budgets were slashed, after which they handed over the SHGs they had formed and trained to the Rural Development Department, which had broader objectives.

As a transition strategy, however, the SHG movement was a success, as CMG/SHG members managed the last mile between the SHG and the bank branch. The bank staff did not need to go to the SHG for repayments: one SHG member was selected to visit the bank weekly to deposit or withdraw money. This built the confidence of SHG members to deal with bank staff, who began to respect them for their discipline and their performance on repayments. As a result, in the 1990s, thousands of SHG members even opened personal bank accounts. Gradually several of them approached banks for larger loans than the amounts SHGs were willing to provide: the banks could assess their credit history in the SHG before deciding on larger personal loans. In a survey asking SHG members to prioritize the benefits they valued, after their access to credit for any purpose, they listed the respect from bankers and their confidence in them.

Insights and Learning: The Critical Role of Transition in Reform

The insights and learning gained from the SHG financial transition strategy are many, but the importance of putting in place a transition process, in which all the stakeholders are involved is relevant today in the context of the recent farmers' protests. Here, a transition strategy, which would provide a gradual transition across a period of about five to seven years, was not put in place. The traditional relations of trust and face-to-face interaction which guide farmers' transactions with middlemen (*arthiyas*) who operate in the agricultural system today, are not limited to marketing of commodities (as is often assumed), but extend to a much larger basket of services. The middlemen provide lump-sum loans for any emergency, or for social/religious functions, which small farmers require throughout the year, often urgently: they require cash immediately after disposing their produce to invest in the next crop, which the middlemen provide at the farm gate. One farmer told me that if he needs to go somewhere urgently and transport is not available, he calls the arthiya who sends his son on a scooter to give him a lift. Further, the small farmer is not able to cope with the (often unreasonable) demands of Agricultural Produce Market Committee staff; the arthiyas cope with this. To shift him/her abruptly (without a transition strategy) to direct interaction with the formal sector, driven by mega markets, distorted by speculation, and controlled by large faceless corporates, which will not support such diverse requirements, is once again trying to fit a square peg into a round hole. The marginal and small farmers are unable to relate to, leave alone trust, large corporates, or even the complex relationships that dominate this macro marketing system into which the agricultural reform laws seek to place them.

The protests against the agricultural reform laws ended in a stalemate not because the laws are not relevant (they are), not because the farmers did not understand the consequences (they did), not because they were manipulated by a small number of rich farmers and *arthiyas* (small farmers comprising 85 per cent of all farmers in the country, are most vulnerable and they formed the core of the protests), but because there was no transition strategy, especially for small farmers; a transition strategy, in which they were involved in designing and in which they had confidence. This is required—to enable them to either adjust to or to opt out from a market system which is faceless, too complex for them to influence, and which, in the final analysis holds all the cards. It should be noted that elements of such a transition strategy had been included in the papers prepared for the Twelfth Five-Year Plan, which was shelved.

In Hindsight

Would we have done things differently? Since the features of the CMGs emerged from the people, the more relevant question would be under what conditions do such bottom-up initiatives emerge? The micro-environment created by MYRADA provided space for the CMGs to emerge. The macro ecosystem created by RBI, NABARD and the state WDCs enabled the transition strategy to be institutionalized in official policy and to spread. Is it still possible for an NGO to create such a supportive environment at a micro level? NGOs today are increasingly constrained to adhere to their donors' project designs, and civil society is often considered anti-development when it raises questions or is critical of policies and programmes. Can the features of the macro ecosystem that supported the institutionalization and spread of SHGs as a transition strategy be replicated?

There is a strong trend today in designing development programmes, to impose uniformity as the basis of scale, in contrast to the SHG model that incorporated diversity and took it to scale. The number of leaders willing to institutionalize innovations seem to be decreasing. There is an increasing rejection of positions that are not in sync with one's own and a reduction in spaces that allow for true debate. All these do not inspire confidence that a supportive ecosystem for bottom-up ideas exists, but without such spaces it is unlikely that we will be able to make significant dents in the lives and livelihoods of those who lie at the margins of society.

3

Seva Mandir: Exploring the intersections of *Seva*, *Sadhna* and *Kranti*

NEELIMA KHETAN[1]

SEVA MANDIR WAS FORMALLY INCORPORATED in 1968, though its foundation stone dates back to 1931. The founder, Mohan Singh Mehta (a former bureaucrat and diplomat),[2] founded two organizations through regular interaction with the local governments in Udaipur in 1931: Vidya Bhawan Society and Seva Mandir. In pre-independence feudal Rajasthan, Vidya Bhawan Society was to focus on creating a school that would be open to all religions, castes, classes and genders and work on producing socially responsible citizens, and Seva Mandir was to focus on working directly with communities. While the work on the school began in earnest the same year, the concept of Seva Mandir was not formally realized until the late 1960s.

In the five decades that have passed since, Seva Mandir has come to be recognized for its deep community work and for its introspective culture. It made a conscious choice to stay focused on southern Rajasthan and has developed strong insights into community development, arising in part from a very long engagement with villages in the area. Currently, its work reaches 1,300 villages in two districts of south Rajasthan, with an impact on nearly 5,00,000 lives. However, even as Seva Mandir's direct work has focused on a particular region, it has impacted the development discourse at national and international platforms. In the words of Raj M. Desai[3] of Georgetown University and the Brookings Institution, 'Seva Mandir has established itself as one of the world's most innovative and effective organizations in addressing the problems of resource management, livelihoods improvement and village-level governance.'

The Core of Seva Mandir

Seva Mandir draws much of its inspiration from Mahatma Gandhi in terms of ideas and approaches to service. In fact, of the seven chief executives that Seva Mandir has had since its inception, at least two have been committed Gandhian scholars.

The core of Seva Mandir's approach has been the belief that change from within is the most essential ingredient for building a more just, equal and caring society. As one of Seva Mandir's oldest song goes, the very first change must be within the self, moving then to the family and the community. An extension of the same belief has been a constant attempt at aligning the means and the ends, which has meant that for Seva Mandir, what happens to the value systems of its own staff members has been as important as what happens within the communities it seeks to serve. This inner transformation is the *sadhna* (sustained practice) that has been a constant in the organization.

Another core element of Seva Mandir's approach has been its belief that constructive work is the most enduring lever for change, that values are formed (and changed) through engaging in action. Hence, service or seva, has been a strong thread that has run through all its efforts—whether it is in terms of running a pre-school centre or doing community forestry. It is only when one is engaged in action that one's values are tested and challenged and formed. Running a preschool centre or managing a village pasture requires a community to work on constantly holding each other to account, ensuring equity in efforts and rewards as well as transparency in operations. It becomes a journey in which people occasionally slip, but given Seva Mandir's belief that everyone can be fallible, a setback is usually converted into an occasion to reflect and improve. *Seva* and *sadhna* thus go hand-in-hand for Seva Mandir, each remaining incomplete without the other.

And then there is *kranti*. There is no sequence to these three elements and almost always the three are deeply intertwined. However, both seva and sadhna are in some ways incomplete if they do not ultimately lead to kranti (defined as a deep/significant change in the way things are done or organized). In that respect, kranti is the only one in this triad which is both an intervention and an outcome. In several small and big instances of mobilization and protest—both individually and collectively (but always non-violently)—Seva Mandir has used this third element very effectively over the years. The only question open to interpretation would be whether and, to what extent, kranti as an outcome has happened.

Impact over the Years

Seva Mandir, like several other organizations of that vintage, came into being when organizational credibility and worth were not assessed in terms of targets and numbers. Given the organization's belief in its core purpose of working towards building democratic, just and caring communities, the tools for assessing progress towards this goal are often blunt and qualitative in nature. However, even before the development context became more metric-centred, Seva Mandir had repeatedly made efforts to develop surrogate indices (such as the Village Cohesion Index, or a way to assess the health of community forests) that are objective and quantitative. Other than this, there are intermediary but more tangible indices such as the hectares of land regenerated or the number of children provided access to education and women involved in self-help initiatives, among others. Most of this data is available on Seva Mandir's website.[4]

However, to pick a few of Seva Mandir's more lasting contributions to the development landscape in the country, one should mention the following:

- Seva Mandir has been a leader in the area of adult education (in the 1960s, 1970s, and into the early 1980s), contributing much to its theory and practice.
- It was among the first few organizations in the country to partner with the government in its efforts to bring about a people's movement around afforestation in the 1980s. Seva Mandir then worked intensively on bringing communities together around common lands (community pastures and community forests). During the 1990s and 2000s, it was a national voice on these issues, including

being part of the government's Committee on Land Reforms and heading the sub-committee on common property resources. Over the years, Seva Mandir has stayed steadfast on strengthening communities around shared natural resources and has demonstrated its feasibility in hundreds of villages.

- Persuading and supporting communities towards protecting and preserving community forests despite a dominant paradigm push towards privatization, has probably been one of Seva Mandir's biggest successes.
- Its innovation (and detailing) of the Gram Vikas Kosh (GVK) or Village Development Fund concept as a nucleus of community cohesion and autonomy has now become part of several government and non-government initiatives across the country.
- Seva Mandir's model for provisioning of early childhood care has been mentioned in the country's Five-Year Plan documents and is still referred to by those working in this field.
- Its twelve-year partnership (beginning in the late 1990s) with The Abdul Latif Jameel Poverty Action Lab and Nobel Laureates Esther Duflo and Abhijit Banerjee has led to a slew of breakthrough research in the areas of healthcare and education provisioning, adding to the richness of debate on the balance between intrinsic and extrinsic motivation in ensuring good service-delivery initiatives.
- The formation of Sadhna (a women's craft enterprise) and Udaipur Urja (a member-based organization working on meticulous carbon-offsetting initiatives) as two independent well-functioning entities has been another huge source of satisfaction and a reaffirmation of Seva Mandir's investments in these ideas over the years.
- And finally, Seva Mandir would like to believe that, through its work, it has kept alive the conversation around the value of constructive work. This is important given that much of the development discourse over the last two decades has tended to tilt more towards rights, often overshadowing the matter of responsibilities.

What Makes for Seva Mandir's Success?

Seva Mandir has had a long journey—with its share of ups and downs. But on the whole, the organization takes satisfaction in having made a difference. Institutions are as much art as they are science, and distilling the variables that go behind positive outcomes can be difficult. At times it could be just some fortunate break or some outstanding individuals, but if one were to look for underlying and steady factors, the following need to be mentioned (not in any particular order):

Recognizing the inseparability of means and ends

Building 'social capital' has been both a means and an end for Seva Mandir. In almost all its programmes, Seva Mandir attempts to bring in a community dimension. Most programmes that are chosen are for community benefit, like community forestry, community pastures, community watersheds, and others. Even for programmes which could be individual-focused in nature (agriculture, sanitation, etc.), the approach used is such that the community is involved in selection, supervision, and so on. A truly wonderful innovation birthed and nurtured at Seva Mandir was the idea of the GVK. It began in the late 1980s when Seva Mandir started supporting farmers to do afforestation and land development on private lands. Since a few families would benefit more than others, the idea of beneficiary families contributing towards a common fund was born. They would contribute both from their immediate wage earnings as well as from the longer-term productivity benefits. This principle gradually extended to cover almost every intervention undertaken in the community.

Over time, the GVK emerged as a strong virtual 'commons' offering continuous practical lessons in democracy. Not just this, the GVKs also grew to become a nucleus of very significant core financial autonomy for the village. As in 2022, about 735 village groups have a total fund of approximately Rs 6.8 crore, which is managed by the villages as an endowment. The fund's earnings pay for several local services (like a day care centre, a teacher for children out of school, protection of the local forest, etc)—indeed a vibrant example of functioning rural republics.

The GVK is only one example of how the means and ends get blended, but this belief in an alignment between ends and means is something that permeates everything that Seva Mandir does, and lies behind its programmes, processes and culture.

Who does 'development'?

For a long time, there has been a societal perception that social change or development work can only be undertaken by those who are idealistic and exceptional. It has also often meant that 'doing development' and looking after one's family cannot happen together. Of course, the recent past has seen a swing to the other side with the emergence of development as a 'profession', and with large non-profit organizations at times paying salaries at par with other sectors. However, between development being a preserve of the idealist to development needing professionals, we tend to miss out on the very large bulk of the average lower-middle class that bring everyday continuity and much-needed long-term stamina to organizations such as Seva Mandir. These are people who did not always come to an organization like Seva Mandir with a sense of mission, but more in search of a job or livelihood. However, many of them then found a sense of purpose and dignity in a Seva Mandir kind of place, began to identify with the mission and stayed on to play long meaningful innings. A large number of them in fact come from the very same communities where Seva Mandir is working, making them both the 'community' and 'the agent of change'.

An important factor that makes for Seva Mandir's continuing strength is its recognition of this latter set of development workers as an important and unique set of people. A recognition of their strengths and potential meant that organizational systems, processes, rhythms and cultures got built not just around the occasional exceptional individual, but around these stable, long-term members of Seva Mandir.

Not only did this approach lead to an organization that was more true to those who composed the bulk of it, it helped establish a more fundamental point, which is about non-exclusivity—that it is not just inspired leaders, but every one of us who can contribute to building a better society. In fact, this formulation not only means that everyone can contribute, but that everyone has the responsibility to do so—the onus for the creation of a better society lies not only with leaders, but with each one of us.

Recognizing contradictions internal to communities

During the early 1990s, the shift in Seva Mandir's funding arrangements made it possible for the organization to actually practice bottom-up planning and execution. However, in the first few years after receiving the new kind of funding, Seva Mandir found that it could not spend the money that had been budgeted based on plans submitted by the villages. Even though the community may have submitted a proposal, but when it came to actually carrying it out, often internal differences would surface making it difficult for the programme to be undertaken. These conflicts were most evident whenever the work involved any village commons (pastures, ponds, etc). All these helped Seva Mandir better understand that constraints to development come not only from the outside (such as through adverse policies or lack of resources), but also from inside. Seemingly homogenous tribal communities were also divided internally, eroding their own ability to cooperate or hold others to account. A clear and early recognition of these issues helped Seva Mandir factor these internal contradictions into the way it approached its work of rebuilding communities.

Acknowledging failures

For a very long time, Seva Mandir has been known for its honest, introspective culture—certainly not perfect, but one that nonetheless stands out in a context where most non-profit organizations feel pressured to only present successes. Even though everyone would agree that it's not possible to succeed all the time, yet, somehow the discourse among civil society organizations is mostly centred around successes. However, Seva Mandir was able to build a microculture where honest reflection was the norm, not just internally but also with its donors and supporters, or with visitors. Credit for this goes equally to the leadership within Seva Mandir and to its very unusual set of donors, who encouraged such honest conversations.

This culture of honest introspection is what has helped Seva Mandir build some truly strong programmes, especially in the areas of natural resources development, education and building community institutions. Acknowledgement of its failures and a constant review of its own beliefs and interventions have enabled Seva Mandir to remain relevant and adaptive to the constantly changing context.

Winds from all lands ...

Seva Mandir, from its very beginning, has believed in an openness to ideas, which Gandhiji stated so well: 'I do not want my house to be walled in on all sides and my windows to be stuffed. I want the cultures of all lands to be blown about my house as freely as possible. But I refuse to be blown off my feet by any.'[5] Its founder Mohan Singh Mehta believed in bringing in good people from everywhere and providing them the space to explore their ideas. It is not an accident that the institutions founded by him attracted a host of such people, several of whom then went on to establish their own organizations. These different world visions and backgrounds of those who came to Seva Mandir have also occasionally collided and caused internal tensions, but to the organization's credit, it has managed to retain its openness and diversity.

The same mental openness was evident in the generosity with which Seva Mandir welcomed volunteers from all over the world, at times hosting over 100 interns in a year. This would often be a strain on the small team that had to create meaningful spaces for volunteers and help them learn and contribute, but Seva Mandir stayed with this, almost as a commitment to a greater good. Most of these volunteers would end up questioning Seva Mandir and its approaches, thereby helping the organization reduce several of its blind spots.

And finally, it is this DNA that has also helped Seva Mandir build partnerships with researchers from both within and outside India.

External enablers

Two key external factors that helped Seva Mandir enormously in its work have been the rootstock of social capital that exists in tribal communities, and a set of exceptional donors during a critical phase of the organization's evolution. Southern Rajasthan—Seva Mandir's area of focus—while extremely deprived and challenging in many respects, is also very congenial in others. Unlike the Indo-Gangetic plains, southern Rajasthan is blessed with largely homogenous villages, with limited inequalities and almost no landlessness. The villages consist of mostly tribal populations, who still have relatively high degrees of social capital and strong systems of cooperation. Gender ratios are among the best in the country and women enjoy relatively greater freedom and choice. All of these have greatly helped reinforce Seva Mandir's work on the commons.

And then the kind of donors Seva Mandir has had, especially from the late-1980s to the late-2000s (almost twenty years), would be any organization's dream. In the mid-1980s, as with most other voluntary organizations then, Seva Mandir worked with a large number of donors, each of whom was supporting specific 'projects'. And somehow, it had to keep alive the space to work towards its larger goal while trying to stitch together the (at times disparate) requirements of the various projects and donors. This was not always easy, and just the administration of the projects took up a lot of quality time at the senior levels.

In this context, Seva Mandir was fortunate to work with The Interchurch Organization for Development Cooperation (ICCO) and Evangelische Zentralstelle für Entwicklungshilfe. They introduced a completely different paradigm of partnering by asking Seva Mandir to make its own full and comprehensive plan for three years. They would then underwrite the plan to a significant degree (even up to 80 per cent of total budget in the initial years).

Seva Mandir seized this opportunity and put in place processes whereby every village developed its plan and budgets, which were then factored into a larger goal and direction. The next twenty years were in some ways a time of the richest thinking, experimenting, action and consolidation at Seva Mandir, where the trust reposed in it by the donors enabled it to truly carve out its own identity. What made this trust even more remarkable was that it came immediately on the back of a particularly bitter internal power struggle that Seva Mandir had gone through.

Questions without Easy Answers

Looking back can be both easy and difficult—there is hindsight-enabled clearer vision and one can forget the reality of actions and decisions taken while being on the 'dance floor'. However, the exercise is still useful for the very important guidance for the future this may provide. We are sharing here some thoughts which are more like questions to ourselves. And even though these reflections may appear specific to Seva Mandir, these are issues and dilemmas that most organizations face at times.

Conducting conversations around the ethics/morality of the sector's functioning

The mid-1980s were traumatic years for Seva Mandir. An intense power struggle within the organization led to several senior- and middle-level colleagues leaving, and setting up their own non-profit organizations, often in the same geographic areas where they had worked while at Seva Mandir (as that was where they had built deep community connects). Seva Mandir felt that this was unethical, which led to these small organizations further distancing themselves from Seva Mandir. The late 1980s and the early 1990s was also a time when greater funding became available for social development leading to a sudden increase in the birth of new organizations. The socio-economic profile of the founders of these organizations was often very different from the profile of those who had founded Seva Mandir—they came from more middle-class backgrounds and had often accidentally strayed into this work. Due to the strong moral position taken by Seva Mandir on the issue of overlapping areas of work, communication often broke down with these organizations and it is likely that Seva Mandir lost an opportunity to truly mentor and help these new entrants. And while the moral and ethical aspects should have been kept on the table, was it also the case that Seva Mandir did not fully appreciate the pressures and realities of these fledgling organizations and their founders?

Indeed, even in recent years, Seva Mandir has not been able to have conversations about the ethics of 'overlapping' with other non-profits without this becoming an overtly moral subject, which in turn hampers a forward-moving conversation. Since the moral dimension is never far from decision-making in non-profit organizations such as Seva Mandir, and since the moral dimension is often the internal compass, it is hard to know where the balance lies in such conversations.

The balance between constructive work and the struggle for rights

This is something that has no simple answer and is also an issue that Seva Mandir has always struggled with—how does one balance seva and kranti? The power struggle of the 1980s was also in part a struggle between these two internal pulls, with those in favour of a stronger rights-based approach ultimately leaving the organization. The same ambivalence was apparent in Seva Mandir's reactions to the most prominent rights movements in the 1980s and 1990s.

The Right to Information movement and the Employment Guarantee movement both started in Seva Mandir's very own neighbourhood, and yet the organization's involvement in either was limited. Its position in both these movements was that, while they were good causes, these movements did not speak of the need for citizens themselves to also change (alongside asking for the state to change).

In constantly pointing to what was lacking in the citizen, Seva Mandir at times may have come across as lacking in its support for these rights movements. As one looks back, one is reminded of Seva Mandir's own logo which says that seva (and sadhna) and kranti are not sequential steps—one does not stand for rights only after the inner self is completely purified. Both need a lifetime of effort and often go hand in hand. But it is certainly easier said than done, and the struggle is in finding the elusive right balance between seva and kranti.

Understanding community aspirations, influencing community aspirations

The work of organizations such as Seva Mandir is ultimately located in the space of community aspirations and beliefs, with an attempt to both understand those aspirations and influence them. But there are always multiple realities, and it is difficult to know how much of our own self gets projected in what we see. There is also the danger that the community begins to read our expectations and presents a version of reality that matches that expectation. The community may do this out of politeness or out of self-interest. Given its long years in one region, one can say with a fair degree of confidence that Seva Mandir has a deep and layered understanding of the communities it works with. However, it may be useful to share one big shift within communities that Seva Mandir possibly missed out on. Seva Mandir has mostly worked among the tribal communities of south Rajasthan. Traditionally, they had depended on forests and agriculture for their livelihoods. However, gradually, with the push of diminishing forests and lower agricultural returns, coupled with the pull of improved connectivity with the external world (roads/transport), migration and labour work began to contribute more to the household kitty. The experience of going to urban centres was often not pleasant from a dignity and quality-of-life perspective (or even from a safety perspective), and many migrants spoke yearningly of options nearer home.

Most of Seva Mandir's focus was on strengthening options in the village (through forestry, agriculture and even some small enterprise development), and it kept receiving positive reaffirmation on this direction from the communities. However, the reality was also that migration continued to increase. In its fixation with looking at the problem through its lens (of creating local livelihoods), coupled with villagers possibly telling the organization what they felt it wanted to hear, Seva Mandir failed to notice this social shift. Better understanding of the shift may not have changed the focus of what Seva Mandir was doing but could have helped contribute to a better understanding of the communities' aspirations.

Often when communities sense a wider chasm between their belief systems and those of the outside agency—and where they feel that engagement may only lead to disharmony—a kind of 'weapons of the weak' syndrome begins to work in the shape of overt agreement and acquiescence. There is no sure way to avoid this, except to keep working on one's ability to listen and look beyond one's own perspectives.

Societal change and institution building

This is another dilemma that has been a constant at Seva Mandir—where do the boundaries of the institution end and where does it merge into the society it is a part of? The tension becomes obvious when it comes to defining what is acceptable within an organization, especially when it is at odds with what is acceptable within the society in which the organization is located. For example, Seva Mandir has never had a zero-tolerance policy on any financial or ethical violation on the part of its staff. Instead, it has believed that people need to be counselled and given opportunities to reform, especially since the larger context has often not affirmed these values consistently. People can behave differently within an institution (due to respect or fear) and be different in their own personal and social spaces. Does an organization (specially one like Seva Mandir which is trying to bring about social change) worry only about how people behave within its institutional boundaries or should it also worry about how they behave beyond the organizational boundaries?

This has been a difficult dilemma and one that is ever present. Being conscious of it has led to Seva Mandir adopting more of an approach of reform (and not just a punitive one). This has resulted in the creation of a far more caring organizational environment and has led to (maybe) values which have permeated into spaces beyond the institution. However, it may also at times have given out signals that were confusing for people—both external and also internal.

Concluding Thoughts

Seva Mandir's experience suggests that there is need for a paradigm shift in the way we think about development. It is not enough for the government to make large allocations of funds for poverty alleviation and rural development. What is needed is that villagers themselves and civil society be empowered to play a significant role in the conceptualization, execution and governance of development. In this approach of autonomous development, the differences in education and class backgrounds can give way to more wholesome identities of shared purpose.

At another level, Seva Mandir has also discovered that those who are oppressed are often complicit in their exploitation. They tolerate the poor quality of public services—such as health provision, education and stable property rights—as well as the arbitrary behaviour of the authorities. They often seek benefits to which they are not entitled and thereby bend to those in power rather than seeking to transform their relationships. Realigning self-interest so that it supports, rather than undercuts, the common good is the challenge for development, not just improving individual wellbeing in terms of health, education and income. Seva Mandir has found that constructive work programmes can bring this change. It, however, needs time and patience and a vision for development that acknowledges the damage being done by development sans democracy.

4

The Jamkhed Model: Sowing the Seeds of Community-based Primary Healthcare

APARNA THOMAS, SHOBHA AROLE AND RAVI AROLE

JAMKHED, A TOWN IN CENTRAL Maharashtra, is in a drought-prone area. It is surrounded by villages, with the nearest city of Ahmednagar more than an hour away. In the 1960s and 70s, people here were extremely poor, with high rates of malnutrition, infectious diseases, infant and maternal deaths and occupational injuries. They lacked basic healthcare services and access to appropriate curative care. Social injustices such as the low status of women and caste-based prejudices contributed significantly to the chronic state of ill health of the village communities.

The Comprehensive Rural Health Project (CRHP) in Jamkhed[1] was set up by Drs. Raj and Mabelle Arole, who were doctors working with India's rural poor and marginalized people. The Aroles had graduated from the Christian Medical College in Vellore and obtained their residency training in medicine and surgery and master of public health degrees as Fulbright Scholars at Johns Hopkins University in the USA. During their time there, they devised an innovative project based on comprehensive community-based primary healthcare to effectively meet both the immediate as well as the long-term needs of poor and marginalized people, especially women.

In 1970, the Aroles returned to India to establish the CRHP in Jamkhed. CRHP is a comprehensive, community-based primary healthcare programme, focused on community empowerment. It became known as the 'Jamkhed Model', where community cooperation and participatory development were found to be most welcome and needed. Initially covering eight villages with a combined population of 10,000, CRHP rapidly expanded in its early years across village communities, spreading to cover over 300 villages.

The programme aimed to involve the community in addressing its health problems, to prevent and treat most of their health conditions using simple techniques and to tackle the root causes of health ailments—such as poverty, the social status of women and the caste system. Its focus was on the poorest people but involved the whole community. Since 1978, it has been recognized by the World Health Organization (WHO) and United Nations International Children's Emergency Fund (UNICEF) as an effective way to deliver healthcare to marginalized populations while simultaneously addressing social injustices.

Its strategy was to develop a healthcare delivery programme suited to the needs and resources of the area. An essential element was community empowerment; from the outset, village communities were involved, and they participated in partnership with the project staff. The focus on equity, integration and empowerment of people were key to effecting change, leading to overall sustainable development and in turn to better health.

The goal was to build the capacity of communities to participate actively and responsibly in primary healthcare activities in order to improve the physical, mental, emotional, psychological, social and economic health of the whole community. A multisectoral approach was seen as important, as health services needed to be integrated and appropriate technology used.

Key Principles of the Jamkhed Model

Equity: This ensures that the needs of the poorest groups are addressed. They are brought into the fold of the larger community, ensuring their participation in identifying and addressing the root causes of their problems in order to resolve them. Even if not everyone receives equal healthcare, it is possible to ensure that everyone has access to it.

Integration: CRHP's approach to healthcare is multisectoral. The core belief is that health does not exist in isolation, but it is intrinsically related to education, the environment, sanitation, socioeconomic status and local traditions. Additionally, sometimes non-medical interventions are more effective and have greater impact on wellbeing. In fact, health and development are two sides of the same coin: people may be advised to wash their hands, but if they have neither the money for the soap nor enough water, how can they observe hygiene? These basic needs need to be addressed first.

Empowerment: This is one of the most important principles of the Jamkhed Model. Working at the grassroots with village health workers (VHWs) and community groups initiates a process of empowerment, of women in particular and communities in general. Once people have information and can make informed decisions, they have the power to consider constructive ways to transform their communities. They can also learn skills for themselves and to help others. This builds capacity in the community, enabling people to jointly assess and identify their problems, analyse the causes, decide what to work on and develop appropriate solutions. The focus is on helping the community to 'heal' itself and to gain control of their lives for the wellbeing of all.

Appropriate Technology: This applies to people (through on-the-job training), facilities (simple hospitals, community halls, home healthcare), supplies (basic and easily available), equipment (locally made and maintained), medicines (limited to an essential list), education (simple, through local media) and energy sources (renewable). Locally available resources such as people (labour, knowledge and ideas), money and materials are used as much as possible, including effective traditional methods and remedies. Equipment is technically appropriate and easily made, so it can be maintained and repaired locally.

The village communities are involved through the use of simple and traditional media for health and education, and the VHWs use basic equipment and traditional, simple and effective remedies for prevention and treatment of illnesses. Examples of employing appropriate technology include utilizing VHWs, delegating duties to others less qualified but capable of performing tasks adequately and training persons with little formal education to do various tasks.

The Process Involved in the Jamkhed Model

Step 1: Identifying villages that are willing to collaborate.

Step 2: Getting to know the community, building rapport, identifying socially minded people as well as leaders. There is an important difference between political leaders and leaders the community listens to, and the trust of both needs to be gained. Simultaneously, learning about government programmes and other resources and agencies in the area.

Step 3: Organizing community groups, holding focus groups, listening to the community and addressing their problems.

Step 4: Selecting and training a VHW.

As the community becomes knowledgeable and more capable of managing its own problems, the project's role shifts to enabling, facilitating and training. The staff facilitates the process, trains the VHWs and other villagers, provides backup for difficulties, encourages and supports the VHWs and community groups and shares information. The mobile health team (MHT)—consisting of a nurse, social workers, paramedical workers, an agriculture specialist and sometimes a doctor—provides the VHWs with knowledge and skills through weekly classes and practical demonstrations at the village level.

The project staff learns how to work with the communities in new ways—including participatory methods through adult learning techniques and qualitative research methodologies—which can be adapted by both staff and villagers, irrespective of literacy.

Key Players in the Process

The project works at different interrelated levels, which include the village, the MHT and the health centre. The key players in this process are the VHW, the community and community groups, the MHT and the health centre. These groups operate at the primary level, for it is the building of the community's capacity to deal with its own problems that will ultimately improve their health in a sustainable way. Here, the emphasis is on the VHW, the women's and men's clubs and the adolescents' and children's groups. Nearly 80 per cent of the health problems can be taken care of by the people themselves in their community.

Village health workers

To improve the health status of a community, there is requirement for a health agent who will consistently reach out to the local people—especially the poor and marginalized—to facilitate the prevention and early detection of serious diseases and bring about positive change in their habits and attitudes towards illnesses. Thus, the qualities needed for the agent are not the mechanical ability to store information and hand it out like a robot, nor mere technical ability, but a sensitive human ability to recognize other people's needs, patiently promote health knowledge and gently and compassionately care for the sick. The aim is not to train a cadre of health workers who become another level in the healthcare system, but a cadre of facilitators or change agents who share what they learn with others in their villages and who are motivated by service and not by financial reward.

The VHW is selected by the community and is accountable to it. The role is usually given to a woman, and even those without a formal education are eligible. They are partners with the organization as representatives of their villages. The main aims of these volunteers are to improve the health of the village community through sharing knowledge and skills, as well as providing minor medical care. Their roles include that of health educator (which is the most important role); provider of basic medical care (including prenatal care, safe childbirth practices, infant care, family planning advice and treatment of minor illnesses); organizer and facilitator of community groups; mobilizer of people for activities planned by the community; and others, such as motivator, mentor, supporter, role model and as a source of information.

They initially receive basic training and thereafter are trained once a week at the health centre in their village. They are mentored by an experienced VHW, who gives on-the-job training at their village. Follow-up training is also provided during the project staff's village visits. At first, most of the training is dedicated to the personal development of the VHW in order to build their self-esteem and confidence, and equip them with the skills necessary for community organization and effective communication; the rest of the time is spent developing their clinical knowledge and skills.

The training covers basic knowledge and skills to respond to community needs in the fields of women and children's health, tuberculosis, leprosy, eye care, care of the disabled, HIV/AIDS, environment, sanitation and social issues such as women's status and caste-based prejudice. They are also taught to understand the root social, economic, cultural and political causes of social justice and developmental issues. As a value-based system, the training also covers universal concepts such as care, love and harmony.

The training of the VHWs is based on their interests and experiences in their villages, using adult learning principles. Thus there is no set curriculum, and they often learn more from each other than from the project staff.

Community groups

Alongside the VHWs are community groups for men, women, adolescents and children. These are organized around members' interests, so they are motivated to participate in meetings and joint activities. As people undertake more activities together, they expand their concerns to health, social and cultural issues. They learn to assess problems, analyse causes, select a problem to work on and develop appropriate solutions.

Both the farmers' clubs and women's clubs work together in supporting the VHWs by helping in keeping records, promoting health activities and mobilizing villagers for community action. Community groups monitor births and deaths in their village and the progress on common health indicators. They are involved in the surveillance of endemic diseases—such as malaria and TB—within their village. The men's and women's groups also cooperate in improving the environment.

Farmers' clubs

Young socially minded men across caste groups who are eager to improve their villages are encouraged to organize themselves into farmers' clubs. Care is taken to ensure that the membership includes people from all socio-economic backgrounds, but the majority is drawn from the poorer communities. They learn to work together to plan and carry out programmes that benefit the community, especially the poor and the marginalized.

The groups focus mainly on agricultural and environmental development, which also influence health. The programmes also cover issues such as employment, agricultural methods, development of water resources and improved housing, among others. They have been successful in bringing fallow and wastelands under cultivation.

Women's clubs (mahila mandals)

One of the most important organizations to evolve from the project is the Mahila Mandal. Since one of the greatest social injustices in villages today is the low status of women, the primary goal of the women's clubs is to bring about social change, especially those which will improve the lives of women and children. In each village, women from different caste groups come together to form groups, which initially often focus on issues of income before gradually expanding to include health concerns. The women work with different economic programmes to improve their families and homes, which have a deep impact on health.

Their ability to earn money gives a boost to their respective positions in their own families and in the community. Since most health problems are related to women's reproduction and young children, the women's clubs concern themselves with these health issues. Over time, they become skilled and knowledgeable about prevention, early detection and care, including dealing with harmful practices, improved antenatal care, safe childbirth, childhood diarrhea, respiratory infections and malnutrition.

Adolescents' and children's clubs

The adolescent programme is mainly for girls aged twelve to eighteen. They participate with the aim of improving their knowledge about health, personal development and sex. The main aims of these groups are to encourage girls to stay in school and to delay their marriages and first pregnancies, in order to develop them as strong young women.

The child-to-child programme focuses on sharing health knowledge with children and improving their self-esteem in creative ways. Many children are left to look after their younger siblings, so the skills and knowledge they acquire in the programme improve their caretaking responsibilities as well. They can also influence their parents in the adoption of healthy practices.

Mobile health team

This is an interdisciplinary, multipurpose team created to address all the components of health and development for the community. The primary focus is on building and maintaining a rapport with the community, training and supporting VHWs, gathering data, responding to requests from the community and, when necessary, referring people to the health centre for their legal, social, economic, agricultural and health concerns. The team consists of a doctor, nurse, social worker, paramedical worker and an agriculture consultant (and an experienced VHW after a few years), all of whom are trained across disciplines and can perform several functions. Its function is to support the VHW, supervise development activities in the village and to act as the liaison between the village and the health centre.

In the early stages, the team visits a village weekly, reducing the frequency of visits in later stages; eventually, the village can manage without regular visits. During the visits, the staff meet the families together with the VHW and members of the various clubs, and discuss specific health, social or economic issues. Problems needing solutions beyond the MHT's level are referred to the centre. In the evenings, the team meets with various community groups and discusses relevant issues or facilitates assessment and analysis of problems.

The health centre

The centre consists of a training wing, consulting services and demonstration farm. Sometimes, there is a hospital or clinic. There are provisions for legal services for referrals for medical care. The centre also offers training, networking and administration. If there is a hospital, it handles medical problems that cannot be dealt with in the village and provides low-cost, high-quality, cost-effective secondary care. The hospitals are equipped with modern diagnostic equipment, surgical facilities and inpatient beds for surgery, obstetrics, pediatrics and other specializations. There is a referral system for cases that cannot be handled within the hospital. The health centre also networks with the government and other agencies to identify resources for training and community projects.

The centre keeps costs low by having a basic facility (building, furnishings, equipment and supplies) with adequate, appropriate technology, limiting its use to necessary functions, using effective but inexpensive essential medicines and basic low-cost materials in surgery and other areas. Staff are trained in various disciplines, and tasks are also delegated to the lowest-trained person (including family members) who can do an adequate job. The patients' relatives help the nurses in the care of the patients, which improves the healing process and allows for earlier discharge to home care by the family, where the VHW and MHT conduct follow-up visits. Patients pay very basic fees to support the hospital as well as to avoid issues that could arise from providing free care.

The training wing provides basic training in knowledge, skills and personal development to VHWs and other villagers. It also organizes seminars on various topics, including health, agriculture, credit, loans, income-generating programmes, government schemes and watershed management.

Proliferation of the CRHP Approach

As the village residents see the changes taking place in their community, they share their experiences with their relatives and friends in other villages, organize more farmers' clubs and women's groups, and select a larger number of VHWs. As people become more self-reliant, they volunteer to go to other villages to initiate new programmes, and there they become facilitators for change. It becomes a people's movement, with villagers encouraging other villagers to start programmes. The villagers are themselves best equipped to explain the process and motivate other villages to emulate their experiences. Thus, community-based primary healthcare becomes a movement, spreading from community to community.

Projects that develop successful programmes feel the obligation to share this transforming experience with others through visits and training. The Jamkhed Institute has trained thousands of grassroots workers, project managers, health and development workers and policymakers from India and abroad. Hundreds of thousands of people have realized this energy and potential and are responsible for a worldwide movement for social change. The undergirding principles of equity and justice have resulted in changes in the lives of people. Empowered women from poor and marginalized communities have taken their rightful place in society.

Most health problems in rural areas are preventable or amenable to early detection and simple treatment, but get exacerbated and could become fatal if not identified and treated early on. Sustainability of healthcare involves working with the communities and health centres through an integrated approach, dealing with promotive, preventive, curative and rehabilitative services and keeping in mind people's economic situations. Sustainability is defined not in financial terms, but through knowledge, attitudes, practices, values and the development of caring and sharing communities, where all people are included.

Impact of the Jamkhed Model

The impact of the Jamkhed approach can be seen at all levels, whether local, national or international. At the local level, the infant mortality rate in the project villages has fallen from 174 per thousand in 1970 to 14–16 per thousand in 2015. Similarly, prenatal coverage in the project villages improved from 0.5 to 99 per cent. In 1970, immunization rates were less than 1 per cent; currently, over 95 per cent of all children are fully immunized. These changes have greatly impacted the health of families and communities and resulted in more children going to school.

At the time of the project's inception in 1970, people in most villages suffered from water-borne illnesses such as cholera, malaria and typhoid. By mobilizing communities to change their hygiene habits, eradicating open wastewater and emphasizing and demonstrating the benefits of a clean environment, many of these illnesses were minimized within five years. In project villages, most of these illnesses no longer exist. Similarly, the number of leprosy and tuberculosis cases were reduced by similar interventions of breaking down stigmas and disseminating knowledge.

There is no doubt that the Jamkhed Model has strengthened the local health system. But it has greatly influenced state and national policies as well.

A prime example of this is the Accredited Social Health Activist (ASHA) worker programme under the National Rural Health Mission (NRHM), which is based on CRHP's VHW programme. Many other states have also adopted the Jamkhed principles into their own health and development programmes.

Its dynamic nature enables the Jamkhed Model to be used in non-health settings too. One example among many is a programme in Nigeria. A delegation from Nigeria visited CRHP, studied the model and sought CRHP's help in implementing an agriculture-based programme. The issue they were facing was that while there was plenty of fertile land, communities were oppressed and lacked agricultural skills. Through the basic principles of equity, integration, empowerment and the application of appropriate technology, people were trained, communities were mobilized and a large-scale agricultural programme was implemented in two provinces in the country. The Nigerian government replicated the model later in other regions. Apart from Nigeria, Sri Lanka and Bolivia have implemented the Jamkhed Model, and several leading public health and global health institutions have applied it as an example of an efficient, sustainable health and development model.

Furthermore, since health is not isolated from other socio-economic factors, it is important to highlight the broader impact of change in some of these areas. Early on, CRHP experimented with strategies to ensure sustainable economic empowerment while also emphasizing nutrition. For example, during the green revolution in the 1970s, the state government of Maharashtra encouraged the planting of sugarcane in the hope of economic growth. But the Jamkhed area is too drought-prone for sugarcane to flourish. Through the creation of farmers' clubs, the CRHP started educating traditional farmers on the benefits of planting crops such as onions that would survive in their region. Later, these clubs began making their own decisions and growing specialized crops.

Similarly, women's self-help groups were initially created so women could share their experiences with each other, eventually creating close bonds among them. This led to the creation of income-generation groups; as the initial bond had already been established, it was easier for the two groups to successfully engage in joint activities.

Another example of the impact of this approach is seen in the adolescent groups, where young adults were taught about the links between health and overall economic development, and also other matters such as the importance of saving money and opening bank accounts.

Conclusion

In its fifty-second year of functioning, the Jamkhed Model continues to be viable and comprehensive. A key aspect of its uniqueness is its initial insistence on the sharing of knowledge across groups—including village communities, the mobile health team and those at the centre. The CRHP's philosophy of equity, integration and empowerment of people was a key component in the successful implementation of its various programmes, specifically focused on improving the social status of women over the years. This approach results in people's overall development, including their holistic health, in a sustainable form.

The organized groups in the villages pass on the knowledge to younger residents with the hope of inspiring the next generation of active farmers' club and women's group members. In this way, knowledge multiplies across larger groups of people and across generations. The initial VHWs who learnt and shared their knowledge and later became trainers of the next generation are part of an ongoing process. The third and fourth generation of health workers are now working in their villages, mentored by their older colleagues.

The project's impact can be assessed by the statistics, which show substantial results achieved over a long period of time. But beyond the numbers, we can find self-confident women and men who were once on the fringes of society now taking leadership positions in their villages. They have become individuals capable of making their own decisions, empowered to take charge of their own health and wellbeing.

It is not only the quantitative changes that are important, but also the qualitative transformations of people and communities, which lead to harmony, health and peace.

5

Eklavya's Journey of Adaptation and Evolution in Public School Education

HRIDAY KANT DEWAN AND TULTUL BISWAS

THE EKLAVYA FOUNDATION[1] (HENCEFORTH EKLAVYA), is a non-government society registered in 1982. It was set up to seed and develop academic programmes for curricular change in elementary education at the micro level and to mainstream these programmes through government and non-government agencies. It was driven by the need to change a dormant education system and address the triangle of equity, quality and quantity in relationship to education. While it was registered forty years ago, it has been in existence for over fifty years, with its first intervention in middle school science teaching taking place in Hoshangabad district of Madhya Pradesh.

Kishore Bharati and Friends Rural Centre, the two organizations that initiated the Hoshangabad Science Teaching Programme, chose Hoshangabad as a base because it was part of the heartland and representative of a large part of the 'Hindi belt'; their aim was for the initiative to work as a model for other regions. The objectives of these founder organizations were diverse, ranging from the improving of science teaching in resource-starved government schools to the seeding of education programmes that could lead to social transformation. The genesis of Eklavya came from the ideas being discussed by the diverse people involved in the Hoshangabad Science Teaching Programme (HSTP).

Eklavya has mainly focused on contributing to the public education system and transforming classrooms and schools, both public and private. The context in which it started was of mainstream education being fraught with multiple maladies of rote learning and top-down, didactic teaching. The classroom neither offered any scope for children to bring their knowledge and interact with each other or with the teacher, nor any avenues for teachers to learn and innovate. Eklavya has worked to alter this and to simultaneously develop platforms of interaction among children and teachers to create shared learnings and a sense of togetherness.

As an organization committed to the values of the Indian Constitution, Eklavya has worked on social and scientific awareness, fostering rational and critical thinking as well as encouraging dialogue. It promotes social dignity and respect for all and follows principles of tolerance and inclusiveness in all its work. A strong belief in collaboration and the need for a larger movement has propelled it to develop collaborative networks with like-minded organizations and forums to share knowledge and learnings. For this reason, Eklavya's publications are available freely for all to access in the webspace.

Eklavya is known for its work on reforming educational processes in the country, its vast body of publications and for setting up forums and structures for interaction among those concerned with children's education.

With a large number of people participating in and contributing to Eklavya's work without formally being a part of the organization, many view Eklavya more as a movement than an organization. The numbers keep growing as more join to contribute voluntarily to work they find meaningful, interesting and challenging.

Diversity as well as respect for every contributor are part of the essence of the organization, encoded in all its actions. Keeping the interest and motivation alive among these diverse people continues to be a major concern for Eklavya, as their participation enriches the organization and is a key aspect of its existence. It is the social ideal Eklavya works towards: a society that cultivates open-mindedness and creative, independent and scientific thinking.

Defining the Various Points of Impact

Working with the public school system

Eklavya's school intervention programmes were the first comprehensive curriculum reform interventions in India. It laid out most of the elements that needed to be included for making change feasible, including acknowledgement that little to no change was possible by changing individual elements such as syllabi, textbooks, teacher training and pedagogy. These elements needed to be aligned to the principles of pedagogy and the nature of training, otherwise the inertia of the system could not be challenged. The reform process required ensuring respect for teachers and keeping them central to the process.

The programmes were aimed at bringing the needs of the students, teachers and the school to the forefront, and modifying the role of the administrative structure from that of an inspector to an enabler and facilitator. The structures and processes to ensure dialogue among the various levels of educational system functionaries were set up, to enable the public education system to continue to reform itself.

A salient feature of the curricular programmes was to avoid setting up parallel systems and to act as an empowering catalytic agent. This involved developing a sense of agency in those working at all levels of the public system. There was a requirement for systems that enabled and empowered teachers and local-level educational functionaries to act. This was made possible by abolishing inspectorial monitoring and by ensuring respect and support for teachers in the programme. By building their capacity and helping them develop as trainers and resource contributors, the teachers could eventually become ambassadors of the programme.

From this experience, many concrete working principles were drawn, and they continue to be an intrinsic part of Eklavya's work. A few examples are:

- Teachers are as central to the classrooms as the students. Most have vast experience and wisdom, and can make learning possible if guided appropriately, supported in their efforts and given the agency and space to design how learning happens.
- All children can and want to learn; they have the capability of finding meaning in and learning from all situations.
- Children bring their life experiences, understanding, wisdom, language, culture and knowledge to classrooms; this needs to be recognized and to become the foundation of learning.

- There needs to be more emphasis on developing learners who are curious, capable of learning on their own and excited to learn instead of focusing on just content delivery.
- Assessments of learning need to happen concurrently, and not only at the end of the term/year; they must also be holistic and participatory in nature.
- Classroom materials are a gradually evolving process; they need to be developed through active engagement with schools and students, and support from teachers.
- Crucial structural and functional hurdles that obstruct the possibility of reform must be addressed simultaneously.

Initially, Eklavya's primary task was to transform the public education system. The direction for this was provided by HSTP, which at the point of closure of the intervention in public school system, was being implemented in over 1,000 schools in thirteen districts (and a proposal to expand it to the entire state was under consideration). By evolving simple locally available science kits with help from teachers, HSTP demonstrated that science could be taught well even in ordinary rural schools. It showed how systems for continuous learning for teachers and the programme itself could be set up, and how teachers could be supported in their classrooms. These systems for teachers were introduced in two other school interventions – an integrated and holistic primary school programme and a social science programme for middle schools.

The former programme was called 'Prashika', and was the first to emphasize the use of home languages of children in the classroom. It developed materials that focused on the children's capability to learn and analyse rather than to memorize content. It focused on foundational abilities in the primary classes and considered classes 1 to 5 as two distinct phases: classes 1–2 (foundational) and 3–5 (upper primary). It was developed with rigorous theoretical and conceptual inputs as well as extensive practice in over 100 schools. Its elements and imprint can be seen in many books and syllabi across the country, including in National Council of Educational Research and Training (NCERT) materials.

The social science programme was developed through rigorous work with schoolchildren over six years and aimed to make the subject accessible for the learner. It transformed social studies from memorizing a bagful of facts to learning about changes in the world and exploring possible reasons for these. The pedagogy encouraged dialogue and discussion in the classroom to enable rational ethical development and thinking about choices. These foregrounded constitutional values were imbued with a spirit of humanism.

These principles, materials and methods—and those who participated in their development—have continued to inform efforts at educational reform across India. These are reflected in particular in the pedagogical materials of many states, as these are simplest aspects to tackle. It is not as if these were original ideas in education, but more that the stated desirable ideas were concretized pragmatically and put into operation, thus making them pathfinders.

These ideas may have emerged eventually, given the concern over inequalities in education and the increasing understanding about the nature of human learning, but Eklavya undoubtedly pioneered the development and implementation of these ideas and brought together concerned academics, ordinary schoolteachers, students from deprived backgrounds and those who made it their goal to be a bridge among these. This ensured that voices from the ground were heard and respected.

Widening the avenues for learning—beyond classroom initiatives

Our work in schools brought into focus the fact that a school is located in a social space. Children spend far less time in school every day than they do outside it, and they need spaces for interaction away from schools. The same applied to teachers, as their training sessions and meetings were not conducive to free interaction among them. Discussion forums for teachers and children's clubs were set up to be platforms of meaningful interaction.

Eventually there were over 100 children's clubs, which—after initial support from the Eklavya team—were run by the children themselves. Initially focused on reading and an exploration of their own interests, the clubs evolved to include many activities such as theatre, ecological awareness and responsible journalism. Many of these clubs continued to function long after Eklavya had stopped working in the region. They saw generations of children coordinating and leading their activities.

Publishing and access to reading

Our work with schoolchildren revealed the dearth of study materials for students. There were very few books for children and teachers, and few schools had libraries. The process of populating school libraries with books further revealed the lack of interesting books written for children: they did not have content that could extend a conversation or give children an opportunity to express themselves.

Starting with a monthly magazine on science for children called *Chakmak*, Eklavya's publications expanded to include periodicals for teachers (*Sandarbh*) and for the general community on the confluence between science and society (*Srote*), along with a variety of children's books. Eklavya now has a large bank of books on different genres for elementary school students of all ages, as well as materials teachers can use to add to their understanding on education and pedagogy. It has also worked on ensuring these materials reach children through libraries, fairs and their schoolteachers.

Sawaliram—encouraging children to question

Eklavya started a postal forum called 'Sawaliram' to respond to questions from children arising from the classroom or from their outside experiences. The intention was to help children develop the confidence to ask questions and also to continue a dialogue around the responses. The avenues for conversation included handwritten postcards and inland letters. Sometimes response envelopes were received with explanations about the experiment or the instrument made from local materials. The handwritten responses to each individual writing were also sent by post. These were a source of great joy for the receiver, and were often read out loud in the *Chakmak* clubs.

Sometimes the letters were written by a group of children and could be based on what happened in the science classroom or what they observed outside, or related to social issues. Teachers sometimes wrote to seek answers to their questions or to questions children had asked. The forum was coordinated by the Hoshangabad district education office, which received and posted the replies.

Why Eklavya Was Started

Apart from its historical roots in the reform of science teaching in the public education systems and bringing experiments to classrooms, there were other factors that supported Eklavya in its initial stages. In the 1980s, there were concerns about the quality of school education and the growing need for encouraging a scientific temperament. The central government's Department of Science and Technology was keen to promote the development of a scientific temperament; at the same time, the government's interest in education was shifting from adult learning to ensuring education reached all children. Questions were being asked about the low rate of enrolment and retention of children in schools. There was also a view that non-government organizations could help fulfil the task of education and development in the rural areas; in this climate, the HSTP experiment and Eklavya's work became meaningful ventures to support.

The 1970s and early 1980s saw enthusiasm and desire to make a difference and create change spawning several groups applying different strategies. They were imbued with a sense of purpose and energy in hope of achieving what seemed impossible. It was a period which saw the promotion of science and the development of a scientific temperament as a harbinger of rational understanding. In 1981, a special meeting was called by the Planning Commission to discuss the idea of setting up Eklavya. In response, the Department of Science and Technology (Government of India), Department of Education (Government of India) and the Department of Education (Madhya Pradesh Government) came forward offering full financial support for Eklavya (each put in one-third of the total). The open-ended nature of the support meant there were no stipulations, which seemed like a miracle. This sustained support from the government helped Eklavya build a robust core team, programmes and a set of principles, along with in-depth capability in selected areas.

Impact of a Changing External Environment on the Direction of Eklavya's Work

The government's attitude toward NGOs started changing in the 1990s, and this caused a lot of churning within Eklavya. The closure of the scheme extending comprehensive medium-term support for Eklavya meant that it had to adapt to different patterns of support, monitoring and reporting. This led to adjustments in the geography of its work as well as the direction of evolution of the programmes and, to some extent, the organization's structure also changed.

Changed relationships with the organizations providing financial support and the lack of continuity and absence of long-term support threw up many challenges. It led to readjustments in Eklavya's way of working. There were intense discussions on the organization's purpose and whether the adjustments being visualized were contrary to its essence. However, the new developments also led to many alternative avenues and methods of reaching students and teachers being explored. Structures and forums outside the school—such as the Shiksha Protsahan Kendras, reading rooms, voluntary teacher groups, children's fairs and learning activities with adolescent children—emerged, as did the collaborative support to many organizations that wanted to work in education.

The scope of Eklavya's work at its founding covered all aspects of school education from primary to senior secondary, gradually spreading to cover the entire state. The goal was to build capacity to act as a watchdog at all levels and to ensure the system worked as closely as possible to its intended design. Its main principle was from the title of its guiding document: 'From Micro-level Experiments to Macro-level Expansion'.

With experience came a realization that the path for macro dissemination had to be different from the path taken by the micro experiment, and the acceptable divergence from the elements of the original model was a subject of intense debates and contentions. The somewhat one-dimensional nature of Eklavya's engagement with the formal school system and the need for more open spaces of interaction led to various explorations across the organization. Apart from the publication and dissemination of two periodicals (one each for teachers and for children), its interventions remained small, as the organization continued to focus on its in-school programmes.

However, the beginning of the 2000s brought more intense resistance to external intervention in the public education system, leading to the curricular programmes being stopped abruptly in 2002. This led Eklavya to develop other streams of work, such as partnering in an advisory role with the State

Councils for Educational Research and Training (SCERT) and with the government education departments in different states. With the changes in its funding sources and the closure of its formal school programmes in Madhya Pradesh, Eklavya shifted from being an inward-looking organization to becoming more accommodative of the external environment. A different and perhaps richer understanding of the concepts of 'quality' and 'dilution' emerged.

On reflection, the curtailing of its intervention in government schools seemed inevitable, but what has been surprising is that Eklavya's programmes were allowed to continue for so long, given the tensions they generated by placing pressure on the system to reform, by challenging the hierarchies and by highlighting the lack of concern for the plight of teachers and the quality of education reaching the under-served children.

Core Principles

Changes in the external environment, the size of the organization and the nature of its people required some elements of continuity to keep the idea of Eklavya alive. Since its inception, the variety of people engaging with the idea and goals of Eklavya has required a consensus on the framework and outlines of its work strategy. This is an evolving consensus, rooted in core principles and structures that are dialogical. These core principles include:

- Avoid setting up parallel systems and transform and strengthen the public system instead;
- Those working in the organization are responsible for all aspects of everyday details, including raising support, conceptualizing new programmes, planning and implementation, with the governance structures functioning as advisors and watchdogs;
- Exploration with structures meant for planning, review and functioning (for example, teams or groups) and periodic realignment based on a review of the internal and external environments;
- A democratic style of working through a 'non-hierarchical' approach, shared forum-based leadership and developing and nurturing new leadership within the organization;

- A low and comparatively flat highest-to-lowest salary ratio inclined towards the interests of the lower salary brackets;
- Respect for all categories of work and the expectation of participation of all Eklavya members in all tasks, including decision-making; and
- Open sharing of learnings and materials across organizations and promoting free and open access to resources within partnerships.

These principles are nuanced. For example, it is not as if there is no leadership or differences in responsibility and decision-making within Eklavya's structure. The implication is that despite their different roles and responsibilities, members are treated as equals with space for their views, concerns and suggestions to be voiced and heard.

Multi-dimensional Learnings

The essence of the school interventions was a collaboration between a reluctant state machinery provoked into action by the presence of some 'maverick' officers who wanted to reform the system. These officers went against routine and existing processes to enable the school programmes and helped Eklavya initiate the interventions to achieve its goals. However, the sustenance of these often required persevered nudging from the HSTP and Eklavya teams.

A long struggle led the erstwhile government to release a manual of rules for academic, administrative and financial functioning, informing people of their roles to ensure automatic allocations. Though approved at the highest administrative level, it could be over-ridden by an administrative order. The struggle to have it circulated and implemented confirmed its limited use. All such experiences highlight the short-term reform memory of the system. Reform statements in policy documents can only enable those who want to act. The extent to which an idea will be pushed depends on those behind it within the system. The crucial members in this chain were the schoolteachers, as it relied on their understanding of the tasks and strategies. However, the culture of officers taking radical decisions (which had initially helped Eklavya) started a trend which later moved the system in directions orthogonal to the spirit of Eklavya's work, dismantling all that they had wanted to build into the system. The teachers imbued with Eklavya's ideas struggled for a while but eventually succumbed.

Our other learning relates to Eklavya's own sense of itself. The special treatment it had received—being fully funded, with a bounty of external support—gave us a false sense of grandeur. We felt unique and different, with the naive belief that we understood education and its context, due to our close relationship with the grassroots. We were also 'fearful' of being absorbed by the system, of 'getting co-opted'. In Eklavya's relationship with the government, we were their partners, but also strong critics of their actions. Our relationship was driven by our confidence that we knew what needed to be done; the subsequent realization of this 'foolishness' took time to sink in as a collective. However, the feeling of doing something unique and different, and not what others tell you to do, both as an individual and as a group, persists, which perhaps is common to many non-governmental organizations. It is this urge that determines the openness of an organization to partner with others, learn from them, and even change their own direction of work. For Eklavya, this sense was balanced by a strong sense of realism, and recognition and respect for the contribution of people in the system. Its belief in keeping the doors open and its networking also helped it keep its feet on the ground.

Its partnerships and joint efforts with different government structures and non-governmental organizations led to a nurturing space for mutual adjustments and learning. While there was always space for volunteers to contribute and a respect for outside wisdom, the extent of flexibility and accommodation was low. Eklavya started as a fully funded organization with complete freedom to chart its own path. The journey from there to having to raise money and be self-sufficient was difficult. At the conceptual level, the idea of 'micro to macro' was reluctantly altered. Since the macro expansion could not have the same format as the pilot, modified forms, not merely clones of the pilot, emerged through seeding at different locations. A newer theory of change emerged that did not depend on Eklavya's presence to ensure close replication, which gave a deeper understanding of a pragmatic framework of change.

The struggle to balance the pressures to follow certain trajectories, keeping sight of our ideals, intents and purposes was very intense. It was difficult to keep aligned with our organizational and work principles, and constantly re-define them in view of then-relevant purposes and strategies. The challenge continues to be of listening to outside messages and assessing them for their intent and possible impact.

Questions that remain are: To what extent can the organization be flexible enough to adjust? How does one balance 'core work' with expectations from short-term, output-directed support? Which of the principles are really core? There is a need for flexibility and change, but where do the boundaries lie?

Concluding Reflections

Eklavya had to revisit its initial vision of the 'change theory' from 'micro to macro' when, within a few years, it became clear that the theory was not working on ground. Interventions are not planned packages that can be automatically scaled up, as they require motivation, conviction, ownership and a personal stake. An understanding of what is needed and is possible in a certain context can come only from the opportunity to explore, experiment, make mistakes, learn from them and reconstruct the model and its strategy. What can be retained are the key principles of functioning, but many details would emerge from the ground through collaborations of shared ownership and mutual respect.

The strength of Eklavya has been in these collaborations and its ability to draw academics from universities, teachers from schools, the youth and the elderly from the communities and many others in the form of volunteers, interns and researchers. The sense of ownership, belonging and commitment to the concept of Eklavya all of them carry is a strong scaffold for the organization.

6

Beyond Cerebral Palsy: The Growth of Spastics Societies and Their Contribution to the Disability Movement

RAJUL PADMANABHAN

IN A DEFINING MOMENT FOR the birth of the spastic society movement in India, a doctor in one of Delhi's premier institutes had this to say of Malini, Mithu Alur's baby daughter affected by cerebral palsy. 'Once the brain is damaged, it is damaged for life. Nothing can be done about it.' He then added that Malini won't go on to achieve much and will remain 'a vegetable'.[1]

The bleak prognosis, pronounced matter-of-factly after Malini was born in 1966, reflected the prevailing attitudes within the medical and educational communities in India with respect to cerebral palsy. Brain damage was a severely limited and hopelessly inadequate way of coming to terms with the complexities and granularities of this condition, which is classified by major types (ataxia, athetosis, spastic), which can be attended by a mix of other dysfunctions, and can vary from mild to moderate to severe.

Luckily for the Alurs, there was an opportunity to pull Malini out of this seemingly hopeless situation. There was family, in the form of her sister Mita Nundy and her doctor husband Samiran, two key figures in the dawn of the movement, who were able to organize her assessment and early treatment in England. The Alurs also had access to resources for relocating to England to oversee Malini's education and put her on a path that has seen her become a leading disability rights activist, the author of an autobiographical book, and the subject of film that is loosely based on her life.[2]

The Birth of a Movement

Alur trained as a special educator in England and returned to India with a sense of purpose and a recognition of possibilities. 'What about the other Malinis?', namely those who cannot avail of the same services, was a recurring thought. And so, in a modest way, one that possibly could not have foretold that it would spawn a major transformation, a small centre was started, modelled on the Cheyne Centre in London. What began in 1972 in Bombay with three students was a 'second birth' for Alur—the Spastics Society of India (SSI), later renamed ADAPT (Able Disabled All People Together).

Alur's fledgling would grow quickly, and over the years, it would seed progeny, of which I focus on three other institutions—the spastics societies that were set up in Calcutta, Delhi and Madras. Today, there are a large number of institutions that admit children with cerebral palsy, in virtually every part of the country. But there is a case for believing that the Spastics Societies set up in the four cities (which have now all been renamed) acted as a major catalyst in training teachers, therapists and parents, and imparting the technical expertise required to provide a rounded and holistic education for children with cerebral palsy.[3]

It is possible to maintain that India was extremely late in setting up centres for children with cerebral palsy, but it is important to recognize that there has always been a worldwide gap between identification and rehabilitation. The term cerebral palsy coined by Dr William Osler entered the lexicon as early as 1887, but the underlying condition was known even a few decades earlier thanks to the work of Dr William John Little, who published a series of lectures on the 'nature and treatment of deformities to the human frame'. Even so, one of the largest health organizations in the United States, the United Cerebral Palsy Association, was founded only in 1950. In Britain, the National Spastic Society, renamed 'Scope' in 1994, was established in 1952.

Influencing a Systemic Response

Another similarity between the Indian experience and that abroad is that the critical push for setting up schools, founding associations, and pressuring government to take notice came from parents of children with cerebral palsy. In Britain, it was parents in the early 1950s that raised money and were at the forefront of challenging attitudes towards disability. It was 'a growing network of parent-led organizations, which were united through membership of the National Spastics Society' that created the conditions for children with cerebral palsy to have better access to education.[4] In the United States, the United Cerebral Palsy Association was co-founded by Leonard and Isabelle Goldenson, after their daughter died from the condition at the age of twenty-nine.[5] In short, it was parents that led the battle to establish that many children with cerebral palsy were unfairly dismissed as unsuitable for education.

Likewise in India, parents led the push to create the conditions for the education of children with cerebral palsy. One distinctive feature perhaps was that, despite the size of the country, the other three pioneering spastics society schools—Calcutta, Delhi and Madras—were linked, in one way or another, to the one in Bombay. In Calcutta, Sudha Kaul founded the West Bengal Spastics Society and set up a Centre for Special Education in 1974, a couple of years after Bombay (It has since been renamed Indian Institute of Cerebral Palsy [IICP]). When her son was diagnosed with cerebral palsy, Kaul took him to Scope in England. After returning to India, the IICP began operating from a couple of rooms in the Ballygunge Military Camp. Kaul was able to avail of help from Scope, a close circle of friends in Calcutta, and benefit from listening to the experiences of Alur over a fortnight during a trip to Bombay ('She told me all that was needed to start a centre').[6] In Delhi, it was Alur's sister and Malini Chib's aunt, Mita Nundy, who, with friends Meenu Jalan and Anita Shourie, founded, in 1978, the Delhi chapter of the Spastics Society of Northern India, later re-christened as AADI (Action for Ability Development and Inclusion). And in Madras, a branch of the SSI (now called Vidya Sagar) would be set up by Poonam Natarajan, the mother of a son with cerebral palsy and one of the earliest to complete the special education course run by the SSI in Bombay.

Garnering Government Support

Two things emerge from the narratives of the founding of these four institutions. Deeply affecting personal circumstances were the catalyst for creating the momentum and the environment for what became a professional and socially-conscious mission. Second, that although the first steps were taken without government support, this would come quickly—and in the form of an invaluable asset when it comes to institution-building in large Indian cities—land. To some extent, it helped that most of the people who led the mission were socially well-connected. But the move from smaller centres, which ranged from a garage in Natarajan's residence to rented premises in a small Colaba bungalow, could not have taken place without governments—both at the state and central level—being sympathetic and supportive of the cause.

There were those such as former Prime Minister Indira Gandhi who were extremely supportive of the initiatives taken in Bombay and Calcutta. The backing of governors and chief ministers was also critical for the growth of these institutions. At that time, there were no government schools for children with multiple disabilities. There was also a lack of technical expertise in the knowledge and application of rehabilitative techniques in this area. In such an environment, there was possibly an underlying pragmatic consideration as well for ensuring the viability and success of non-government initiatives in this area. In Bombay, the state government came forward to help with land and grants; together with assistance from a clutch of international donors, a brand-new building, customized for people with disabilities, was constructed in Bandra West. In Calcutta, a long lease facilitated by the then chief minister led the IICP to move to its current location on Taratala Road. AADI in Delhi was allotted land in the prime Hauz Khas area, thanks in no small measure to then Lt. Governor Jagmohan. In Madras, Natarajan had to struggle somewhat harder as government offers of land had to be withdrawn six times as a result of legal complications. But after a six year wait, she secured land in Kotturpuram in the heart of the city.

Education and Empowerment

The initial years had a twin focus—children and their parents. Children were provided rehabilitation services in the form of special education and therapy. There was also attention paid to extra-curricular activities, an attempt to impart as holistic an education as possible. This was a small but important part of the overall programme, going as it did a long way in demonstrating that schools for cerebral palsy could be happy, vibrant places with smiling and excited children. This helped to dispel public misconceptions that such schools were essentially gloomy places, the educational equivalents of treatment centres.

At the same time, a lot of attention was given to the education and empowerment of parents. 'In the early years, in some ways, they were the main stakeholders,' reflects Kaul.[7] It was apparent that parents needed to come on board as partners for rehabilitation to be effective. It was important to treat them with respect and to acknowledge their contribution to their children's development. Their socio-economic backgrounds were irrelevant. One of the critical values of the four spastics societies was that parents only paid what they could afford, something that helped in the shaping of institutions that catered to a diverse set of families. It was recognized that parents needed to come to grips with the condition of their children, and its implications for the future. And that it was natural for parents to be confused or simply bewildered with what they were up against. Getting them to understand the condition was a priority and empowering them to take charge of the situation was an absolute necessity. In time, this helped to create a pool of resource people in the community—some who were trained informally, and others who had completed courses in special education run by the four societies.

There was a recognition that formal education and the presence of a skilled multi-disciplinary team was critical to going forward. In Bombay and Calcutta, the presence of two British physiotherapists (Pamela Stretch and Tessa Hamlyn) helped in creating a measure of this. And while Alur, Kaul, Reena Sen (Calcutta) and Meenu Jalan (Delhi) went on to register and receive doctorates in England for their work in special education, it was essential to formally train staff in India. The first formal course, a postgraduate diploma in special education (Multiple Disabilities: Physical and Neurological) was set up by ADAPT in Bombay in 1978.[8] Similar courses were started at the spastics societies after their founding in Calcutta, Delhi and Madras. Around a decade or so ago, they became two-year courses, a part of the bachelor of education (BEd) programme, that has university recognition.

But even before this, the formal one-year course had begun to attract students from other parts of the country. A number of them went on to start schools of their own, for example, Deepak Kalra in Jaipur, Ketaki Bordolai in Assam, Manjula Patankar in Gwalior. There is also Ishwari, an unschooled parent who received only informal training at the Madras centre, who went on to start and run a centre in Mayiladuthurai in Tamil Nadu. Parallelly, she studied to complete her schooling. All these organizations became a part of a loose and informal network that learnt and benefitted from each other.

Expanding the Network

Another way the network expanded was through community-based rehabilitation (CBR) programmes. These took rehabilitation services to smaller towns and villages around the country, to places where people had no access to them. In a pioneering venture, AADI in Delhi in 1980 launched a project that offered rehabilitation services to children with multiple disabilities in rural Dayalpur, a village near Ballabgarh town in Haryana.[9] The project was undertaken in partnership with the All India Institute of Medical Sciences in New Delhi. In Calcutta, CBR programmes began with a collaboration with Visva-Bharati University and local youth clubs, which together ran monthly clinics in rural areas of Birbhum district.[10] In Madras, Vidya Sagar's impact was far and wide, reaching far-flung areas of rural Tamil Nadu, a result of its decision to partner with a wide array of NGOs, engaged in education and development, that were already working at the grassroots. Over the years, the focus of CBR programmes expanded with the spastics societies getting involved with issues such as health, nutrition and access to mainstream or inclusive education. The Madras and the Delhi centres went a step further by including mental health in their CBR ambit, a decision that involved training the staff in this area. One result of the CBR programmes was that the four organizations changed from being smaller outfits into considerably more complex ones. The expansion of their footprints—in terms of geography and the widening nature of their work—was a result of the expertise they had developed internally over the years.

It is undeniable that some of this expertise owed to developments of new techniques and approaches in the West. The organizations maintained links with institutions and experts in the West and availed of their services with the help of government and non-government funding. One important consequence of this was the introduction of programmes such as Alternative and Augmentative Communication (AAC), essentially methods, sometimes with help of devices, that help people with limited or no verbal skills to communicate with others.

But new techniques and approaches, including AAC, often needed to be creatively adapted to suit the Indian environment and circumstances. For example, in India, the emphasis on family-based rehabilitation was far greater, given that the larger family—siblings, uncles, grandparents etc—was often involved in providing support to children and their parents. At another level, support from families was also critical to the founding of the centres in Bombay, Calcutta and Madras. In interviews with the author, Alur, Kaul and Natarajan said it would have been difficult, or almost impossible, to have done this without the support of extended family. For instance, Kaul's parents, her sister-in-law and niece were some of the members of her family that assumed responsibilities for looking after her son.

The Push for Inclusivity

But spastics societies (as well as other agencies dealing with disabilities) would undergo an arguably more radical change—one of outlook. These were a result of the idea of inclusive education taking hold around the turn of the century. This idea of course predates this time by a long way. For instance, in 1974, the Integrated Education for the Disabled Child was launched to provide children with mild disabilities the necessary infrastructural and financial support for an education in mainstream schools. It was launched all over the country and an attendant programme to train teachers for this purpose was also instituted. The programme had its limitations, and was eventually withdrawn. However, it played a role in acquainting policy makers with the concept of integration, a nascent first step in getting them to review educational services with an eye on inclusion.[11]

The global effort to push for education for all as a fundamental right culminated in a gathering in 1994 in Salamanca, Spain. Representatives of ninety-two governments and twenty-five international organizations gathered under the umbrella of the United Nations Educational, Scientific and Cultural Organization (UNESCO) to declare that inclusion should be the rule when it comes to the education of children with disability. In short, physical, intellectual or verbal abilities should not be used as a measure for denying them access to mainstream schools. One result of the Salamanca declaration was the globalization of the idea of inclusive education. As for organizations that ran special schools, this idea implicitly contained the intimations of their own mortality, at least theoretically. At a practical level, the enormous challenges to implement a true and thoroughgoing inclusivity still remains, and so the special schools still retain an enormous relevance in the rehabilitation of children with multiple disabilities. It would eventually lead AADI of Delhi to take the revolutionary step of shutting down its special school and sending its children into mainstream schools, both government and private. It was a bold and arguably controversial decision, but one that took the idea of inclusion to its logical end. They did, however, carry on their advisory and assessment centres and support to parents, states Meenu Jalan.

A year after Salamanca, India, passed a legislation called Persons With Disabilities (Equal Opportunities, Protection of Rights and Full Participation) Act, 1995, also known as the PWD Act, 1995, which underlined that all children with disability should have access to free and adequate education. While this was another step forward, the act became a catalyst of sorts for a larger movement. There were two aspects to this. The first was focused very specifically on the shortcomings of the 1995 Act. It was criticized on many counts, starting with defining the notion of disability in much too narrow a way. Ironically, it was this very shortcoming that spurred or gave an impetus to a larger cross-disability movement. Rather than focus on specific impairments or their 'own' disabilities, there was both an ethical as well as a pragmatic ground for being in favour of a cross-disability effort. First, such a position rose above a certain self-interest and strengthened their moral case against segregationism. And then, at a practical level, there was strength in numbers; according to some conservative estimates, disabled people in India number nearly three crore.

The growth of a distinct advocacy movement among, and for, people with disabilities got further entrenched in the language of rights. The disabled were no longer asking for state benevolence, they were merely asserting their fundamental social and economic rights. Parallelly, there was a paradigmatic shift from a view that regarded the disabled as socially dysfunctional, a narrow medical view, to one that regarded the disabled as the collective responsibility of the community. It was no longer the disabled that needed to adapt. This was the task of society.

The growth of the cross-disability movement and the increasing emphasis on advocacy as a tool for social and economic reform led the United Nations General Assembly to adopt a Convention of the Rights of Persons with Disabilities in December 2006. It stressed individual autonomy, non-discrimination and full and effective participation and inclusion in society. India ratified the convention a year later, but the move to radically overhaul the PWD Act of 1995 had already fructified. The Rights of Persons with Disabilities Act, 2006 (RPWD Act, 2006), a more comprehensive legislation, which expanded the definition of disability by including, among other categories, people with mental illness and autism, and providing for reservation in government and government-aided institutions of higher education and government jobs for those with benchmark disability, defined as at least 40 per cent of those disabilities recognized under the act. Work on this legislation had of course begun some years earlier. Sudha Kaul, from IICP, who was chosen as chairperson of the committee to formulate the provisions of the new bill, played a critical role in seeing it through. Natarajan, who was chairperson of the National Trust for Welfare of Persons with Autism, Cerebral Palsy, Mental Retardation and Multiple Disabilities, at the Ministry of Social Justice and Empowerment, was a part of this committee.

The final shape of the RPWD Act, 2006, owed to the inputs from many people, not the least from that of the late Javed Abidi, who was at the forefront in trying to mobilize different organizations from the early 1990s to create a pan-Indian cross-disability rights advocacy campaign. In 1999, he founded the National Disability Network. Vidya Sagar became the south zone partner of the organization, setting it on a path of advocacy and campaigns for appropriate laws and policies for people with disability. Each of the four organizations discussed here had their own approaches to the advocacy question, but there was no doubt that there was a marked shift from service delivery to campaigning for the rights of the disabled. Since such advocacy called for people with disability to fight for their rights and assert their independence, it was probably no accident that they became increasingly involved in the campaigns. Many children who were educated in these organizations—for example, Malini Chib in Mumbai, Jeeja in Kolkata,

Alok from Delhi, and Rajiv from Chennai, to name only a few—formed a youthful vanguard of the advocacy movement.

Still Miles to Go

But has that involvement of people with disabilities been enough? Has enough attention been fostered to creating an environment where such people can play critical decision-making roles in organizations? It is here that some disability activists feel, and perhaps with some justification, that the four spastics societies, and indeed other organizations working on disability, have not done enough. While there is an acknowledgement that these organizations have played a vital role in foregrounding cross-disability discourse in India, there is a feeling that they could have done more to break down the barriers to full participation in the movement. For instance, Meenakshi Balasubramanian of the Centre for Inclusive Policy and co-founder of Equals (Centre for the Promotion of Social Justice) acknowledges the central role played by the spastics societies in promoting the cross-disability movement. At the same time, she feels they should have played a greater role in influencing the legal and administrative framework. 'Though people from these organizations have been on consultative bodies of the government, there was not a great deal of influence exercised on the policy front. For example, in the making of the RPWD Act, there should have been greater heed paid to what people with disabilities wanted.'

There is a feeling among disability rights activists that changes in the overall framework could be effected more quickly if those with disabilities are made the primary stakeholders within organizations such as the spastics society. Rajiv Rajan, a Fellow with the Global Disability Summit Team of the International Disability Alliance, believes it is important for them to have people with disabilities at higher levels, on the executive as well as the board. 'Decisions are made at the top. And we need people at this level as well,' he says. One way to do this could be to lend greater support to Disabled People's Organizations, namely those established by and for disabled people. The support is needed because most often these are smaller organizations which find it difficult to sustain themselves. For instance, Vaishnavi Jayakumar, co-founder of The Banyan, an NGO working with homeless and mentally ill women in Chennai, argues that after having done so much to bring diverse disability groups together, there is a case for the spastics societies to get—paradoxically—'a little selfish'. 'It is not sufficiently acknowledged that cerebral palsy is a multiple disability. It continues to be recognized as a locomotor disability. As a result, those with the condition are being left behind,' she says.

The call to foreground the disabled in the disability movement is something that cannot be ignored by the spastic societies and other centres working with people with cerebral palsy and multiple disabilities in the long run. It will be an important step in the battle they have waged towards changing attitudes, reforming policies, and introducing more equitable laws. Even so, the dream of a thoroughgoing integration and inclusivity remains distant.

In India, the challenges for inclusive education are numerous and created by a number of issues such as inadequate teacher preparation, poor physical infrastructure and inadequate financial resources. While there are many more children in mainstream schools today than before, there has been a parallel growth in the number of special schools, which are a sober reminder of how much remains to be done. But the important thing is that the spastics societies and the disability movement at large have begun to force a change in mindset, by advocating that inclusiveness is not something granted by benevolence or a sense of altruism, but a systemic problem that can and needs to be fixed. It is from such progressive ideas that real changes are ushered.

7

Gram Vikas and the MANTRA for Inclusive Community Development

LIBY T. JOHNSON

GRAM VIKAS[1] EMERGED FROM THE work of a group of university students from then Madras, among the Kondh Adivasi communities in Ganjam district of southern Orissa. Invited by the district administration in 1976 to set up a dairy unit and promote commercial dairying among the rural/Adivasi communities, the group found that earning money from animal husbandry was not among the priorities of the villagers.

The communities were struggling with problems of debt caused by the exploitative nexus of moneylenders and liquor merchants. It led to bonded labour and alienation from their own resources. Poor health and nutrition—particularly among women and children—was another issue, as was abysmal access to primary education. Thus, dairying was far from being a priority for these communities.

Gram Vikas decided to start by first mobilizing village communities. Initially, it tried to understand and claim their legal and social entitlements, and later began to manage inclusive and dignified development processes. This became the core of Gram Vikas' work, and over the last forty-three years, it has impacted 1,10,000 households in 599 gram panchayats of twenty-seven districts in Odisha and Jharkhand.

Community Mobilization—Gandhian and Conscientization Approaches

In the late 1970s and early 1980s, Gram Vikas tried to address the immediate needs of Adivasi villages through its interventions in healthcare and literacy while also taking a long-term view on other issues. Its work in healthcare spanned the preventive, promotive and curative aspects. It also conducted the training of community health workers and helped villages set up and run *balwadis* (preschool centres), non-formal education centres and adult literacy centres in present-day Ganjam, Gajapati and Kalahandi districts of Odisha. Its work in these areas helped Gram Vikas connect with and build trust among the local communities.

Over time, with the spread of the Integrated Child Development Services (ICDS) Scheme—a pan-India scheme that seeks to improve the nutrition and health of children aged six and below—and other public primary health programmes in the villages, Gram Vikas' work shifted from delivery of health services to building awareness and access. Gram Vikas soon realized that non-formal education was not sufficient and that there was a need for quality education facilities in remote villages. In 1982, it established the Kerandimal Middle Education school in Kankia, Ganjam district. It was a residential school for Adivasi and Dalit children. In 1999, it was expanded to a high school named Gram Vikas High School.

Three more residential schools were set up in remote locations in the Ganjam, Gajapati and Kalahandi districts between 1992 and 2003. They continue to attract many students, with over 1,200 children enrolled at present. The schools, which are managed by independent trusts, have set high standards for quality, and offer affordable education to children from remote villages.

In the late 1970s, a people's organization called Kerandimal Gana Sangathan—led by young men from the villages—started a campaign to challenge the moneylenders. Gram Vikas lent legal and organizational support to the campaign, which became significant in helping communities from over a hundred villages in Ganjam free themselves from debt and secure their land rights. Gram Vikas also helped with the formation of women's self-help groups, which apart from savings also addressed issues of rampant alcoholism in the rural areas. Efforts in afforestation—which leveraged the national programme in wasteland development in the mid-1980s—helped bring together village communities to address common concerns such as deforestation and regulating the practice of slash-and-burn agriculture.

Gram Vikas' early efforts in community and social mobilization were aimed at building local capacities, improving quality of life and enabling the Adivasis to make choices that helped them to live with dignity. The approach was a mix of Sarvodaya principles from Gandhian thought and the conscientization process advocated by Paulo Freire. Gram Vikas applied this approach for about twenty years with satisfactory results. However, one of the key shortcomings was the absence of tangible and clearly measurable markers of short-term outcomes.

Four decades later, it is evident that Gram Vikas' early efforts in human development have led to substantial improvements in the overall social and economic situation in these areas. The difficulty in attributing reasons for the change persists, as it would with most social development processes.

Technology for Development

Gram Vikas' failed attempt at promoting dairying in its early days gave rise to another stream of work: promoting biogas as a renewable and environment-friendly source of energy for cooking. The biogas programme was launched in collaboration with the Government of Orissa and was one of the first instances of a non-government organization working with the government to provide technical inputs and implement a last-mile intervention to rural communities on a state-wide scale. Between 1982 and 1993, Gram Vikas helped more than 54,000 households in nearly 6,000 villages—covering twenty-five of Orissa's thirty districts—build biogas plants, and trained about 6,000 people from rural communities as 'barefoot technicians' during the programme.

All along, small adjustments were made to the technical processes to adapt them to local conditions. Before Gram Vikas exited from the programme in 1993, it helped most of these trained people to become self-employed mechanics who could provide technical services for building and maintaining biogas plants. Several of them set up development organizations to promote renewable energy in rural Orissa and later diversified into other aspects of development.

Gram Vikas decided to withdraw from the biogas programme for various reasons: the intervention focused on households which already had some assets, cattle in this case, and by extension were 'better off' than others. A large part of the biogas programme was implemented in villages predominantly non-Adivasi, with a very different social structure from the Adivasi communities. Inequality and exclusion were the norm, and work on the biogas programme offered Gram Vikas very little scope to engage with the village community as a whole. By then, the biogas programme had also become a standard government scheme and there was little value addition that Gram Vikas offered. By exiting from the biogas programme while it was at its peak, Gram Vikas demonstrated the importance of leaving at the appropriate time and undertaking role transformation to continue to be relevant to the community.

Lessons from Two Conflicting Approaches

The first two decades of Gram Vikas' work demonstrated how a community-focused grassroots organization can balance two seemingly conflicting approaches to development. The first approach—through social mobilization—focused on the rights of rural communities and worked towards their empowerment through intensive and deep engagement in 'softer' aspects of development. This often required standing up to the local administration and enabling the communities to question agencies of governance. The second approach—through 'demystified' techno-managerial solutions—focused on mobilizing rural communities around building physical infrastructure to enable a better quality of life. This required working with government agencies and mobilizing public resources. These approaches are examples of how small non-governmental organizations can innovate, build systems and deliver results at scale.

Towards the end of the first two decades of work—which coincided with the start of the new millennium—Gram Vikas attempted to integrate its experiences with the 'social mobilization' and 'techno-managerial' approaches into a holistic process of development. The Rural Health and Environment Programme in the mid-1990s was developed to become Gram Vikas' flagship intervention, with water and sanitation as the entry point. The principles of MANTRA, the Movement and Action Network for Transformation of Rural Areas—which emerged from lessons learnt over these first two decades—have guided Gram Vikas' work since the early 2000s.

Water and Sanitation for Inclusive Community Development

One of the common and persistent problems in villages was the increasing incidence of morbidity and mortality arising from the consumption of unclean water created by the unsafe disposal of human faeces. Human waste in its raw form found its way to the same water bodies people depended on for their daily needs. As the problem affected everyone in the village with no regard of wealth or caste, it presented the opportunity to explore community-owned and managed integrated water and sanitation solutions as a means of bringing communities together to solve a common problem.

There were additional factors which convinced the team this was an idea worth intervening in. In the absence of proper mechanisms for sanitation, women bore the indignity of defecating in the open. To have some level of privacy, they rose before dawn and had to endure the humiliation of searching for discrete locations to defecate. Women also spent the better part of their day fetching water for their household needs, a drudgery which became more acute during summer, when they spent hours traversing four or five kilometres to fetch water. In many villages, the women took their girl children with them to fetch the extra little water they could carry, or gave them other household responsibilities. This meant that sending girls to school was given lower priority, and as a result school enrolment and attendance for girl children were abysmal.

In the villages of Orissa, social exclusion—of Dalit, Adivasis, backward castes, widows and women in general—had grown into a deep-rooted hegemonic system, where the excluded believed that it was their fate to be excluded, and those excluding them believed it was their right to do so. Clearly, to improve their health status and quality of life, it was necessary to have a process where communities went through an experiential learning of social inclusion. For the individual and collective good, it was important to have a 'win-win' solution for all the stakeholders in the village. Every person's demand for drinking water was more or less the same, making drinking water an 'uncontested domain'. Thus, water and sanitation was seen as a critical entry point through which the village community could come together to have their first experiential learning of 'inclusion'. Those who had been previously excluded from most development activities, now become part of the progress of the entire community. Even those who had been perpetuating exclusion benefitted, since from the point of view of environmental sanitation, it was in their interest that every individual in the village has access to a means of safe disposal of human waste.

Gram Vikas realized that institutional mechanisms could be developed around this programme, which would be the first instance of a community jointly managing their own village institutions and financial resources. The marginalized sections of the community got the opportunity to sit together with the more powerful groups and negotiate village-related issues on equitable terms. In the integrated water and sanitation programme, the following institutional and infrastructure systems were established in the participating villages:

- Twin-pit pour flush toilets and bathing rooms for every family
- A piped water-supply system with a source (borewell, sanitary well or spring), pumped using electric or solar power or gravity flow into an overhead water reservoir or sump and distributed through two or three taps per family
- A village development committee or village water and sanitation committee handling the ownership and management of the water and sanitation system
- A village corpus fund, set up with an initial per family contribution of Rs 1,000, maintained in a bank fixed deposit, whose interest income was to be used by the village committee for financial assistance to new families in the village, to build toilets and access water supply to ensure full coverage at all times

- A maintenance fund managed by the village committee to pay for the regular upkeep and repairs of the piped water-supply system

The MANTRA Principles

The integrated water and sanitation programme was built on the five principles collectively known as MANTRA. Its approach has since become the basis of Gram Vikas' work in all sectors. The five principles are:

- *'All or none'—100 per cent inclusion*: This is not only necessary for effectiveness in public hygiene, it also ensures that poor people and those socially excluded are not left out. If not included from the beginning, it is very likely that poor people would find it difficult to join up later, especially in the more sharply stratified villages. Besides ensuring equity, this approach creates a unique opportunity for the entire village to work together towards a shared purpose.
- *'Share costs'*: Everyone needs to make a significant contribution to the initial capital cost and bear the cost of running and maintaining the facility. This helps build people's stake, and ensures they continue to look after the facility, individually as well as by making demands on the village organization.
- The insistence that people *'take responsibility'* from an early stage to generate consensus, mobilize local contributions, manage construction, and take charge of operations and maintenance ensures long-term sustainability. This creates an experience in the community of negotiating with each other and with outsiders, and of working together.
- The programme actively promotes the *'participation of all'*, and takes affirmative steps to ensure that women and poor people are included in the management. Besides empowering marginalized people even if in a limited way, such inclusive processes are essential to ensure that development processes continue to be managed well and for the benefit of all.

- The creation of a *'corpus fund and maintenance fund'* ensures there is 'inbuilt financial sustainability,' that there are sufficient resources for major repairs and to upgrade infrastructure facilities, and that future generations would continue to be served.

Assessment of Gram Vikas' Work in Water and Sanitation

By September 2021, the water and sanitation programme covered 84,000 households in 1,458 habitations of 545 gram panchayats in twenty-five districts of Odisha and two districts of Jharkhand. The programme has received wide recognition at the national and international level. Several independent studies have established the overall efficacy of Gram Vikas' approach. A team led by Esther Duflo had, in 2015, estimated[2] the impact of the integrated water and sanitation improvement programme in providing water connections, latrines and bathing facilities to households in approximately 100 villages. The estimates suggest that the intervention was effective in reducing treated diarrhea episodes by 30–50 per cent. These results are evident in the short term and persist for five years or more.

A matched cohort study in 2019[3] by researchers from a consortium of research institutions led by Emory University compared the intervention villages with non-intervention villages in the area and found that the programme increased toilet coverage (85 per cent vs 18 per cent), toilet use by adults (74 per cent vs 13 per cent) and child faeces disposal (35 per cent vs 6 per cent). Children in the intervention villages also had lower helminth infection and improved height-for-age scores.

Gram Vikas also carried out an internal assessment survey to check the status of the institutional and infrastructure components it had helped set up in villages where the water and sanitation programme had been implemented from 1997 to 2017. The survey was also to identify gaps and obtain necessary information to plan corrective action. It was conducted between August 2018 and January 2020 in two phases. The first phase covered 846 villages in sixty-nine blocks across ten districts; it collected data on governance and management of community institutions, financial mechanisms such as the corpus and maintenance funds and functioning of the water supply system. The second phase, covering 626 villages of the 846 from the first phase, collected data on household profiles, physical status of the toilet–bathing room structures and tap connections, availability of water and the use of toilets and bathing rooms. It covered all the households in the village at the time of the survey, irrespective of whether they were part of the Gram Vikas' intervention in the village. A quarter of the households in the survey were 'new'—i.e., they were not present at the time of the Gram Vikas intervention; 31,255 were 'old'—i.e., existing at the time of the intervention. The key findings of the survey were:

Access and use of sanitation infrastructure: 75 per cent of all the households had a toilet and a bathing room, 4 per cent had only a toilet and 17 per cent had neither. Among households that had been part of the Gram Vikas intervention, 95 per cent had a toilet and a bathing room, while the remaining 5 per cent had had these earlier, but not any longer. A substantial number of households without a toilet had emerged in the village after the Gram Vikas intervention.

The behaviour pattern related to toilet use did not vary substantially between earlier households and newer ones. Overall, 77 per cent of the households in the survey who had access to the infrastructure used the toilets and 76 per cent used the bathing rooms. In households that had been part of the Gram Vikas intervention, usage of toilets was 78 per cent and bathing rooms 76 per cent.

Access and functionality of piped water supply: 75 per cent of all households in the survey were connected to the piped water-supply system in the villages; 24 per cent had never been connected. In households that were part of the Gram Vikas intervention, 92 per cent had access to piped water supply, 6 per cent had never been connected, while 2 per cent had been connected earlier, but were not anymore; 87 per cent of households with a tap connection reported receiving water through the tap.

The Swachh Bharat Mission claims to have achieved its target of making all villages open- defecation free. There are no reliable, realistic and independent sources of data to verify this. The figures from our status assessment of toilet access and use and of functional tap connections look promising, considering the overall situation in Odisha, but for Gram Vikas it was a sobering assessment, given that the 100 per cent coverage principle, fundamental to its approach, had not been achieved.

The survey allowed for a better understanding of factors contributing to the lack of full functionality of village and household infrastructure. In the piped-water system these included failure of the water source, seasonality in water availability, issues with the village electricity supply, inadequacy of a pipeline to cover all households and physical expansion of the village that rendered the system non-functional in the expanded areas.

Failure of household-level sanitation infrastructure was caused by damages from natural disasters such as cyclones, landslides or floods, deterioration of the structures built and a lack of repairs, as well as insufficient motivation among households to continue to use the facilities. An overall factor contributing to the failure is the lack of leadership in the village to address the shortcomings and limitations of the institutional mechanism.

Demonstrating a Way of Doing—Our Role in Government Interventions

Gram Vikas' approach to integrated water and sanitation for every household in a village was initiated two decades before the national government started its mission to end 'open defecation' in villages. Its experiences from Odisha had contributed substantially to the formulation of the Nirmal Bharat Abhiyan, a precursor to the Swachh Bharat Mission launched in 2014. Five years later, the government launched the Jal Jeevan Mission with the aim of providing a functioning tap connection to every rural household. It prioritized community ownership and management of the facility. Here again, the Gram Vikas model for water and sanitation was acknowledged.

Gram Vikas actively contributed to national-level policy platforms as a member of the Working Group of the Planning Commission on Rural Domestic Water and Sanitation for formulating the Twelfth Five-Year Plan (2012–17). The organization was also a member of the National Task Force set up in 2019 by the Jal Jeevan Mission to review the implementation of rural drinking-water schemes.

Social Inclusion and an Improved Quality of Life

Gram Vikas has had fair success in its work in water and sanitation from a technical perspective, but has its work led to improvements in the wellbeing of the village communities? In many villages, the water and sanitation programme has been an entry point for a comprehensive social development process. The experiences of villages such as Samiapalli[4] and Tamana[5] have received wide attention. About 50 per cent of the villages where the programme was introduced are socially heterogeneous and have a mix of caste groups. In many such villages, the programme contributed to increasing the participation of socially weaker groups in village-level decision making, leading to several instances of lower-caste groups asserting their right to be part of village affairs. The impact of the programme on the condition of women has been positive, even though a lot more can be done. Access to toilets, bathing rooms and tap water has reduced their drudgery and physical toil. In many villages, women now have a prominent role in village-level decision making and community leadership.

These successes can be attributed to the strong focus on building community-level capabilities and institutional processes. Wherever the focus on the MANTRA principles was not diluted, the results have been remarkable. The work of Gram Vikas is almost entirely dependent on grants from donors or programme funds from government schemes. Over the past several years, the scale and time-bound results-orientation of such funds have become more prominent. Our undiluted focus on the MANTRA principles requires that sufficient time is spent on each village, depending on its social and economic conditions. This gets short shrift in time-bound large-scale project funding, where completion of the water and sanitation infrastructure, rather than institutional process, assumes greater importance.

Ensuring Sustainability

There are three aspects of sustainability that need to be examined in the context of Gram Vikas' work with water and sanitation as the entry point.

Institutional: This includes creating village-level managerial and technical capabilities, ensuring social and gender equity as well as access to financial resources for maintenance, expansion and upgradation of the social infrastructure. A critical area where non-government organizations such as Gram Vikas have not done well is in engaging with panchayati raj institutions and building citizen-level capabilities for more effective participation in local governance processes. The effective convergence of village-level institutions and panchayati raj institutions will enable greater sustainability. At the same time, there is need for affirmative and conscious action to ensure social and gender equity at all levels.

Environmental: This is related to the availability and use of natural resources, particularly water. Gram Vikas advocates environmental sustainability at all levels in its programmes. Mountain springs comprise about one-third of the drinking water sources that it had helped harness. The conscious effort to promote springs rather than deep borewells has helped in creating greater understanding and awareness among the village community on the need for sustainable management of hill slopes. Changes wrought by climate change have emerged as critical areas that need attention. Interventions of any kind are bound to have a short shelf-life, given the rapid pace at which changes are taking place in the natural environment.

Behavioural: Access to safe sanitation and clean water can lead to improved health and nutrition outcomes only if the infrastructure components are backed up by strong individual and social behaviours. These include addressing areas of personal hygiene, handling of drinking water, kitchen sanitation and child faeces management. With changes in consumption patterns in rural areas and the resultant increase in the proportion of non-biodegradable waste, the creation of individual, household and village-level systems and appropriate mindsets towards waste management are emerging as areas requiring attention.

Lessons and the Way Forward

Gram Vikas' greatest strength as an organization is its community 'rootedness', which we have sustained over the last four decades. Similarly, the ability to work at significant scale and deliver high-quality results has been consistent. However, we have not been equally rigorous about efficiency: our internal abilities have not matched our growth and this needs to be addressed, along with other critical areas such as quality consciousness, time- and cost-efficiency, and better communication with communities and external stakeholders.

In the current context, state and market appear to have acquired the ability to reach the last mile to address community-level development, and grassroots organizations are not considered as important anymore. The resources to develop and demonstrate innovative solutions to development challenges have shrunk substantially for such organizations. At the same time, improvements in physical connectivity and increased opportunities to migrate and explore the world, have enabled the rural poor, particularly the younger generations, to aspire to a world different from the one their parents lived in. This poses a challenge to Gram Vikas in terms of understanding the changes in the aspirations of rural communities, and continuing to remain relevant to them.

Engaging with local governance and community development

Grassroots organizations like Gram Vikas have not yet effectively found ways of engaging with the local political processes led by the panchayati raj institutions. There continues to be a conflict about who represents citizen interests and how these are taken up at higher levels of governance. Internal capacity building and realigning of work processes will be necessary to resolve this. The constitutional mandate of panchayati raj institutions—particularly the gram panchayat as the local government—cannot be wished away under the guise of 'doing good'. The devolution of funds for development to the three-tier panchayati raj system has accelerated in the past decade or so. While there are many social and political constraints that hamper true and democratic decentralization of power, it is important for organizations like Gram Vikas to make sure that the citizen community, especially those who are from the traditionally weaker sections of society—are made capable of engaging with local governments and local development resource allocation decisions, with knowledge and confidence.

The challenge before Gram Vikas is to scale its successful experience of building people's self-governance institutions to the gram panchayat level to help them become true citizen bodies. This requires working with all habitations within a panchayat. The Water Secure Gram Panchayat Programme is currently being developed to build upon the work done in water, sanitation, livelihoods, technology and building village institutions, and uses natural resource management as the fulcrum for promoting the engagement between citizens and local governments. Gram Vikas aims to work with 1,000 gram panchayats in Odisha by 2030.

Engaging with new aspirations and dreams

Gram Vikas also has to strengthen its work with younger village inhabitants. The aspirational and generational category of 'youth' has been absent in most villages in which Gram Vikas has worked. Boys and girls grew up, took over primary livelihood or household responsibilities and transitioned directly to adults. It is only in the last ten years that adolescents and youth have emerged as a key component of village society, aided by better access to education and information. They now have a distinct identity and voice in community affairs.

Migration for work to locations that pay better wages has emerged as a preferred choice for young men—and, increasingly, women—from south and southwestern Odisha. This is a shift from the traditional forms of migration from Odisha, most of which was driven by distress. This new form of 'aspirational' migration has the potential to change the quality of life and livelihoods for poor communities if sufficient facilitation for safety and dignity is enabled. Studies by Gram Vikas and its partner organizations in four blocks across four districts show that in one-fifth to one-third of the households, there is at least one member who is a migrant worker. Annual bank remittances by migrants to their families back in the villages range from Rs 28 to 60 crore per block, and in several blocks this is equal to the developmental spending of the panchayati raj institutions.

The increasing incidence of migration also introduces many challenges for households and communities. Women who stay behind—mothers, wives or daughters—face emotional issues and difficulties in accessing healthcare services, social protection schemes and simple daily items such as fuelwood. The limited reach of banking services limits the ability of migrants to send money home and of their households to use the money efficiently and effectively. Occupational issues related to wages, payments, benefits and workplace safety and the low skill levels of the migrating people have direct effects on the safety and dignity of the migrants.

Whether or not to migrate for work is an individual decision. A meaningful intervention would ensure that no one in the programme area is left without a choice and having to resort to migration out of distress. The primary focus needs to be on adequate and appropriate livelihood opportunities in the villages. The decision to migrate must be a conscious and informed one made for the overall benefit of the household. The Safe and Dignified Migration Programme has been initiated to address these issues and enable better livelihoods for rural households in twenty-two blocks of six districts of Odisha.

In Conclusion

Despite the seemingly bleak circumstances for grassroots, community-centric development organizations, Gram Vikas has managed to stay ahead of the challenges and remain a pioneer in many ways. Its work will continue to be driven by its core values of inclusion, equity and dignity. The ability to be relevant to rural communities comes from being embedded in the community, seeing people as the most important asset, being open to new ideas and different viewpoints, being transparent about decisions, valuing collaboration at all levels and being flexible enough to respond with agility to changes in the environment.

8

Dastkar: A Crafted Route to Development

LAILA TYABJI

FORTY YEARS AGO, A FEW women friends sat talking about why the skill sets and knowledge systems of craftspeople—India's unique asset in an increasingly industrialized and monocultural world—were being marginalized. Artisanal products had been reduced to cheap tourist bric-a-brac and gift items, their makers regarded as unlettered and redundant. These shared concerns, interspersed with personal memories and laughter, were the genesis of Dastkar.[1]

Dastkar's strength is that it was created out of these varied life experiences and perspectives, rather than being the singular vision of one individual. One of us worked with slum women, another with a Government Handicrafts Corporation, a third with a rural development project in Rajasthan. Bunny Page, the catalyst who brought us together, had worked with and seen the impact of craft as income generation in poverty-ridden Bangladesh after its independence from Pakistan. I was a designer, obsessed with the deterioration of the extraordinary craft and textile traditions I had grown up with. The result was an integrated holistic strategy, incorporating our varied viewpoints, and the needs and potential of the producers themselves.

Four decades on, Dastkar remains as relevant as it was when it began. The Indian craft and handloom sector is the second-largest source of employment after agriculture, and as long as millions of Indians remain dependent on handicraft for a livelihood, they will need support to keep their place in an increasingly professional and demanding marketplace.

Dastkar has grown organically with the craft communities that are its heart and motivating core. Starting with fourteen crafts groups, we work today with 750-plus artisan communities and over 1 lakh craft families in every corner of the country, organizing, training, professionalizing them; adapting and re-designing traditional craft techniques into contemporary products; helping craftspeople hone skills, materials, and production systems and bringing them to the market.

Dastkar's Contributions to the Crafts Sector

Our work and outreach are not visible, but Dastkar and Dastkar-developed crafts are in most shops and homes all over India. Assisted by us, Dastkar craftspeople are now entrepreneurs in their own right, procuring and producing bulk orders, exporting, dealing with retailers directly, owning their own retail outlets, sourcing fabric from each other, developing their own linkages, skills and products on international fashion ramps and trade shows. Over the years, Dastkar has played multiple roles as a:

Bridge between craftsperson and consumer, from Jawaja, Ahmedabad Study Action Group, Mahila Patchwork, and Baan Utpadak Samiti, nervously but triumphantly selling for a few thousand rupees in Delhi for the first time in 1982—to assisting over one lakh artisans to achieve crores of annual sales today. The Dastkar Nature Bazaars in Delhi and other metro cities attract over a lakh visitors and annual sales of over Rs 30 crores. It has become a brand name that is now a catchword for authenticity and quality—in Delhi and all over India.

Designer, supporting artisans from Tilonia, Rajasthan; Self Employed Women's Association (SEWA), Lucknow; Urmul Trust, Rajasthan; Bharati Vikas Manch, Bihar; Sandur Kushala Kala Kendra, Karnataka; Berozgar Mahila Kalyan Sanstha (BMKS), Godda; Banas Crafts, Banaskantha; Naie Kiran, Kashmir; Ladakh Ecological Development Group; and Disha, Rajasthan.

Networker, linking craftspeople all over the world, through the Threadlines International Embroidery Workshop, the OXFAM Craft Study Workshops, the Commonwealth Festival Manchester, the Asia Society Exhibition in New York, the Boros Museum in Sweden, World Craft Councils, etc.

Researcher, documenting crafts and crafts issues, such as the Dastkar OXFAM Study of Post-Independence Indian Craft, Voluntary Health Association of India (VHAI)/Kutch Design Directory, and documentation of Madhubani and Indian embroidery techniques.

International spokesperson representing the Indian craft sector: keynote addresses at International Federation for Alternative Trade; the World Assembly of Alternative Trade Shops, Netherland; the Cumulus Design Conference, Utrecht; the Mainz Conference on Tourism; the Asia Society International Meet, Shanghai; the World Craft Council Conference, China; and so on.

Advocate, for including craft in mainstream policy, including in the Ninth Five-Year Plan in 1985 and the National Council of Educational Research and Training (NCERT) Curriculum Review.

Activist, campaigning against the 1985 Textile Policy and the 2005 excise on handlooms, for the abolition of the Handicraft and Handloom Boards, and supporting the Pashmina Project.

Educationist, linking design and craft through design workshops and diploma projects with National Institute of Fashion Technology, National Institute of Design, Indian Institute of Craft & Design, and Pearl Academy; and with the Dutch/Kutch project with Design Academy Eindhoven, Craft Design Institute Srinagar, and the Indian Institute of Craft & Design. Dastkar is also on the board of prominent design institutions.

Friend in need, mobilizing funds and supportive interventions for the Bihar floods, Kutch and Latur earthquakes, Odisha cyclone, Covid-19 pandemic, through the Dastkar Artisan Support Fund.

Facilitator, for short-term loans to artisans, assisting craftspeople access government schemes and other programmes, and sourcing raw material.

Trainer, honing systems for production, developing production and costing/pricing systems, skilling artisans and creating leadership.

International designer/curator, developing artworks and wall hangings for Aid to Artisans and the Asia Society, New York; the Victoria & Albert Museum, London; Boras Museum, Sweden; Tarshito Warrior of Love series, Italy; Indian embassies abroad; and the Taj chain of hotels.

Consultant and mentor, developing strategies for the United Nations Development Program, VHAI, Rajkot Urban Development Authority, OXFAM, and Aid to Artisans (ATA); evaluating the impact on the craft sector of natural disasters such as the Kutch earthquake, Odisha cyclone, and Covid-19 pandemic; incubating the Commitment to Kashmir project; mentoring SEWA Ruaab and VIRSA Punjab.

Awardee: SANSKRITI Award, ATA Award for Preservation of Craft, the Federation of Indian Chambers of Commerce & Industry (FICCI) and NIFT awards, Padma Shri 2012, and the Crafts Council of India Kamala Lifetime Achievement Award.

As a result of Dastkar's work, incomes are earned, houses are built, villages redesigned, children educated, fed and clothed, and there is sanitation, medicare, and housing. Even more significant is the human growth—the entrepreneurs created, self-esteem built, hope generated, cultural identities preserved, creativity brought forth, thousands of women in control of their lives, the skills and creativity of their hands channelled into empowerment and earning.

Addressing Challenges and Catalysing Change in the Crafts Sector

Despite all this, and while craft remains the second-largest employment sector, lakhs of craftspeople remain marginalized—earning wages lower than unskilled manual labour. Crafts remain a story of skilled but unsung, anonymous hands, their voices silent in public forums, their needs ignored in policy and plans, their tools and traditions seldom upgraded by new technology, their products absent in the burgeoning urban malls.

A Banjara tribal woman, mourning the destruction of her home in the Latur earthquake, said sadly 'From our hands no one will buy. We are no one.' Banjaras are among the most skilled embroiderers in the world: their red skirts, backless cholis and veils are ornamented with mirrors, shells, coins and silver beads, embroidered in appliqued layers of motif and colour. Connoisseurs search for their textiles in antique shops; designers used them as design inspiration. But they themselves have no place in the urban marketplace—no way to benefit from the demand. They work in the fields as casual labour, unaware that if they were to replicate their old pieces, they could be wage earners.

Like most craftspeople, these rural women are the last to benefit from their own traditional skills. This is the paradox that Dastkar seeks to address. Our Latur, Kutch and Sandur projects, and work with the Banjaras, Lambanis, Rabaris and other tribal women, have shown how they can become a successful part of mainstream retail.

Dastkar means 'one who works with his/her hands'—it is the craftsperson rather than the craft that is the focus of our work. Helping develop skills and products is the catalyst and entry point for the economic and social development of the craftspeople. Starting as that informal group of concerned women forty years ago, Dastkar is today a professional organization, working with crafts people all over India, and communities as diverse as the Vankars in Kutch, bead makers from Varanasi, and reclusive, burkha-clad women in Lucknow. Brahmin Madhubani painters as well as Adivasis come from Bihar to participate in the Dastkar Bazaars and workshops, wide-eyed at the unfamiliar city scene. So do Bodo women from the Northeast, mustachioed *regurs* (leatherworkers) from Rajasthan, *kalamkari* artists from Machilipatnam and Kalahasti, victims of insurgency in Kashmir, displaced agricultural labour in Ranthambhore, isolated sheep-herders from the foothills of snow-bound Ladakh, and others.

Dastkar workshops and training help develop both the product and the producer's skills, and the Bazaars help them understand and learn about the market—the needs and usages of the urban consumer and the power and potential of the skill in their own hands. Through Dastkar's design, product development, skill-upgradation, management and production training inputs, they translate that skill into products that are based in tradition yet contemporary, fitting them for the national and global mainstream. The Dastkar Shop and online website, run on a non-profit basis, is a lifeline for several thousand craftspeople—sustaining incomes and livelihoods, as is the permanent Gali-e-Khas at the Dastkar Nature Bazaar.

From Increasing Incomes to Changing Social Equations

Increasing economic returns to the craftspeople helps them feed, clothe and educate their children, dig wells, get proper hospitalization, start bank accounts; it also motivates them to learn to cipher, read and write, changing their own perception of themselves as marginalized, dependent, second-class people. Women who had no names except 'Indira-ki-maa', 'Kalu-ki-aurat' (so-and-so's mother, so-and-so's wife), have turned into Rameshwari, Nafeesa and Sundari. Not only have their names changed, they have too.

In 1985, Dastkar went to SEWA in Lucknow to work with the local *chikankari* women, who were earning about Rs 100–150 a month, housebound and dependent on the local *mahajan* (moneylender) to fetch their work or pay them for it. Sitting with them, embroidering and teaching them new skills and designs, was also a forum for discussing gender, caste, religion and women's rights.

Today, those few dozen SEWA women have grown to over 7,000! They travel all over India, happily doss down and sing bhajans in a dharmsala, or cook biryani at the Mumbai YWCA. They interact with equal ease with male tribals and sophisticated buyers in cities. They march in protest against dowry deaths as well as Islamic fundamentalism, demand financial credit and free spectacles from the government, and confidently refuse to give VIP politicians a discount! They earn in thousands of rupees rather than hundreds, have their own savings bank accounts, and have thrown away centuries of repression and social prejudice along with their burkhas.

When I think of our years with Dastkar, I remember Dhapu, a woman in Rajasthan, whose lack of economic alternatives, fear of the future, family pride and prejudice, had driven her to burn herself to death. I ponder the tragic irony that a few years later Dhapu's daughters were among the most sought-after brides in Sherpur village, due to their earning power and educational possibilities that working as craftswomen in the Dastkar Ranthambhore project had brought them. The local doctor here says he can recognize a Dastkar craftswoman from half a kilometre just by the way she walks and holds her head.

The Journey of Personal Transformation and Finding Purpose

Forty-five years ago, I stepped off a train and found myself in Kutch—flung into the heat, dust and colour of an exciting new adventure—as a visiting designer for Gurjari. In 1978, Kutch was still a mythic, exotic destination, and I was a young, very urban professional. I found it extraordinarily moving that, in this barren landscape, people who toiled all day in the harsh sun still had the motivation to create something beautiful for their homes and themselves. Their thatched, conical mud houses were a reservoir of creativity and craft—every utensil, textile and surface covered with motif and colour—from the carved wooden spokes of their camel cart wheels to their own elaborately embroidered cholis and ghagras.

Working with them to translate these skills into merchandize for the contemporary urban market was a challenging, humbling experience. Sitting cross-legged on a mud floor—without measuring tapes, scale drawings, paper patterns, drafting tables—all the paraphernalia a city-bred designer takes for granted, I learnt a love and respect for rural craftspeople that altered my life.

Returning to Delhi after those catalytic six months, I was plunged into something entirely different. It was early 1979, and the Taj Group was launching Khazana, their retail outlet at the Taj Mansingh Hotel. They invited me to be their chief merchandizer and designer. At the time, there was no one-stop shop for Delhi's culturati other than the Central Cottage Industries Emporium on Janpath. It was a wonderful opportunity to create a new Indian aesthetic and look. Indians were just beginning to move away from imitative western interior décor and re-discovering their own culture and style. We introduced them to handspun home furnishings, folk art, hand-carved

Shekhawati and Sankheda furniture, bidri, brass, mirror-work cushions ... Shopping at Khazana became the 'in' thing.

But as we became more successful, there was pressure from top management to bring in products (diamond jewellery, leather luggage, designer garments) that had higher per unit prices—no more basketry or potted plants; Kashmiri carpets rather than cotton durries—sourced from suppliers who could afford to give goods on a sale or return basis. The imperatives of retail economics meant that both craftspeople and consumers were denied something: the former of employment and earning and, the latter, something they were willing to pay for. It seemed such a paradox. I knew, from my Kutch experience, how much rural craftspeople needed orders and work; and yet the hard logistical and economic realities of urban retail also made sense.

At Kutch began my love affair with crafts and craftspeople; the Khazana experience prompted my joining those other women in conversations that led to Dastkar. If craft was to survive, craftspeople needed to be helped to enter the market directly themselves. Very few commercial retailers, and not even the Government Handicrafts Development Corporations, were willing to invest the time, human resources and money required to turn a traditional craft into a viable mainstream commodity. One needed a non-profit organization like Dastkar, without short-term imperatives or narrow sales margins, to act as a bridge between the craftsperson and consumer —guiding craftspeople in design, product development, skills training and capacity building, and ushering them into the metro market at their own pace.

Forty years later, the success of Dastkar projects like SEWA Lucknow, Berozgar Mahila Kalyan Samiti, Kala Raksha, Dastkar Ranthambhore, Sandur Kushala Kala Kendra, Urmul, Anwesha, Disha, Naie Kiran and many, many more, proves that we were right. Chikan, Lambani and Kutchi embroidery, woven *tasar*, hand-block printing, tribal jewellery, *shibori* and *pattu* weaving, and handmade *juthis* (shoes), are out there on the street, on the fashion ramp, on page three, and all over town—their presence there facilitated by Dastkar interventions and marketing, the artisan groups now sustainable.

Pupul Jayakar, the doyenne of Indian crafts, once said, 'Craft is an economic activity before it is a cultural activity. The centre of the development process is marketing.'

Lessons in Connecting Craftspeople with Markets[2]

Ironically, bazaars and exhibitions were not part of Dastkar's original intent. When we began helping craftspeople develop their skills, we thought that if the product was right a buyer would automatically appear. We had no idea of the invisible wall that separated craftspeople from customers; that a dhoti-clad weaver with the dust of the village on his juthis cannot even enter most export houses, let alone meet the marketing manager. This led to the first Dastkar Bazaar, with craftspeople coming to the Bazaars in Delhi, Bombay, Bangalore, Calcutta—all the metro cities—selling their own products, interacting directly with customers.

In India, much of the labour in the unorganized rural non-farm sector is extremely skilled—possessing unique techniques and traditions that can be tapped for domestic and international markets, generating export and tourism. There is a curious paradox though, that while both government and corporate social responsibility (CSR) schemes are willing to fund projects creating rural employment and vocational training centres abound for carpet weaving, tailoring, embroidery, wood and metal craft, and so on—there is seldom money available for marketing and promoting the finished products. As a result, micro success stories, like those I have mentioned above, are not converted into macro international block blusters.

Globalization and liberalization have changed the face of the Indian market and the psyche of the Indian consumer, putting new pressures on the craft sector and small producers. These new pressures need a new perspective. If traditional craft techniques and their producers are to survive, they cannot remain static—locked in mindsets, production systems and marketing strategies now outdated. A failure to classify craft properly lies at the root of much confusion and failure. Focal needs get confused; inputs get diffused.

Working in a craft community, we need first to identify and classify both skill and product; where change (in materials, functions, technology, or markets) would benefit the craft, and where it would inextricably do damage. Having established the core value system and context of the craft, we should not cross this line. Training and sensitizing NGOs and government staff working in the sector to these issues and to the cultural and technical aspects of the crafts with which they work is crucial. Finding new opportunities to suit the tastes of the contemporary market without compromising traditional aesthetics, while leaving space for individual creativity and cultural meaning, is the test of a successful craft intervention.

We need also to be aware that there is often a conflict when buyers have wanted products tailored to current trends or lower prices. Simultaneously, we cannot ignore the need for alleviation of poverty, or the need to create more employment. 'We want work, work and work. If we have work, we live. If we have work, we eat. No work, no future,' reminds Rani Bai, a craftswoman from Anternes village in Gujarat.

Therefore, part of our role is to also sensitize the buyer. Crafts are not just part of our aesthetic and culture, they are the bread of life for millions of craftspeople. Ironically, while figures show that sales of craft, both domestic and export, have doubled or tripled over the last decades, we are simultaneously losing 10 per cent of our craftspeople every ten years. In a period where we are worrying about rural migration to overcrowded cities, we need to build on these existing skills and invest in their makers. However, we should also be aware that not all crafts and skills are immediately viable. Where there is a need, there is not necessarily a potential. Stockpiles of unsold goods made in good faith lead to disillusionment and further hardship, while subsidizing the unsellable alienates the consumer. Strategies need to be long term, with marketing research to support them.

Another important point to remember is that craft is not one sector—it is a multiplicity of skills, communities, traditions, needs. Lots of us get upset when craft is called 'a product', we need to be equally sensitive about not treating craftspeople as products. As the veteran master craftsperson of bronze icons, Parameshwar Acharya, indignantly spluttered at a crafts seminar, 'They lump us together with cobblers and pot makers!' Baskets and brooms, furniture, folk art, garments and jewellery do not all sell in the same craft emporium—functional products get edged out by high value ones. Creating a new product range and finding a market for it are part of the same cyclic process. There is need to talk about the importance of 'institutional innovation' in the craft sector.

Dastkar Bazaar became the inspiration for Dilli Haat and similar spaces all over India. There had of course been exhibitions of handicrafts in the past, but never one with craftspeople themselves (from all over India) selling their own products. How dependent the craftspeople were at the time! We picked them up from the railway station, set up their stalls, organized accommodation and food—on some occasions even bedding and warm clothing; so different from the confident world travellers of today.

The Benefits of Bazaars[3]

What are the pros and cons of craft marketing through bazaars? Firstly, and most importantly, it is one occasion where the craftsperson is the centre of attention—getting the kind of exposure, publicity, visibility and focus that artisans otherwise do not get in urban metros. They are an opportunity to highlight not only crafts products and skills, but the problems and potential of the sector. Infographics, craft demonstrations, workshops for children ... mixing awareness along with sales pays dividends.

The second advantage is the ability to attract a wide cross-section of buyers, including those who would not normally buy craft—the kind who do not frequent craft emporia or up-market exhibitions in art gallery venues. There is otherwise a caste system in shopping: people who go to the Santushti complex boutiques would not go to Khadi Bhandar, and the Sarojini Market shopper feels awkward in Anokhi. There is a false perception that handcraft is 'exclusive'; meant only for 'elite' rich customers.

One of the delights of our four decades in the business is seeing more and more people actually buying and enjoying craft—realizing there is something for everyone. As one east Delhi buyer delightedly exclaimed: *'yeh toh Sadar Bazaar se susta bhi hai or sunder bhi hai!* (this is cheaper than Sadar Bazaar and prettier too!)' At our first 1982 bazaar our mailing list consisted of 250 names, all known, recognizably 'craft-y' types—big bindis, 'ethnic' sarees, chunky silver jewellery and chauffeur-driven cars. Today our Delhi mailing list runs into thousands, ranging from Patparganj academics to Punjabi Bagh traders—students, diplomats, housewives, yuppies, the media, activists, wholesalers, bureaucrats. Creating a space where the young can discover craft (60 per cent of Indian consumers are now under the age of thirty) is also important; otherwise GenNext goes to the malls.

Most importantly, the Bazaar is a learning place. Craftspeople realize the value of their own products, but also the importance of quality, functionality, and finish. Discovering that a product being colour-fast and correctly sized is as important as its ornamentation, can be a tube-light moment. Learnings are also about packaging, presentation and display, and how to talk to customers. Craftspeople interact directly with consumers, learning about tastes, trends, and colour preferences. Instruction passed on at workshops and trainings, in letters or lectures, about quality control or sizing, suddenly comes home in the most direct way possible. There is nothing like seeing others make sales to drive home a message! Interacting with other crafts groups in the Bazaar and at the dharamsalas or guest houses where they stay gives collective confidence, and is its own learning. The knock-on exhilaration from another craftsperson's Rs 15 lakh sale is a great catalyst for a crafts group participating for the first time in an urban milieu.

How an exhibition looks, and how it is advertised are also important. Our distinctive displays, combined with visually attractive and evocatively worded mailers, press releases and advertisements, have been influential in establishing Dastkari Bazaars as a recognized brand name all over India, synonymous with good craft. When the internet and social media took over urban mindsets, Dastkar was the first to jump on that wagon. Today we have several lakh followers on multiple platforms. We no longer send physical cards—emails, WhatsApp, Facebook and Instagram have replaced them.

Mega craft success stories like SEWA Lucknow, Sandur, Banascrafts, BMKS, Dastkar Ranthambore, Urmul, Kala Raksha, Chirag, Anwesha, Naie Kiran, Disha and the ant, all had their first market exposure at a Dastkar Bazaar. I remember Urmul fearfully bringing stock worth Rs 1 lakh to a Dastkar Bazaar in 1988; they sold Rs 85,000 worth of it and never looked back.

The Bazaar is a good place to test-market products, and discover what moves and what does not. It can help set targets for your own effectiveness and impact. It provides immediate data—on growth, sales variations and customer preferences. Only when you understand your potential market, and build both your production and product ranges, should you venture into your own shop or into solo marketing. Craftspeople must remember that great turnovers may not necessarily result in great profits. They need to calculate hidden expenses and unsold goods, do proper costings and understand the intricacies of goods and services tax. Fixed prices, proper bills and no bargaining, are something that is very important if crafts, and craftspeople, are to be respected.

The Bead-work Craftswomen of Hapur: Reluctant Entrepreneurs

A few years ago, Dastkar was approached to help a group of village women in Hapur, one of the poorest districts in Uttar Pradesh. The women were bead-workers—burkha-clad and illiterate. Their village had five masjids but no school! They strung glass beads for the export market for Rs 10–15 per day. An international mega-chain had sponsored the training, but backed out of giving the promised orders, resulting in frustration and bitterness. Dastkar invited the women to Nature Bazaar, then two months away, and also developed some new products targeted at the Indian retail market. Raw material was bought with a small loan from another Delhi NGO.

Come Nature Bazaar, the women had to be forcibly pushed into the jeep bringing them to the Bazaar. It was 'against their culture'; 'what would the community say?', 'who would look after the children?', 'how would they speak to customers?' Dastkar insisted that if they did not go, their products would not either. They reached the Bazaar three hours late—giggling, scolding, nervous. By evening, all their stock had been sold; they worked all night making more pieces, which sold out the next day. After fifteen days, they had turned from passive, exploited labour into confident entrepreneurs. Today they travel all over India to bazaars, investing their own savings to make stock, including new craftswomen each time. A couple of years later, they came to the Dastkar office, demanding new designs. 'We need something new for our customers. If you design us some new necklaces, we'll pay you a fee out of our sales,' they proudly told us.

Lessons the Crafts Sector Still Needs to Learn

Today weavers form a large section of the rural poor. Ironically, our history books tell us that they were once among India's wealthiest professionals. Weaving guilds built some of the major temples in south India, and even maintained their own armies. What are the tools craftspeople today need to recover a place in the economic mainstream? Exposure, information, awareness, education (technical and otherwise), as well as the resources and access to use them.

We cannot also ignore the market and customer. Product development, design and functionality, and skilful merchandising are crucial to the success and survival of craft traditions. However exquisite the workmanship, however beautiful the object, if it does not meet a need or fit contemporary tastes, it will not sell. People do not buy out of compassion.

Craftspeople must learn how to reinvent designs and products, while simultaneously maintaining their own identity and unique selling proposition in the competitive mainstream market. It is the artisan's distinct craft skill and design tradition that gives him or her an edge. Our experience is that a quality product, however expensive, is easier to sell than a cheap, ordinary one. Craftspeople, instead of imitating and undercutting one another, should attempt to go one better! Local markets may want mill products at a low price, but metro and export markets are willing to pay high prices for handcrafted tradition, given it has been adapted for contemporary lifestyles and fashion-led colours. Today 'handmade', 'organic', 'eco-friendly' and 'natural dyes' have all become desirable international labels.

In India, craft is a cultural and creative manifestation, it is also a mainstream commercial product. This duality is a source of strength, a reason craft has survived into the millennium; but it has also caused confusion and conflict. To add to the confusion, craftspeople themselves —despite there being a couple of hundred million of them—are not active players in either policymaking or marketing craft.

Economic liberalization has added further pressures and new dimensions to both the marketplace and the position of craftspeople. Our strategies and interventions with artisans need some re-thinking. A more sophisticated, demanding customer means that crafts need re-designing, as well as new packaging and promotion. The new trendy young consumer, head filled with images from cable TV and multinational advertising, needs to be made aware of craft's unique qualities and potential.

The development of product, producer and market must go hand in hand. Unless those of us in the sector pay heed to the economic and social problems and realities that confront craftspeople, and unless craftspeople themselves are part of this process, they will remain marginalized, disadvantaged, and forgotten. Our centuries-old craft skills will dwindle and die, and the craftspeople who make them will die away too.

In the two years of Covid-19 pandemic and lockdowns, craftspeople, hitherto tempted by the bright lights and aspirational potential of the city, were witness to the devastation caused by returning migrant labour, factory closures, overnight terminations and huge unemployment. They realized their own fortune in having skills and knowledge systems that enabled them to generate their own incomes and livelihoods. Craftspeople too suffered hugely from the loss of markets, orders and sales, but had the resilience to recover more quickly than any other sector with relatively little investment.

Today we see many young craftspeople recognizing the inherent value of their ancestral trades. This reaffirms Dastkar's strong belief that the continuing existence of an extraordinary diversity of craft traditions and skilled producers is one of India's great strengths, as it searches for its own identity in a world that is increasingly uniform and technological. But this goldmine needs excavation, as well as assistance, and investment to profit from its ore. Craft, as everything, must move with the times, and we must partner with and give social and economic value to its makers.

9

Meals That Educated Generations: Lessons from Tamil Nadu

CHANDRA MOHAN B AND A.R. MEYYAMMAI

MAHENDRAN (SIXTY-EIGHT) OF SINGAMPATTI IN Tirunelveli district, a father of two sons, smiled as he ended the call with his son, a software engineer in the USA. His son had been blessed with a child and he looked forward to travelling to their home to celebrate the arrival of the newborn. His younger son had just graduated from a reputed college. Mahendran himself had recently retired as a senior officer in the service of the government of Tamil Nadu and was happy that things had indeed turned out well. As he counted his blessings, his thoughts drifted to his childhood and his village where it had all begun almost six decades ago.

Born into the Puthirai Vannan community, considered 'untouchable',[1] he remembered the many days that he had gone to sleep on an empty stomach. His family's traditional occupation was washing the clothes of Dalit families in the village. For this back-breaking work from dawn to dusk, they were often paid in kind with food grains at harvest time. In the years when the rains failed and the harvest was meagre, it would be difficult to even have two square meals a day. With his survival at stake and even two meals a day being uncertain, school seemed a distant dream for him. Much as he longed to go to the village school, his absence from work would mean going hungry for the day.

In 1956, poverty was rampant in India, with up to 73 per cent of the population in rural areas living below the poverty line. The total number of children enrolled in schools was an abysmal 5.6 lakhs in the age group of 11–14 years and 1.81 lakhs for those aged 14–16 years for the entire state.[3] The chief minister, K. Kamaraj, was acutely aware of how poverty and hunger were conspiring to keep children out of school. He sought to address the issue by introducing a hugely ambitious and transformational scheme of serving an afternoon meal in all schools of Tamil Nadu. Kamaraj overcame opposition from many quarters to ensure that the government started providing hot meals to students in schools. For many impoverished children, it often became the only meal of the day. School enrolments saw a dramatic increase.

Among the new students was Mahendran, who ran barefoot to the elementary school in his village early every morning. The noon meal at school not only satiated him but also gave him a respite from his strenuous work. The meal made it possible for Mahendran to break the shackles of hunger, go to school, study and reach for the skies. It was his ticket to freedom from hunger, illiteracy and deprivation, and would go on to change his life forever. He went on to become the first postgraduate from his community. Mahendran says, 'If the school had not served me a hot meal, there was no way I would have gone to school. I would have continued to wash clothes for a living.'

The noon meal programme of the Tamil Nadu government is still in force and is making a difference to lakhs of poor students who would otherwise have found it difficult to attend school. Like Mahendran, generations have benefitted immensely from this scheme, and it has changed the destiny of many from a life of stark poverty and hunger to dignity, self-respect and a life-changing education. The noon-meal scheme not only eradicated hunger from classrooms but also substantially improved student enrolment, retention and education levels in Tamil Nadu, laying the foundations for the state to emerge as an economic powerhouse.

Origins of the Noon Meal Programme

The early 1900s saw many swift and dramatic political and social developments in the then Madras Presidency. Established power structures were challenged, and long-suppressed communities found their voice with the self-respect movement gaining traction. The South Indian Liberal Federation, which would later go on to become the Justice Party, was responsible for ushering in many of these sweeping social and political changes in Tamil Nadu.

One of the Justice Party leaders was P. Theagaraya Chetty, who also served as the president of Madras Corporation. He found that boys studying in a corporation school came from very poor families and constituted an insignificant proportion of the student population. After much deliberation, the Madras Corporation council passed a dramatically progressive resolution in November 1920: it would provide free tiffin to the students of the corporation school at the Thousand Lights area. The daily cost was capped at one anna per student. No one could have guessed that this small beginning would in years inspire one of the largest programmes for social transformation in the state.

Madras Corporation later made concerted efforts to introduce and expand the noon meal programme and included four more schools. There was an increase in enrolments by children from poorer communities who were earlier reluctant to attend school. Policymakers were pleasantly surprised when the attendance in these five schools doubled in just two years—from 811 in 1922–23 to 1,671 in 1924–25.

However, the colonial British government played spoilsport by refusing to allot the required funds to support the scheme and it had to be suspended in 1925. Sustained pressure on the government from various quarters eventually forced it to revive the funding after two years. This time the scheme was further expanded to cover about 1,000 poor students in twenty-five schools in the city.

The Architect of the Noon Meal Programme

After Independence, C. Rajagopalachari—then chief minister of Tamil Nadu—tried to introduce the Varnashrama-based 'Kula Kalvi', a system that would retain birth-based vocations for all. Senior Congress party leader Kamaraj stridently opposed it, and the issue led to political turmoil within the ruling Congress government. Eventually, Rajagopalachari resigned and Kamaraj was appointed as chief minister in 1956.

Kamaraj was deeply disturbed at the sight of malnourished and emaciated children when he visited a school in Madurai district. Despite the state facing a severe financial crunch, he immediately resurrected the noon-meal scheme in 1956 in an attempt to bring all children who remained out of classrooms to schools. Political commitment coupled with administrative leadership led to the scheme being successful. Buoyed by this, the government decided to provide midday meals to school children from poor families for 200 days a year.

The proposal initially sought to cover 65,000 students in all the primary schools in the state by establishing 1,300 feeding centres. The chief minister was strongly committed to expanding the scheme, but the state's financial situation was a major constraint. His ministerial colleagues opposed it as being unviable. The Union government was also reluctant to extend support. It seemed an uphill task for the state government to act on the chief minister's mission.

Undaunted and undeterred, Kamaraj made a fervent plea to the public to donate liberally to this project. Public funding was the last resort for the scheme that had been turned down by the Centre and discarded by his ministerial colleagues as impossible and impractical. The state government's contribution amounted to one-and-a-half annas per meal, while the rest was to be borne by the people living in the area where the school was located. The people of Tamil Nadu did not fail him, and generous donations started flowing in. A school in Nagalapuram was the first to embrace the scheme. Local philanthropists were more than happy to provide food free of cost to those children who attended school.

With the help of public donations, Kamaraj first introduced the scheme in government schools in Madras and later extended it to all districts. In July 1956, the first state-sponsored school outside Madras implemented the scheme. It was in Ettayapuram, the village where the Tamil poet Subramania Bharati was born. Kamaraj found it appropriate to launch the scheme to honour the poet who had written the immortal line: 'Even if one person is deprived of food, we shall destroy the world'.

This was followed by many other initiatives by the state government—such as the distribution of free uniforms, which led to the revamping of the entire school education system. These measures laid a strong foundation for the state's growth and development of education.

After Kamaraj, Chief Minister M. G. Ramachandran (MGR) extended the scheme to preschool children in the age group of two to five years in 1982. Later that year, children between five and nine years of age studying in primary schools in rural areas were also included. By 1984, the scheme had been extended to all children from two to fifteen years of age studying in government and government-aided middle and high schools in both urban and rural areas.

The Noon Meal Gets a Makeover

Originally focused on satiating the hunger of children at school, the noon meal programme soon transformed into one that addressed the holistic nutritional requirements of children. The government of Tamil Nadu launched the 'Nutritious Meal Scheme' in 1982 as a full-fledged government programme to cater to the nutritional requirements of the 68 lakh children in the state. The scheme sought to eliminate classroom hunger, reduce school dropouts, increase school enrolment and promote literacy.

When M. Karunanidhi was elected as chief minister in 1989, he not only continued the scheme but also improved it substantially. Boiled eggs were added to the menu with the aim of increasing the protein content. It was hoped this would address the problem of 'protein-energy malnutrition' that was widely prevalent among children in the state. The programme started with one boiled egg every two weeks for students aged two to fifteen.

In 1997, sweet pongal was provided to children on birthdays of eminent leaders. Over the next few years, the number of eggs increased and by 2010, children in all government and government-aided schools were being provided eggs on all five working days of the week. Bananas were provided to children who could not eat eggs.

In 1991, Chief Minister J. Jayalalithaa renamed the programme to 'Puratchi Thalaivar MGR Nutritious Meal Scheme'. In 2013, she introduced different types of rice and flavoured eggs to the menu, eliminating the monotony children felt at having the same food on all days. From then on, children have been getting to taste a variety of delicious and nutritious meals.

In 2021, the nutritious meals programme became one of the flagship schemes of Chief Minister M.K. Stalin. It is closely monitored by him in real-time through the newly established 'chief minister's dashboard'. While the focus all along has been on the food, Stalin enlarged the scope of the programme to include the provision of purified drinking water. Water purifiers were installed at 1,000 Nutritious Meal Centres (NMCs). This is expected to improve the quality of food and reduce the incidence of water-borne diseases, which will go a long way in reducing morbidity and absenteeism among children.

Concerned about the possible adverse effects of Covid-19 on children, Stalin commissioned an elaborate assessment of the impact of the pandemic on their nutritional status. The results will feed into policy iterations that may be necessary to reset the program. A big thrust has been given to improving infrastructure with the construction of kitchen-cum-storerooms at 1,291 NMCs.

The Scheme Today

The nutritious meal programme now covers schoolgoing children in the age group of five to fifteen years and provides them with a variety of hot meals for 220 working days in a year. It also includes children rescued from child labour and enrolled in 186 special schools under the National Child Labour Project (NCLP), who receive these meals for 312 days in a year.

The quantity of food is calibrated according to age and nutritional requirements by nutritional experts. Rice is provided in quantities of 100 grams per child per day (553 Kcal) for primary school children (Classes 1–5) and 150 grams (734 Kcal) for children in upper years (Classes 6–10). Salt fortified with iodine and iron, and oil fortified with vitamins A and D are used in the preparation of the meals. The menu is specially curated to provide for the various taste and nutritional requirements of children. Meticulous care is taken not to repeat the same dish in a week.

Health camps were organized for children in all schools in partnership with the Department of Health and Family Welfare. Apart from regular health check-ups, children are also screened for anaemia as well as eye and dental problems. Iron and folic acid tablets for prevention and treatment of anaemia and deworming medicines are regularly distributed to schoolchildren. Health cards are maintained for each child and are closely monitored. Staff undergo food safety training and certification, and there is a tollfree number and website for grievance redressal.

Budget and funding

In 2021–22, there were 42.14 lakh students being served by 43,172 NMCs in Tamil Nadu, including 21.3 lakh students in primary schools, 14.35 lakh students in middle schools, 6.45 lakh students in high schools and 4,030 children enrolled in NCLP's special schools.

The allocations and expenditure for the scheme have been rising over the years barring 2020–21 when the Covid-19 pandemic forced the government to close down schools and only dry rations were distributed. Expenditure rose from Rs 1,511.15 crores in the year 2016–17 to Rs 1,870.5 crores in 2019–20 but fell to Rs 1,504 crores in 2020–21. A sum of Rs 2,181 crore has been allocated for 2021–22, of which the state government's share is Rs 1,711 crore and the central government's share is Rs 471 crore.

While the cost of supplying food grains and transport is borne entirely by the central government, cooking costs and staff salaries are shared by the centre and the state in the ratio of 60:40. The central government provides a cook-cum-helper to each NMC while the state government employs an organizer, a cook and an assistant for every centre. Adequate staffing with generous allocations ensured that the children were served a variety of tasty and nutritious meals throughout the year.

Organizational Structure and Mechanism of Delivery

The Department of Social Welfare and Women Empowerment of the Tamil Nadu government administers both the noon meal programme and the Integrated Child Development Service (ICDS) Scheme. The department is led by the minister for social welfare and women empowerment. The additional chief secretary or the principal secretary oversees the functioning of the two heads of department, who are usually senior administrative service officers.

The rice is sent by the central government through the Food Corporation of India and supplied to all NMCs by the Tamil Nadu Civil Supplies Corporation. *Dal*, salt and oil is also supplied in this manner, whereas vegetables and condiments are purchased by the noon meal organizers using the feeding charges grant credited to their accounts. Eggs are procured through tenders. Food is prepared in the kitchen-cum-store located in the school premises by the cook on all 220 working days as per the standardized menu prescribed by the state government.

Nationwide Application of the Scheme

The Puratchi Thalaivar MGR Nutritious Meal Programme has emerged as a pioneering example for the rest of India. Today, it stands tall as Tamil Nadu's contribution to the pantheon of developmental interventions that have transformed India. After the huge popularity and stupendous success of the programme, the central government announced the 'National Programme of Nutritional Support to Primary Education' on Independence Day in 1995. Initially implemented in 2,408 blocks around the country, within two years the scheme was in force in all blocks in all states and union territories. In 2007, upper primary children were added to the programme.

Initially, the states were reluctant to participate in the scheme; but after the Supreme Court issued a directive to all states to provide cooked midday meals in primary schools, the programme's coverage increased manifold between 1999 and 2004. Now, the programme is being implemented across the country by the government of India as the Pradhan Mantri Poshan Shakti Nirman scheme with the twin objectives of ensuring good health of students and securing better educational outcomes.

In September 2021, the Cabinet committee on economic affairs chaired by Prime Minister Narendra Modi approved a budget of Rs 1,31,000 crore for the scheme to be in force at government and government-aided schools for the next five years. It is expected to benefit 11.8 crore children from classes 1 to 8, in addition to covering kids in the 3–5 age group. There is now a mandatory social audit of the Poshan scheme.

The programme has a special provision for providing supplementary nutrition to children in districts reporting a high prevalence of anaemia and other health issues. A comprehensive evaluation of the nutritious meal programme by the Department of Evaluation and Applied Research is on the cards. The health of children in government schools is being monitored and records are being maintained with the help of the Department of Health.

The initiative started in just one school of Madras in 1920 has now not only continued for more than a hundred years but has also become one of the largest programmes of its kind in the world. The journey of a hundred years is a story interspersed with stellar milestones, each of which added substantial value to the programme and its sustainability.

Hygiene and quality are given top priority in the programme. Tamil Nadu has the distinction of being the only state to have registered all its NMCs under the provisions of the Food Safety and Standards Authority of India Act and are renewing their registrations every year. Many NMCs have also received ISO certification. Good infrastructure, supply of quality food materials and effective supervision have ensured that the incidents of children taking ill due to food poisoning are negligible. The government has mandated that the heads of all beneficiary schools check and taste the food before it is served to children.

Vouching for the safety and hygiene in the NMC attached to his school, a teacher at a government high school in Madurai district says, 'The days of complaints of food poisoning are over. Besides the headmaster, we teachers take turns to taste the food served to our students. Moreover, we always have an eye on the kitchen when the food is prepared.'

To ensure transparency and accountability, the accounts of the NMCs are placed in the Gram Sabha meetings in village panchayats. Another interesting feature that enthuses the cooks and assistants to hone their culinary skills and sustain their interest in the work is the introduction of cooking contests. Intra-district competitions are conducted, with winners receiving a cash prize of Rs 5,000 and a certificate. Similarly, the best noon meal organizer of each district is awarded a cash prize of Rs 5,000. Replicating this practice, the central government has started cooking competitions for cooks and helpers to promote ethnic cuisines.

Since November 2019, the state government has been piloting a programme that provides fortified rice containing nine nutrients (Vitamins A, B_1, B_2, B_3, B_6 and B_{12}, along with folic acid, iron and zinc) to NMCs in the districts of Dharmapuri, Madurai, Thanjavur, Thoothukudi and Nilgiris, benefitting over 7 lakh children. Under another pilot project implemented with funds from the central government, the NMCs in Tiruchirappalli district have been receiving rice fortified with iron, folic acid and vitamin B12 since October 2020. From 2021–22, fortified rice is being supplied to all NMCs in the state.

The state government has established kitchen gardens in 17,123 schools and plans to expand them to more than 43,000 schools. This gives NMCs a ready supply of fresh vegetables and further addresses malnutrition and nutrient deficiencies prevalent in children. Moreover, children can gain first-hand knowledge and experience of gardening while learning about the nutritional value of vegetables.

The government ensured that the provision of meals was not disrupted during the lockdown periods after the onset of the Covid-19 pandemic. When schools were closed, dry rations including rice, dal and eggs were delivered to the homes of the students.

The state also implements the ICDS with the aim of reducing morbidity and mortality among children and promote their physical, social and psychological development. Its services include supplementary nutrition, preschool education, counselling on feeding practices for infants and young children, community-based management of severely and moderately undernourished children, health check-ups, immunization services and referrals.

In Tamil Nadu, the scheme operates 54,439 'anganwadi centres', which cater to children under six, antenatal women, lactating mothers and adolescent girls. Through 385 rural, forty-seven urban and two tribal projects in the state, the scheme reached 26,91,208 children, 7,23,890 pregnant women and lactating mothers and 237 adolescent (aged eleven to fourteen) girls in 2021.[4]

A hot meal is provided to children aged two to six visiting these *anganwadi* centres for up to six days a week. Dry rations are provided for the seventh day. Double-fortified salt, oil and rice are used for cooking to address the micronutrient deficiencies. For 300 days a year, a multigrain nutrient mix is provided to children aged six months to six years, pregnant women, lactating mothers and adolescent girls not in school.

Hunger and Education

In 2020, globally, 14.9 crore children under the age of 5 years of age were stunted (too thin for their age), 4.5 crore wasted (too thin for their height and age), and 3.8 crore overweight. More than half of all children affected by wasting live in Southern Asia and Asia as a whole is home to more than three-quarters of all children suffering from severe wasting.[5]

Hunger and education cannot coexist. Hunger adversely affects not only the health of the child but also retards their physical and mental development resulting in poor learning outcomes. Malnutrition also makes children sick, susceptible to disease and vulnerable to exploitation, abuse and discrimination. Studies by the American Psychological Association reveal that hunger causes depression, anxiety and withdrawal, all of which pose serious challenges to children in schools.

Tamil Nadu's unique nutritious meal scheme has gone a long way in fighting hunger among children and enabling better learning outcomes. It has not only eliminated hunger among children but has also dramatically increased enrolment and retention, thereby improving literacy levels and laying the foundation for a just and equitable society.

The astounding success is the result of strong political commitment, visionary leadership and bipartisan consensus that provided a fertile ground for policy coherence, iterative improvements and programme continuity. Competent and able administrative leadership helped achieve program objectives and delivery of quality services.

10

PRADAN and the Idea of a Development Professional

NARENDRANATH DAMODARAN AND SMITA MOHANTY

'What lies beneath this tapestry of successful micro-projects across states and communities is an intangible and yet very critical philosophy of transforming poverty—leveraging community-driven initiatives that are aligned, compassionate, empowering, and sensitive to the human context, and yet are radical in shifting oppressive power imbalances and disenfranchisement within society.'[1]

The PRADAN-ite and the Community

PRADAN,[2] A NOT-FOR-PROFIT ORGANIZATION WORKING for the rural poor was founded in 1983 on the idea that young, educated Indians need to work face-to-face, with poor people, and with empathy, to solve their seemingly intractable problems of poverty and marginalization. It was a radical idea at that time, quite like Gandhiji's call at another time in history, to Congress workers and volunteers to take up 'constructive work' in villages, rather than involve themselves in party politics. The Gandhian idea of constructive engagement can be described as nonviolent action taken within a community to build structures, systems, processes or resources that provide alternatives to a life of deprivation or marginalization. It contributes to self-improvement of both the community and the individual. PRADAN's professionals were expected to engage directly with the community, and use their knowledge and expertise to help communities tackle their very real problems. In the words of the founders, '... for young people armed with a good professional education, there are few more worthy challenges than those posed by poverty.'

With this in mind, the founders of PRADAN paid as much attention to bringing on board the right kinds of people, along with deciding on the vision and mission, structure and systems of the organization. Their belief was that there were no silver bullets to tackling complex problems such as multi-dimensional poverty, or social and political marginalization; these require constructive engagement by sensitive individuals. Funds and technology can be mobilized, but more difficult to obtain were people with the appropriate mix of attributes—of the heart and mind—to give an impetus to enduring social change. Empathetic engagement by the right development professional can trigger basic changes in a village community, in terms of their self-view, attitudes, behaviours and practices. These changes cannot be achieved only through classroom training programmes or investing grant funds, but through close engagement and developing personal friendships. For the development professional, it is a special bond that she develops as a result of her concern for 'the other', and a desire to see a positive change in the life of the other. In the process, she does not remain unaffected; this is an opportunity for her to grow and evolve into a better human being. The bonds and changes the engagement brings into the lives of both the community and the development professional form the basic ingredients of the larger social change that we see.

Major Highlights of PRADAN

Since 1983, over nearly four decades, PRADAN has been growing and evolving in its outlook, in what it does, the way it delivers on its commitments and its structures, and in its systems and processes. Its mission statements have changed across time as the organization has gained in experience and demands have changed. Its first mission statement was the name of the organization—Professional Assistance for Development Action. This was in the early 1980s; the country had several grassroots organizations—they were well-intentioned, but lacked analytical depth and professional capabilities. PRADAN tried to address this as part of its early strategy. Its professionals worked as 'action consultants' to other NGOs working with poor rural communities, which was a learning experience. PRADAN decided to shift to initiating projects, and working directly at the community level, with support and guidance from more experienced colleagues. The mission became 'Building People' to 'Build People'. This later became 'Impacting Livelihoods to Enable Rural Communities', as the organization gained in experience and acquired the confidence of being able to tackle poverty through well-thought through livelihood promotion programmes, keeping the needs and aspirations of the community at the centre.

PRADAN's mission since 2014 has been to, 'enable the most marginalized people, especially rural women, to earn a decent living and take charge of their own lives', with a vision of 'creating a just and equitable society where everyone lives and works with dignity'. This change in its mission was the result of its continuous work on rural poverty and marginalization, and the realization that poverty is complex and multi-dimensional, and requires an integrated approach that builds an enabling ecosystem and enhances communities' sense of agency to chart and traverse life on their own terms.

The changing mission statements over time is an indication of how the organization has continually reviewed its approaches and strategies and tried to renew itself to remain dynamic and relevant. At one level PRADAN has been an effective grassroots implementation organization delivering impactful projects, and, at another level, it has been a learning ground where a variety of innovative ideas have found life. The most important contribution of PRADAN has been the high-quality human resources the organization has been able to build and provide to the wider social sector. The founding idea that PRADAN began with has proved itself in good measure in the thirty-eight years of its existence.

PRADAN founders and much of the earlier leadership have moved on to other avenues, and a new generation of leaders in the organization has taken charge of guiding the organizational evolution. The structure, systems, scale, technologies, outreach and programme content have altered considerably over time. But what has endured is the founding view that places primacy on the development professional as critical to facilitating social change. PRADAN over the years has invested time, energy and money in finding the right kind of person who can connect with poor communities with empathy, and facilitate a change process, which is enriching for the professional, significant for the community and builds the organization.

Nurturing Development Professionals

PRADAN has given to the development sector a large contingent of development professionals through its systematic recruitment and training efforts. Over the years, it has put in place a rigorous process for on-boarding the most appropriate candidates from among the best campuses in India, and placing them as development apprentices in PRADAN. The Development Apprenticeship programme is a twelve-month engagement, where the candidate acquires the necessary skills and capabilities to begin work in a village, as part of a PRADAN team and, most importantly, makes an informed choice about 'development' as her vocation. It began primarily as a programme for selecting people to work with PRADAN. To date, more than 2,500 young professionals have gone through the Development Apprenticeship programme, of which around 1,000 have graduated and became executives in PRADAN, while many have moved on to other jobs and roles, most of them in the development sector. There were 428 professionals in PRADAN as on 31 March 2022. The programme has generated its own ripple effect; it would be reasonable to say that for every young professional who has joined PRADAN on a long- or short-term basis, many others have seriously considered the social sector as a career choice.

Around thirty ex-PRADAN professionals have promoted other grassroots NGOs that are creating their own impact. The recruitment and early training programme that PRADAN initiated for finding talented human resources for itself today evolved into a respected programme for preparing talent for the sector itself.

Working with and Changing the Lives of Marginalized Rural Communities

The scale and impact PRADAN has achieved is significant. As on 31 March 2022, it has worked in seven central Indian states, across thirty-four districts and 9,127 villages, with 9,63,324 families, 65 per cent of which belong to the most vulnerable groups. Over the years, PRADAN has built up a remarkable body of work in these states, which host some of the poorest communities in the country. The tribal pockets in this region are endemically poor and have been historically discriminated against in terms of public policy and investment. PRADAN has deployed its field teams in these areas, and so maintains on-going contact with some of the most marginalized people in the country.

This connect with rural people, especially the poorest among them—Dalits, Adivasis, women, etc—over sustained periods of time has given PRADAN an in-depth understanding of the causes of poverty in the region, and enabled it to innovate solutions in partnership with the people themselves and with a variety of stakeholders. PRADAN is one among a small set of organizations that experimented with the idea of women's self-help groups, around microfinance and empowerment, that has today evolved into a national flagship programme. Millions of women are linked to the mainstream banking system for essential financial support. They also are gaining voice and visibility in society through their solidarity and collective action.

PRADAN's work on rural livelihoods, with a focus on smallholder farmers in the tribal areas of central India, has also received much attention. Like many areas in less-developed economies across the world, this region presents a number of challenges to development agencies. The sustained and persistent engagement of PRADAN professionals in the region, along with stakeholders, has helped develop predictable pathways out of poverty for the rural communities living here. Here, PRADAN's work has been acknowledged as impactful because it could bring effective solutions to these poverty pockets, which have challenged policy makers in terms of effective solutions.

Outreach of all livelihood interventions (households)	Year			
	2018–19	2019–20	2020–21	2021–22
Agriculture and horticulture activities	4,74,367	5,31,428	6,01,845	6,25,250
Forest-based Activities	12,160	12,396	13,259	4,697
Enterprises	11,063	17,630	21,087	25,286
Livestock Rearing	81,400	1,77,706	2,32,573	2,32,175
Total	5,78,990	7,39,160	8,68,764	8,87,408

Integrated Natural Resource Management

PRADAN's innovations around Integrated Natural Resource Management (INRM) have received wide attention. These are simple yet technically sound and effective models of land and water management, in consonance with people-resource relationships in the region. These have been implemented at scale by PRADAN and its partners. INRM is also being scaled up by different state governments through large-scale partnerships with NGOs. It also finds a place in the shelf of works provided by the Mahatma Gandhi National Rural Employment Guarantee Act (MGNREGA).

INRM is an approach which centres on the judicious use of resources that aims at improving livelihoods, agricultural productivity, resilience in agro-ecosystems and environmental services. It recognizes the links among natural resources (soil, water, vegetation) within a natural boundary called a watershed. Action in one part affects the others. For example, deforestation in the upper catchment areas increases soil erosion, reduces moisture conservation and increases runoff in the lower valleys. Uncontrolled, unplanned and unscientific use of natural resources results in their depletion: the consequences are low productivity of natural resources and poor health of people and animals. Managing natural resources calls for their rational utilization to optimize production and minimize risk.

In the central Indian region, where land holdings are mostly small or marginal, where farming has become a challenging and unproductive enterprise, INRM technologies and processes have been found to be most effective in dealing with the issue of resource degradation. PRADAN has over the years participated actively in various resource augmentation and improvement programmes of the government, such as the Integrated Watershed Development Programme, to create more livelihood opportunities for rural communities. In recent years, PRADAN has focused systematically on the MGNREGA in all the central Indian states and helped utilize funds allocated to schemes effectively, to enhance the carrying capacity of unutilized or under-utilized resources which largely belong to very poor households.

As of today, across PRADAN locations, nearly 29,000 hectares of land have come under land improvement measures, additional irrigation potential has been created in more than 38,000 hectares, and nearly 12,500 hectares have come under tree plantation. These have contributed to an augmentation in the livelihoods of tens of thousands of poor rural households facilitated by public investments worth millions of rupees. Today, the INRM approach to realizing the potential of natural resources in a village, with the use of public investments, has become a routine component in major planning processes such as Gram Panchayat Development Planning, Comprehensive Livelihood Planning in National Rural Livelihoods Mission (NRLM) and MGNREGA labour-budgeting.

PRADAN is part of large partnership projects such as Usharmukti in West Bengal, the Mega Watershed Project in Chhattisgarh, the Arresting Distress Migration through MGNREGA project in Odisha, and the Cluster Facilitation Programme in many states where significant expenditure under MGNREGA is carried out through multi-stakeholder partnerships. Thousands of rural poor households are being benefitted through these partnerships between coalitions of civil society organizations, government departments and donors.

Innovations in augmenting rural livelihoods

The path-breaking work by PRADAN on smallholder poultry and *tasar* sericulture (forest-based silkworm rearing practice) is widely acknowledged as having opened up important livelihood opportunities for tribal and smallholder communities. Over many years of experimentation and collaboration with expert agencies and individuals, these livelihood activities have emerged as the most prominent opportunities in the non-farm sector for the rural poor in the central Indian region. Similarly, integrated livestock rearing, commercial cultivation of fruits and vegetables, and other similar livelihood prototypes have expanded the portfolio of livelihood options available for vulnerable, poor communities.

Tasar sericulture: Metamorphosis of a sub-sector

India is the second-largest producer of tasar silk worldwide, second to China. The Central Silk Board estimates that in 2018–19, total raw silk production in India was more than 35,000 metric tons, of which raw tasar silk constituted 3,000 metric tons. A kilogram of tasar raw silk (reeled yarn) costs about Rs 4,200 at present rates. It is mainly produced in a vast contiguous stretch across the states of Jharkhand, Chhattisgarh and Odisha, along with parts of Maharashtra, West Bengal, Andhra Pradesh and Uttar Pradesh. Often categorized as the tasar belt of India, this is also a predominantly poor region, and tasar sericulture is a traditional occupation of the tribal communities living in the forest fringe villages. An estimated 1,00,000-plus families are actively involved in tasar-rearing, and nearly 40,000 more families earn their livelihoods from cocoon trade, reeling, spinning, weaving and associated activities.

Natural factors, poor technology and widespread disease had led to a decline in tasar silk production from 600 metric tons in 1970 to 265 metric tons in 1981; what was produced was not able to withstand competition from cheaper Chinese and Korean imports. At this time, in 1981 the Central Silk Board launched the Inter-State Tasar Project, and PRADAN initiated its tasar sub-sector interventions in 1986. Its objectives were to:

- Promote the plantation of tasar host plants—especially the Arjuna variety—on wasteland owned or controlled by poor rural families
- Promote modern plantation and rearing techniques to reduce risks and ensure high factor productivity
- Promote decentralized reeling, spinning and weaving activities
- Explore and develop new market segments to promote tasar-based fabrics, with marketing support to producers
- Foster organizations at various levels to ensure a flow of inputs and services for the sustained viability of the output, ensuring a fair share of the value added to producers at various production stages.

PRADAN's interventions began with a pilot project in Godda district in Santhal Parganas[3] with support from Interchurch Organization for Development Cooperation (ICCO), Netherlands and the government's National Wasteland Development Project. The programme expanded with active collaboration from the Central Silk Board and partners such as the United Nations Development Program (UNDP) and Ministry of Rural Development, through schemes such as the Swarnajayanti Gram Swarozgar Yojana and the NRLM; it has now grown to cover many more states, such as Bihar, Jharkhand, West Bengal, Odisha, Telangana and Maharashtra.

The interventions resulted in the setting up of a sector-support organization—the Tasar Development Foundation, to promote exponential growth in activities in close partnership with the Central Silk Board. The achievements include: 6,500 hectares of block plantation on privately owned wasteland in Bihar, Jharkhand, West Bengal and Odisha; 550 private grainage entrepreneurs, supported at the village level for the commercial production of tasar seed, producing nearly 17.5 lakh commercial seeds annually; 750 yarn producers managing individual enterprises producing 13.8 metric tons of tasar yarn annually; 17 basic tasar seed production units annually producing 25 lakh units of disease-free eggs (the largest set of private tasar seed producers in the country); four cocoon banks in the yarn production cluster with a capacity to store 200 lakh cocoons for the year-round supply of cocoons to yarn producers; and a yarn bank at the central level with a capacity to purchase and store 5 metric tons of yarn.

All the producers were organized under seven self-sustaining producer institutions, and 550 community resource people were trained and deployed in the tasar-producing clusters to extend services to the producer institutions locally and to the State Rural Livelihood Missions of Jharkhand, Odisha and West Bengal. A separate entity was established at the central level to market the tasar seed, cocoons, and yarn and fabric output.

The interventions have demonstrated a livelihood prototype model for block plantation on wasteland, and cocoon, seed and yarn production, which has been replicated in five major tasar-producing states. In November 2021, the outreach of the Tasar programme extended to 34,276 households in thirty-seven blocks across fifteen districts of Jharkhand, Bihar, West Bengal and Odisha. These models have been adopted by the Central Silk Board and incorporated in the regular sericulture scheme. The stakeholder base has expanded to include NABARD, the District Mineral Foundation, and tribal welfare departments. The interventions have also entered the carbon credit market.

Internal Processes for Growth

PRADAN's success in evolving as an effective organization in the civil society space can be attributed to various factors.

A factor crucial to PRADAN's success was its abiding faith in people. Since the start, the organization has focused on getting the right kind of people to be groomed as development professionals; and, at the same time, fashioned a development engagement based on the community driving change, with the NGO's role being one of a facilitator.

PRADAN's Development Apprenticeship Programme was initiated in 1990 to bring in professionals as Development Apprentices, to help them engage in grassroots development. The year-long programme focuses on the individual, to help her make an informed choice about a career at the grassroots. It provides young graduates an opportunity to experience rural realities, and develop the perspectives and skills to work with rural communities.

Opting for a career in grassroots development, after being educated at a reputed institution, is not easy. Choosing a non-traditional job requires individuals who value their own experiences, and are confident enough to deal with concerns from family and friends. PRADAN professionals are trained to recruit young graduates embodying such attributes, from campuses across the country. Field engagement is often a lonely journey, and each professional has her own unique dilemmas. She could be toggling between daunting challenges of the poverty 'out there', as well as dilemmas 'within'. To help the young stewards along, PRADAN, over the years, has built a support system, where each apprentice is attached to a field guide, an experienced colleague in the field team, specially trained in counselling and mentoring. They are co-travellers in the journey of a development apprentice in her path of choosing a career at the grassroots.

Investments in the professional development of PRADAN staff continue well beyond the first year, across the many years that the professional spends in PRADAN. An ongoing professional development plan caters to changing roles and the various conceptual, technical and human capabilities required at various stages. Every professional also is part of a work unit (team) in the organization, so she always has a peer group for support and collaboration, as well as access to various discussion platforms and learning groups, for professional inputs. Overall, the orgnization has tried to create a collegial and achievement-oriented climate, so that each member can receive adequate support for her professional needs. The focus of PRADAN's human resources development unit is to nurture each professional as a reflective practitioner.

As a reflective organization, PRADAN holds an annual retreat of all its professionals—a space for individual and collective reflection on what went well and what did not during the past year—for resolutions, and to invigorate them for a new beginning. These retreats contribute in no small measure to individual rejuvenation, but also to organization renewal, and have contributed to rearticulating the organization's mission, vision and approaches apart from building a nurturing climate.

PRADAN, with its participatory culture as a non-negotiable, has a relatively flat structure, with functional hierarchy with a lot of autonomy. Decisions are taken where they make the most sense and by those who are most involved. There is a culture of consultation, not only on strategic issues but also on most important operational issues, and all decisions are taken in groups. To underline its quest for equality, PRADAN has also ensured that all professional staff, from new executives to the Executive Director, are on the same salary and benefits' scale. The only factor determining a pay raise is tenure in the organization. PRADAN has only four executive levels—executive, team coordinator, integrator and executive director, which are de facto roles rather than positions of authority. Moving across designations is possible in either direction, as changing designations does not affect pay and benefits.

PRADAN considers itself an organization of its employees. Every PRADAN-ite is considered a trustee and architect of PRADAN. The governing board plays a largely fiduciary role and works as a sounding board rather than a hands-on entity. This gives PRADAN-ites a lot of space in their development tasks, positions and strategies. Every decision of strategic importance and long-term significance is taken by the General Council (GC), a body created for internal governance of PRADAN. All professionals with more than four years in the organization become GC members; its role is to carry forward the organization's values and culture to the next generation, and give it direction for its future. Apart from the GC, there are other bodies like the Management Unit (MU), Consultative Forum, Development Cluster Management Committee, and field teams, which are groups of professional staff who meet regularly and take decisions. The emphasis is on fostering collective leadership.

An important practice in PRADAN since its inception is that the Executive Director (ED) changes every five years and is selected from an internal pool of experienced colleagues, and that the shortlist for the new ED is selected by the GC through a sociometric process. The final selection is done by the governing board. The new ED is selected about 5–6 months before the end of the tenure of the current ED. The new ED also selects a new MU, which is the strategic leadership group, so that there is a smooth transfer of responsibilities.

Even as the PRADAN leadership was building a democratic ethos and participatory governance process in the organization, it accorded the same care to putting in place robust systems—for accounts, finance, audit, compliances, human resources management, and operations review and monitoring. PRADAN's fairly meticulous systems for ensuring transparency and accountability have been appreciated by various stakeholders, especially partners who provide financial support.

A landmark organizational initiative to create a more sensitive climate was to make the organization a gender-sensitive space. The leadership recognized that patriarchy is a deeply embedded strand in our daily lives, and unless each person—male, female or other—becomes conscious of it, trying to shape a gender equal world is not possible. Thus, PRADAN's plans to 'Make PRADAN a Better Place for Women' is a set of sub-initiatives to sensitize men and build male champions for gender equality through special training and awareness on gender for new entrants, nurturing a women's caucus in the organization, and periodic assessment of progress through a systematic gender audit. This has been in place for five years or so, and results are already discernible. Gender-sensitive staff policies have been instituted; there is far more open discussion and articulation of women's issues; and cases of harassment have reduced remarkably. A large number of staff have been trained as gender auditors and trainers, who also function as watchdogs for transgressions. A steering group provides oversight on progress in PRADAN along various indicators on gender equality.

Efforts within PRADAN to create a nurturing climate and inclusive and democratic culture have contributed enormously to people staying in PRADAN for long tenures.

Stakeholder Engagement

An important enabling factor that benefitted PRADAN's work was villagers' ownership of the change processes triggered in their villages. The approach to involve community institutions in defining the problem and evolving a solution, has resulted in considerable ownership and participation by the community on planning and implementation. This has greatly contributed to the sustainability of programme outcomes, whether they are community processes or livelihood assets, and enabled the PRADAN team to move on to other aspects that need attention. As the community takes charge of the development initiatives, PRADAN works on deepening the interventions, strengthening community institutions, building stakeholder linkages and broadening the agenda.

PRADAN's work has garnered acceptance and good will from stakeholders. Government officers at various levels, panchayat office bearers, grassroots functionaries, civil society organizations—all acknowledge PRADAN's contribution and more often than not are happy to cooperate. They appreciate the fact that well-educated, largely urban-bred young professionals work in remote villages with dedication and commitment. Over time, PRADAN has learned to maintain a distance from all political dispensations, which makes it acceptable to all parties, and helped it build functional partnerships at all levels. Examples of partnerships mobilized by PRADAN with a variety of stakeholders can be seen from the panchayat to the state and national levels.

Systematic and proactive partnerships that have evolved with different state governments and civil society coalitions have enabled effective livelihood ideas and models to reach thousands of households in villages even outside PRADAN's direct outreach areas. These projects are unique not just in their scale and reach, but also in evolving new models of implementation and policy guidelines. The projects have not just strengthened NGO-government collaboration but also spawned new ways of inter-departmental convergence around people's plans.

Facing up to Challenges

PRADAN needs to reconceptualize its leadership model. As professionals grow in the organization, it is important to ensure appropriate engagement for those with significant experience and knowledge. In the social sector, the possibilities are enormous, but many of these opportunities may lie outside the purview or reach of an organization aligned in a certain direction. To explore and bring to life any of these possibilities, including PRADAN itself taking on new challenges, calls for experienced professionals to innovate and create, and maybe take risks, rather than seek security and managerial influence within the four walls of the organization. PRADAN's inherent knowledge and experience can be put to work not only in India but also in poverty pockets in other countries in Africa and Latin America.

There are potential avenues in the development space PRADAN has not yet explored. One is the area of primary health. Further, the Covid-19 pandemic has revealed the plight of migrant labourers to our urban areas. Mostly these are young women and men who have no choice but to migrate to cities; a lot can be done in creating more opportunities for them in the rural and urban areas. The activity portfolio of PRADAN today does not address the aspirations of and opportunities for young people who have moved to cities, and is an area it needs to urgently engage in.

Learnings for Others

PRADAN has over these years built a cadre of dedicated and committed development professionals who have seamlessly entered PRADAN's work stream to fulfil its staffing need. This could be a model for other development organizations struggling with high levels of attrition, in tune with their context and needs.

The other important aspect of PRADAN's functioning is its collective leadership. Though this at times may slow down decision-making, today PRADAN functions in line with its vision and mission, because of its participatory processes and collective leadership, which have sustained it beyond its founders.

PRADAN strives to be relevant, and keeps evolving with changing demands in the environment and the organization. It undertakes systematic steps for its review and renewal periodically, and allocates considerable time and energy to the process. This is something that has made the organization remain in tune with contemporary issues, and possibly ahead of the curve.

11

Wealth Creation through Community-owned Enterprise: NSPDT's Model of Cooperative Smallholder Poultry

ANISH KUMAR

Small Producers in an Industrialized Sector

A PRIORITY FOR INDIA IS to alter the low-level equilibrium of the rural economy which occurs due to the reinforcing effects of low investments, low growth, low employment, and a low flow and stock of income. There are emerging opportunities in high-value agriculture (HVA)—animal protein (meat, eggs), vegetables, fruits, milk, etc—which structurally favour small farmers. However, unlike the cereal production-led green revolution, a boost to this sector requires strong business acumen and skills, and investments in a value chain for producers/farmers.

Key to the success of such initiatives is commitment, the right skills sets for farmers, preparing the farm production system for HVA by leveraging private and public investments to develop production and value-chain infrastructure; adapting and customizing technological solutions; building mechanisms for commercial transitions; and reducing concomitant downside risks across the new production systems.

Tapping the soaring demand for poultry

The experience of National Smallholder Poultry Development Trust[1] (NSPDT) is a study of civil society action in the poultry industry that made it possible for first-generation rural producers of poultry meat and eggs to connect with urban markets. The model has grown with public and private investment, and is today the largest producer of poultry, demonstrating the ability of small farmers to succeed on techno-commercial parameters. In the process, it has driven new consumption in the peri-rural segment through a farm and institutional model that addresses industry volatility and risks specific to small producers.

As a counter to the long-run trend in correlations between size, efficiency, and value creation, the model demonstrates an approach of value-capture with producers at the centre. Its implication on rural production systems is critical, given the mismatch between the aspirations of the rural youth for gentrified, urban jobs, with a regular income, and the reality of a rural workforce with asymmetrical gaps in their skills and employability.

The impact of a historical neglect of education, nutrition, health and other quality of life investments in villages is not going to abate in a hurry; and we have to create new avenues for the absorption of the annual growth of about 12 crore young rural and peri-rural workers in line with their aspirations for income and decent work conditions.

Learning Ground: The Kesla Poultry Cooperative

The Kesla Poultry Samity (KPS) was formed in May 1993 as a collective of small poultry producers in Kesla, Madhya Pradesh. It was formally registered on 11 June 2001 under the now-repealed Madhya Pradesh Mutually Aided Cooperatives Society Act, 1997. It has 1,250 members spread over forty-eight villages in Hoshangabad and Betul districts. In 2019–20, KPS recorded sales of Rs 30.42 crore, with over Rs 2.11 crore distributed among its members.

The predominantly tribal Kesla block in Hoshangabad district is characterized by extreme poverty, rain-fed agriculture of low productivity, the collection and barter of minor forest produce and distress migration. It was selected by PRADAN for its non-farm livelihood interventions in 1985. Its work in poultry started with the rearing of low-cost breeds like the cockerel (male rejects of laying hens, hence available cheap); unit-level earnings were low, and farmers treated it as a supplementary activity. Measures such as linking payments to live birds and differential rates based on weight inculcated a sense of accountability and responsibility among the poultry-rearers.

PRADAN drew support from government poverty alleviation programmes such as the Integrated Rural Development Programme which gave farmers loans to construct poultry sheds. Low returns over the next five or six years saw many producers drop out. Servicing debts became a challenge due to low batch intensity (number of batches in a year), inadequate working capital, a steep learning curve, delays in the release of funds by banks and extended credit by buyers. However, there was also significant progress during this phase, which included understanding the business and building rapport with local communities and traders.

In 1994, there was a shift to 'deep-litter broiler rearing' with quality technical support on vaccination, medicines and appropriate technology for rearing broilers. In 'deep-litter broiler rearing', bird flock are reared on a bed of high-absorbency material like sawdust or husk. This led to changes in shed design and management practices and the introduction of rigorous quality parameters. KPS started with the bulk purchase of chicks and inputs, and gradually stabilized the production system. New members were selected jointly by existing members and supervisors, and were given hands-on training through 'learning by doing'. From 1997, new business processes were introduced with linkages to women's self-help groups (SHGs) and a focus on real-time recording of business accounts with the producers themselves, thus introducing a sense of responsibility and integrity in members' transactions with their collective. The process of delinking production from marketing, in which individual producers are insulated from fluctuations in the market price, strengthening governance by instituting a board comprising elected women representatives of poultry producers, and promotion of women's SHGs contributed to growth.

By 2001, women's confidence levels and entrepreneurial skills had soared in over 200 SHGs, and their involvement in democratic processes strengthened their identity and role as owners of their collectives. Over time, quality monitoring systems were introduced for purchases, stores, production and sales. With new management, proficient in both the production and business aspects, the business grew rapidly with vertical integration in supply chain and backward integration.

The first cooperative, set up in Kesla in 2001, has completed twenty years as a formally incorporated entity. The internal systems have evolved across the operating, governance, and membership systems into a structured complement of processes, ensuring 'enduring profitability of the enterprise and providing benefits to the members'. There are well-developed processes ensuring the integrity of member-organization relationships, internal locus of control, and membership processes to exercise control over the operating system, while maintaining the centrality of its women members.

NSPDT's Community Poultry Model: Focusing on Women's Cooperatives

Poultry has been the fastest-growing agri-allied sector over the last two decades in India, growing at about 6 to 8 per cent for eggs and 10 to 12 per cent for broilers. The response to this opportunity has mainly been from the urban and peri-urban capital-intensive industrial poultry farms, including large corporate houses. While 70 per cent of poultry production was at the family level in 1970, today this is less than 8 per cent. The poultry revolution in India is the story of the industrialization of poultry production, with production shifting from a traditional, local family activity to an increasingly market-oriented, vertically integrated business.

This is the context of the intervention of the NSPDT in the poultry value chain. The basic prototype demonstrated in Kesla unpacked and adapted production technology for first-time women farmers and created a socio-techno-commercial model for their transition to producers, able to stand their ground in an industrialized sector. The Kesla model of 'rural decentralized industrial poultry' has spawned nearly 1,000 individually owned poultry units, collectivized into producer collective enterprises. These have been built on the natural advantages of rural knowledge (particularly women's) on husbandry, leveraging decentralized production systems over industrial units, on disease containment, animal welfare and environmental benefits.

Spawned by PRADAN (now spearheaded by NSPDT) the Kesla community poultry model has been designed to enable smallholder—particularly resource-poor (landless or marginal land-owning) families—to participate in the growth in the poultry industry. It has made the small family unit's farm-gate outputs competitive by creating a context-fit across size, investment, technology, input-output linkages, and farmer-driven institutional support architecture. Farmers are organized into business collectives, through systems and processes that support individual farmers to attain production at scale and the resultant efficiencies. The activity is organized to leverage opportunities offered by the industry and build on the strengths of small, decentralized units on three fronts: production organization, input-output markets and financial systems.

In the Kesla model, women from poor families are organized into cooperatives, with each woman rearing broilers in poultry farms built on her homestead. Each cooperative typically has 300 to 500 members, with thirty to forty farmers from one village. A community-based supervisor provides round-the-clock production management and farm support. The cooperative engages a professional manager trained in veterinary or management sciences as its chief functionary responsible for daily management and operational business decisions.

A poultry management system based on a quality-assurance approach and supported by customized Enterprise Resource Planning software provides a detailed template for business decisions and helps in compliance and monitoring. The cooperatives are further federated into two state-level secondary organizations: the Jharkhand Women's Self-Supporting Poultry Cooperative Federation and the Madhya Pradesh Women Poultry Producers Company. The federations provide the benefits of vertical integration, professional and technical support, economies of scale and increased bargaining power with external suppliers and regulators.

NSPDT, the apex organization is a unique trans-sector hybrid organization, combining private development action with a community-based approach. It leverages private and public partnerships to transform first-time women poultry producers into entrepreneurs. As the national-level sector support organization orchestrating and spearheading the expansion of smallholder poultry, NSPDT's vision is to inspire, encourage, facilitate and promote the emergence of an efficient farmer-owned network of well-organized and empowered smallholder poultry farmers, measured by the best standards of professional excellence and development.

Today it spearheads the largest organized family poultry initiative in India and is one of the largest enterprises of indigenous communities globally; uniquely the enterprise is owned entirely by women farmers. Presently, more than 14,000 poultry producers are organized into twenty-nine producer collectives (cooperative societies or producer companies) spread over 456 villages in twenty-six districts of Madhya Pradesh, Jharkhand, Odisha, Assam and Maharashtra.

Phases of NSPDT's Journey

Phases	Keystone	Description
1986–89	The dream	PRADAN sets up Teams for Rural Industrialization and Artisan Development to work on rural poultry production in Bhopal and Kesla.
1989–97	Techno-commercial travails	Struggles related to poultry-production technology, structure of activity, fitting investment risks to the community context, on-boarding farmers, connecting to available anti-poverty programmes (140 farmers launched; 90 failed after a few batches)
1997–2004	Unlearning—making of the Community-owned Producer Enterprise	Techno-commercial model internalizing input-output price volatility, delinking producers from enterprise risks through the pooling and aggregation model—Kesla Poultry pivoted as collective enterprise (280 farmers)

Phases	Keystone	Description
2004–2009	Validation of business model and replication by CSOs	PRADAN replicates the model in Jharkhand and Madhya Pradesh in mainstream poverty alleviation programmes. Business processes and standard operating procedures are systemized. Total strength now numbers 1,500 farmers.
2009 onwards	Fourth-generation institutional framework—leaving the civil society organization (CSO) frame	NSPDT created as an apex sector organization with participation of producer entities and commercial partners with the aim of becoming the largest poultry player in India. 8,000 farmers are part of the programme.
2011 onwards	Private sector partnership and value-chain integration	Commercial partnership with the private VH Group and upstream linkages with feed, hatcheries and parent farms allowing for value-transfer to farmers, ensuring standards above industry, and production stability. State federations such as Madhya Pradesh Women Poultry Producers Company Pvt Ltd and Jharkhand Women Self-Supporting Poultry Cooperative Federation Ltd take over business operations with tighter control, industry competitive supply chain integration.
2013 onwards	Resilience, mainstream funds and growth	External commercial borrowings and local bank credit deepen the integration of the value chain, making it a standardized model with plug-and-play architecture, customized enterprise resource planning solutions and structured business competitive input procurement and sales operations. A total of 14,000 farmers are part of the programme.

Poultry-rearing is essentially a rural enterprise, though it can use fairly complex technology. Apart from knowledge and infrastructure, starting a home-based poultry business requires market assurance. The regular and continuous flow of income helps families meet expenses and contributes to their savings. It also enhances the status of women, who as business owners can negotiate a good deal for themselves within their families and the larger society.

NSPDT's model has demonstrated that small farmers are able to not just participate in this growing industry but also match the efficiency of big farmers and organized integrators. One of the unique elements of the engagement that contributed to this was that women funded most of the value-chain infrastructure themselves, unlike most other similar enterprises that have been supported with development funding.

Smallholder Poultry Model - Cooperative Business

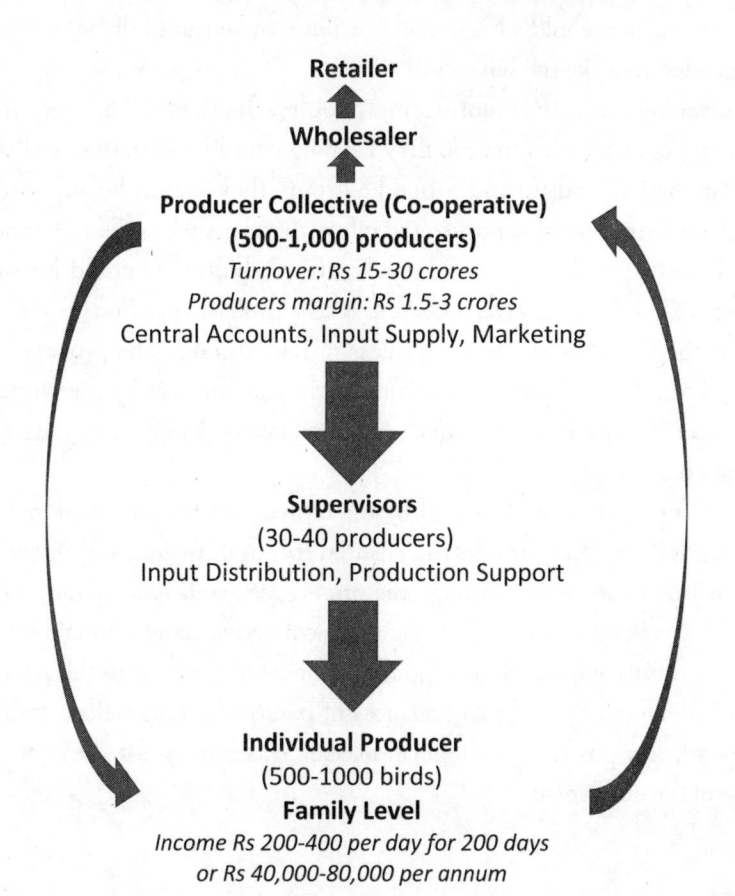

Retailer
↑
Wholesaler
↑
Producer Collective (Co-operative)
(500-1,000 producers)
Turnover: Rs 15-30 crores
Producers margin: Rs 1.5-3 crores
Central Accounts, Input Supply, Marketing

↓

Supervisors
(30-40 producers)
Input Distribution, Production Support

↓

Individual Producer
(500-1000 birds)
Family Level
Income Rs 200-400 per day for 200 days
or Rs 40,000-80,000 per annum

The Endogenous Design Drivers

Defining the boundary conditions

The boundary conditions we identified as important helped us develop a plug-and-play template for replication. These conditions included the following:

Specific criteria for selecting individuals and geographies for intervention. It is necessary to first assess access to markets and availability of basic production infrastructure. As the programme targeted women producers from deprived communities and families living below the poverty line, criteria for selecting these farmer-members had to be established. Those who could be shortlisted had to be young and healthy enough to undertake the physical labour required for poultry farming and be keen to do it. They also needed to have a good sense of hygiene, an enjoyment of basic family harmony and a need for diversification. These criteria ensured that the activity became a critical anchor for the household's livelihood portfolio, and ensured the intensity of effort needed to make the business a success.

The second step was mobilizing people effectively. This required convincing communities that poultry farming could be lucrative, and that once they had signed up and formed a group, they would be supported through the provision of exposure and infrastructure, such as sheds. Farmers were trained intensively for one cycle, after which they could become members of the co-operative. This provided a probation period, as well as an opportunity to assess the seriousness of the aspirant. The process was designed to ensure ownership and an upfront commitment by the farmers. This was critical particularly when large grants were deployed for the start-up infrastructure.

The infrastructure was owned by the farmer, not the community. This reduced conflict among farmers and ensured that performance and efficiency was rewarded adequately through the pricing mechanism on an individual basis. This was critical to ensure member–collective transaction integrity. Gradual growth helped the new poultry farmers to get used to the activity and to understand the risks and nuances of poultry farming before scaling. Commanding a position in the local market was critical for the eventual success of the enterprise.

'Design's' key role in the build-out of the collective enterprise

The superstructure of the federation and NSPDT work in tandem, ensuring that the whole system delivers member benefits. The key elements guiding the design include:

- Benchmarking against the top three poultry houses with the highest productivity and sale margins;
- Self-generated capital reserves to smoothen cyclical and unforeseen market downturns;
- A women-centric focus, hard-coded into all the business processes from skilling, asset creation, membership, share in surplus—and designed to work for women, including production supervision, feed, medicine, vaccination availability, and administration;
- Design principles which include: (a) separating members from the collective enterprise—making individuals responsible for what is in their control/domain of influence; (b) 'small together' becoming a 'big and dominant' player in the market; (c) assured returns with low variability—Efficiency Index-linked grower charge system;[2] (d) internal accruals which fund growth; (e) a balance in institutional focus between women and poultry—realizing the symbiotic synergy, and inter-locked nature of survival and growth; (f) rejecting the use of grants for business funding; and (g) appropriate business structures at all associative levels—primary, secondary and tertiary.
- Processes that: (a) devolve technology implementation with a subsidiarity focus wherein different levels: cooperative, village-groups and producers implement the components of technology within their respective domains (b) benchmark against the best, so provide excellent processes and infrastructure; and (c) encourage performance accountability between members and management based on the practicality of who provides the 'entrepreneurship', without allowing ideology or other considerations to crowd-out the reality of business.
- Central to the producer-ownership of a collective enterprise are the actual experience of being a residue claimant and ensuring member capital infusion.

External Factors Aiding Our Success

The 1980s saw increasing demand for public sector agencies to support rural development and partner with non-state actors. This was the context for PRADAN's initiative Teams for Rural Industrialization and Artisan Development (TRIAD) approaching Industrial Development Bank of India (IDBI) to support its work in Kesla as part of its Block Adoption Programme. The Kesla model continued to draw support from governments across the years, within the ambit of poverty alleviation programmes.

The success of the Amul model of cooperatives provided a template for rural producers to organize themselves; the literature and studies on the Amul model provided easy references to help us develop the Kesla or NSPDT model of smallholder poultry.

Another dimension which has enabled early uptake of our model was the 'marginal-livelihood-inhabit conditions' in the poorer rural pockets, with households typically earning Rs 30,000–45,000 annually. The additional income from poultry represented a significant amount for the women, and led to their increased interest in the model, with low-threshold expectations. The centrality of the model being important to the member and the domain, drove participant engagement, and this was aided by the members, hitherto being women, with low economic participation. The proportion of household earnings or income coming from the activity (member centrality) and income share of this activity in the local economy (domain centrality) greatly determines the participant and stakeholder response and involvement. The 'intervention' was designed taking into account the local economic context to create significant impact both at the member and local economy level.

Looking Back and Looking Forward

Retrospective wisdom can be naïve, as it does not account for the exigencies which drive decisions at the time. The evolution of a programme examined in retrospect while presenting the 'looking backwards' picture could however serve a useful purpose of helping us 'look forward'. In that sense there are some things we could have done differently:

Given the available models for dairy and the additional cyclical and periodic risks in poultry—our model took to value chain integration late in its journey. This integration has proven to be critical to secure, stabilize, aggregate risks and transfer value creation to the base of the value chain, i.e., the producers. This should have been the starting point.

Unfortunately, as a CSO programme, there are inherent limitations, such as: (a) 'bounded geography', which refers to the team's operating area; (b) the donor-funded project approach, which is one of 'bounded delivery'; and (c) 'bounded capital'—the model was restricted to grant capital in its initial stages and within the ambit of the development programme could not raise other forms of capital required for upstream/downstream investments. These facets lead to stunted understanding and enterprise-level actions.

There is need to build for the diversification of risk at the farmer and aggregate entity level—particularly for idiosyncratic (bird flu) or covariant risks (Covid-19), the old dictum of 'keeping all your eggs in one basket' has limits particularly, when production is hit with bigger systemic risks. The aggregate entities like the state federations and NSPDT, while de-risked during regular operations, are hit disproportionately during a business collapse, and could take the entire carefully nurtured business edifice down with them.

The diversification of sources of revenue at this level is critical for surviving such an extreme business collapse. Similarly, with the greater dependence on poultry as a source of income by farmer-members, skipping a batch or two in a poor market situation is not an option. Adding conjunctive portfolio activities will diversify revenue flows at the household level.

The activity has remained in the commodity space and is largely business-to-business, missing the Amul branding trick, and graduating into a product space, so retailing has been half-hearted. The changing demography and technology (like e-commerce) present an opportunity to attend to this shortcoming with vigour and new investment.

What Can Be Learnt from Our Experience?

One of the important takeaways is that accelerated progress on rural livelihoods is critical to India's emergence as a just and equitable society.

There is acceptance that business cannot continue as usual, with the changed dynamics: the Covid-19 crisis has upended the migrant dream; there are tailwinds to place-based economic alternatives that encourage a reverse talent flow to villages; there are also newly acquired skills among the rural youth, with higher digital proficiency, and a change in employment aptitude and orientation; and other proficiencies that can fuel local markets with opportunities and demand. The model of off-farm linked-enterprise presented here can be replicated, with adaptation to enable farm and other local rural economy opportunities to connect with modern markets. We have highlighted the elements that contributed to the making of NSPDT and some of these can be adapted to other contexts. Some facets worth considering are:

A business must pay for itself

The developmental element should be separated from the business, and grants need to be removed from the calculation. Further, fairly early in the process, control of the enterprise should move away from the NGO-promoter, and be designed for sustainability and growth. This allows for a business model that can raise its costs, get the right human resources, get the right partners, and thus become capable of being scaled-up without NGO apron-strings or guardrails. The premise of Kesla Poultry is that the surplus for the 'individual member', the cooperative, the federation and the NSPDT, was specified in detail with realistic assumptions, taking into account all the investments required. While there has been extensive grant support for capacity development and individual asset-building, there is complete clarity on the need for the business to pay for all costs. This clarity guided the creation of the linked-institutional architecture (Cooperative–State Federation–NSPDT) in a manner that a new institutional layer (e.g., State Federation or NSPDT) is added only after there is a clear plan for its value addition role and revenue inflows and not allowing for any parasitic layer/entity to emerge, which would inevitably eat into the revenue flows of the subsidiary level.

Kesla poultry: Financing categories and sources

	Purpose	Source	Node/Entity	Amount
1.	Human resources: acquisition, on-going professional development and incentives	Fixed service-share from cooperatives business	NSPDT	Rs 12–16 crore annually
2.	Value chain investments to secure supply lines and growth (parent farm, hatchery and feed mills)	Internal business accruals and debt	State federations	Rs 120 crore overall
3.	Fixed cost of enterprise and service units (production unit, services and processing)	Business surplus	Cooperatives, federation, NSPDT	Rs 4–5 crore annually
4.	Expansion of member production units	Internal accrual and debt	Members, cooperative	Rs 1,00,000 per member
5.	Start-up member production infrastructure	Grant or subsidy-linked loans under poverty alleviation programmes and debt	Members, cooperative	Rs 1,00,000 per member
6.	Mobilization of farmers, capacity development	Grants and internal accrual	Federation or NSPDT	Rs 5,000 per member

'Design' is key to the viability of a collective enterprise

In the words of Steve Jobs, 'Design isn't just what it looks like and feels like. Design is how it works.'[3] Additional key elements of good design in our experience include: (i) reconciling business imperatives with a focus on purpose (on both women and the poultry); (ii) for collective action to work, needing to strike the right balance in reality and perception between the future and present; (iii) coalescing the challenges of owner-customer, service exchange recipient and residue claimant, typical of member-oriented-firm where member-owner is also customer of services and has the final claim on business profits; this requires clarity on business vision and building robust transaction integrity both to be visible and to be experienced by members; (iv) running businesses only have owners—this is an often neglected dimension. To make the business a going concern and profitable, good business systems are needed, which allows members and member organizations to compete in the market. Striking a balance between member ownership and professional management is very critical. We must not forget that by meeting short-term demands of members, say of cheaper service or better price of produce, we make the business organization weak, and then the same member has no interest or intent to own or associate with the business. The dictum is 'only strong institutions can make members strong'; (v) striking the right balance between a producer-centric and consumer-centric business.

Need for professional management to apply best business processes

Given our size disadvantages, we have to strive to be ahead of the industry. The poor cannot grow with poor managers and systems; we need excellent systems to succeed.

Integration of the value chain is critical to the transfer of 'value' to the primary production system. Depending on the business setting; the cycle of value creation is dynamic and volatile, the risks are also asynchronous for different stages of the value-chain, therefore unless there is some control on the value chain through both upstream and downstream interventions that mitigate the natural size-disadvantage of primary production system particularly when exclusive focus is on small/marginal producers, it will not be possible to stabilize and grow business income. The key insight from the experience of smallholder poultry is validation of smallholder primary producers' growth with 'integrated value chain' like in dairy.

Central to the ownership of collective enterprise are: (a) the actual experience of being a residue claimant; and (b) the infusion of member capital; these are key to building a stake in and contributing to resilience in the enterprise. Government or donor funding, while important for mitigating capital scarcity, the lack of assets and general precarity of poor livelihoods, is no substitute for members having a 'real stake' in the business.

Return per day (RpD) is a key indicator of rural livelihoods/enterprise assessment from a participant lens. Portfolio share is directly related to participant effort intensity. All livelihood programmes must have a bifocal RpD and portfolio share (or member centrality) driving mean income and reducing variance.

Conclusion

India's economy in 2022 is at a critical inflexion point with long-term consequences for its social and ecological life and for the future of its citizens. The extent and intensity of precarity has implications beyond India. In 2021, the country provided almost 60 per cent of its population (i.e., about 80 crore people) with subsidized food. It has the largest number of multidimensional poor and one of the highest number of people living below the international poverty line (less than $1.9 a day). India also has one of the highest rates of inequality and the largest unemployed workforce in the age group of eighteen to twenty-eight and a very high proportion of rural inhabitants.

Land and land-use in the primary sector have provided the bulk of employment historically as well as in present times. Climate variability risks present an unprecedented crisis for primary sector livelihoods. Ensuring a future with basic necessities for all its citizens requires India to grow fast and more equitably, with a net-zero commitment. This requires it to develop a new pathway for its rural and peri-rural economy based on economic opportunities for its growing workforce.

Community-owned enterprises are key to unlocking the rural and peri-rural economies that are at present dominated by gigified production systems across agriculture and livestock. It is the route for small and marginal producers to participate in the market and earn a fair return on their labour, resources and investment, and to be able to invest in increased avenues for growth.

It is critical to have institutional and process innovations that help these community enterprises thrive in the market economy, with declining state support, and grow new tech-intensive enterprises with access to deep capital. The success of NSPDT, in a business domain dominated by large commercial enterprises, with all-women, first-time producers has useful insights for seeding accelerated green-growth in a rural economy.

12

Development Support Centre: Mainstreaming the Idea of Water Users' Associations

SACHIN OZA AND MOHAN SHARMA

DEVELOPMENT SUPPORT CENTRE (DSC)[1] IS a non-government organization (NGO) that provides knowledge-based support to institutions, policies and programmes that promote sustainable livelihoods and participatory natural resource management (PNRM). DSC's initiatives in Participatory Irrigation Management (PIM) brought a change in perspective of the community from short-term, individual gain to long-term, collective benefits.

It led to unprecedented collaboration between communities and the government through a process of dialogue, resulting in local problems being solved and policy issues being addressed. Dramatic improvements in water-use efficiency and crop productivity could be achieved by solving the issues of equity and efficiency in canal water distribution. It led to identification of replicable principles, which enabled creation of location-specific models.

DSC's Beginnings

DSC was established in 1994 by the late Anil C. Shah in response to a demand from individuals and stakeholders concerned with rural development in Gujarat. It now operates in 909 villages in forty-one blocks of nineteen districts of Gujarat, Madhya Pradesh, Maharashtra and Rajasthan, covering 1.44 lakh households across 2.06 lakh hectares. It implements PNRM programmes such as watershed management, PIM, Participatory Groundwater Management and Integrated Water Resource

Management. It also promotes sustainable agriculture and collective enterprise in these four states.

Till the early 1990s, the development and management of natural resources in the country was largely the prerogative of the government, with very little input from the rural communities in the planning, implementation and management of watersheds or canal irrigation systems. After concerted efforts from various NGOs, the central government launched the Integrated Watershed Management Programme in 1994 and the Gujarat government introduced PIM in 1995. These programmes emphasized a decentralized approach at the grassroots, with active participation from communities in developing and managing rural water resources.

However, there were few instances of community-led management of canals or watersheds at the time. Neither the communities nor the officials were clear about processes for translating these programmes into practice. There was clearly an urgent need for an intervening support organization to build the capacities of the stakeholders and demonstrate to them successful participatory natural resource management practices. Only then could they scale and sustain these practices. This need was the genesis of DSC.

DSC visited various regions in Gujarat and interacted with rural communities, NGOs and government departments. It soon became evident that water availability and its management were major problems in both rain-fed and irrigated areas. Many canal networks were dilapidated and caused waterlogging in the head reach and high deprivation at the tail end. This meant that the actual irrigated area was far lesser than it potentially could be.

In the rain-fed areas, farmers could grow only Kharif crops as there was heavy soil erosion, few water-harvesting structures, high production risks and low crop productivity. To tackle these problems with sustainable processes, DSC collaborated with the Gujarat government to promote PIM in Mahesana and Sabarkantha districts and participatory watershed management in Amreli and Sabarkantha districts as its first project interventions.

DSC is now one of the largest NGOs working in the irrigation sector in India. Its PIM projects in Gujarat and Madhya Pradesh have been instrumental in influencing policy at the state and national levels and in developing standard operating procedures for promoting and facilitating Water User's Associations (WUAs). Lessons from DSC's experience in developing self-reliant WUAs can be used as models for other similar interventions.

The Success and Impact of PIM

DSC measures the impacts of PIM at the community, sector and policy levels along the following parameters:

Impact on the community

DSC's work in four states has demonstrated how people-centred initiatives can be successful in the management of canal irrigation. The Dharoi project in north Gujarat and the Man and Jobat projects in Madhya Pradesh are recognized for exceptional improvements in efficiency, equity and sustainability of public irrigation schemes through community participation. Impact assessment studies by the Institute for Rural Management, Anand, and Indian Institute of Management, Ahmedabad, have studied the major impacts of PIM in Madhya Pradesh and Gujarat.

The WUAs have enhanced the access to and supply of water for more than 2,000 tail-end farmers in north Gujarat and to 7,000 farmers in the Dhar district of Madhya Pradesh. They have carried out canal rehabilitation work worth Rs 5.5 crore through grants from the state government in Gujarat and Rs 1 crore through the Mahatma Gandhi National Rural Employment Guarantee Act (MGNREGA) programme in Madhya Pradesh. Further, they have mobilized cash contributions of Rs 1 crore and donated land worth Rs 5 crores for canal construction in the Sardar Sarovar project command area in Gujarat.

About 200 WUAs in Gujarat are now financially self-reliant, with no financial support from the government for operations, maintenance and administration expenses. They meet these expenses through water charges and service fees. The irrigated area in the canal command area has increased by 20–60 per cent due to the improved efficiency in the supply and use of water. The productivity of crops such as wheat, cotton, sorghum and maize has increased by 20–70 per cent, resulting in additional income of about Rs 29,000 annually for each household. This has been made possible by increased access to water for irrigation. PIM has enhanced incomes by Rs 7,000 to 10,000 per hectare, and by a further Rs 19,000 per hectare through the 'PIM-plus' programmes.

DSC has trained a cadre of over 200 paraprofessionals working on various aspects of water management, such as *bhujal jankars*, canal operators and technical supervisors who work with the community. Its strategy is to ensure that income enhancement does not happen at the cost of harming the environment. To achieve this, it has facilitated behavioural change and introduced new technologies for recharging and reducing the use of water in the command area of irrigation systems; these actions have resulted in an increase in in-situ moisture conservation and a decrease in stress on ground water by 20–40 per cent.

Larger sectoral impact

DSC is recognized as a resource centre for PIM at state, regional and national level. It has collaborated with the Water and Land Management Institute (WALMI) in Gujarat to provide capacity-building inputs to functionaries from WUAs, NGOs, CSR organizations and the Water Resources Department (WRD). It was invited by the World Bank to develop training modules and Information Education and Communication (IEC) materials on PIM in Uttar Pradesh and has trained 500 government functionaries from seven states and 447 WUAs in Gujarat and Maharashtra.

DSC has also hosted visits from several states and countries and is working with Shiv Nadar University on a short-term course on PIM for MSc students. The organization develops and disseminates IEC material on PIM in the form of booklets, manuals and videos in Gujarati, Hindi, Marathi and English. These are used extensively to train various functionaries by NGOs, CSRs and training institutes including WALMI.

Research and documentation are an integral part of DSC's strategy for improving practices and influencing policies related to water management and PIM. It has conducted research studies, documented best practices and published research papers on topics such as the impact of PIM on economic growth. Some of its research studies have led to modifications in the procedures and policies on PIM at the state and the centre.

Impact on policy

DSC was a member of the Working Group of the eleventh and twelfth Five-Year Plans, contributing to framing policies on major and medium irrigation schemes and command-area development. The government of Gujarat appointed DSC to committees for promoting, scaling and capacity-building of stakeholders in PIM. The organization was instrumental in introducing PIM in the state through the policy resolution of 1 June 1995, wherein farmers and NGOs were considered partners with the government.

It convinced the Gujarat government to issue a series of government orders authorizing WUAs to award construction work, make decisions and collect water charges, retaining the 50 per cent rebate as irrigation revenue at the minor level. This led to the state government providing 50 per cent rebate to WUAs, 20 per cent to distributary-level committees, 10 per cent to branch committees and 10 per cent to project committees. States such as Andhra Pradesh and Maharashtra have adopted some of these policies.

Internal Enablers

The focus of the organization has been to facilitate strong WUAs by building their capacities. DSC mobilized communities in four sequential phases: formation of WUAs; canal rehabilitation; water distribution; and water and agriculture productivity enhancement. In the initial phase, DSC's community organizers met with individual households—especially the tail-end farmers—to understand their issues with canal irrigation and the impact on agriculture and animal husbandry and to think of possible solutions. The community leaders went on to estimate their costs of continuing as before, which they had been paying in the form of crop loss due to poor irrigation under government-managed systems. They then estimated the cost of restoring the system, which led to the realization that the benefits would outweigh the likely costs.

These discussions were followed by exposure visits to successful community-managed projects. The farmers understood that unless they took steps to change, they would keep losing output and income for years. The role of the government and DSC was to support them in this process of change. Thus, PIM was seen as a solution to their problems rather than as a scheme in which the government wanted to pass on to them the responsibility of managing non-functional canals. Typically, it took about six to nine months for DSC to convince a community and help them form a WUA.

DSC initially developed a few WUAs that had tail-end deprivation as models to motivate other villages. It took special care to ensure that there was a rotational supply of water and that the tailenders received their share in time. Some WUAs made sure that women-headed households were given water during the day. The WUAs were facilitated to prepare an annual budget summarizing their likely incomes and expenditures, which they would use as a basis for deciding water charges. The WUAs acquired the competence to meet their administration, operation and maintenance expenses through revenue earned from irrigation charges.

Since the initial WUAs facilitated by DSC in 1995–96 were part of pilot projects, the learnings from these were shared with policymakers to help them formulate farmer-centric policies on PIM in the state. The Gujarat government allocated funds for rehabilitation encouraged by cost-benefit studies carried out by DSC and the model WUAs.

DSC developed the capacities of farmers and formed a 'farmer spearhead team', which was instrumental in upscaling PIM in the Dharoi, Mazum and Guhai irrigation schemes across 135 villages. Water management is often seen as a technical skill and little focus is given to developing softer skills such as participation, leadership, conflict resolution and 'attitude and behaviour change' (ABC). DSC conducted workshops for senior government functionaries on ABC to sensitize them on enabling factors and barriers to participation, which helped in building a positive environment for PIM.

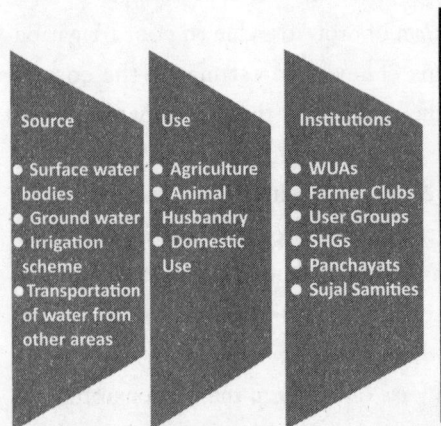

Source	Use	Institutions
• Surface water bodies	• Agriculture	• WUAs
• Ground water	• Animal Husbandry	• Farmer Clubs
• Irrigation scheme	• Domestic Use	• User Groups
• Transportation of water from other areas		• SHGs
		• Panchayats
		• Sujal Samities

- Enhance supply of water and access to water by blending people's knowledge and modern technology
- Reduce the demand for water
- Improve water and soil quality and productivity
- Facilitate and strengthen water governance institutions
- Document & disseminate best practices
- Influence water policy at the state and national level through regular feedback

Water management is region-specific and dynamic. It does not lend itself to a one-size-fits-all approach. DSC realized that the process adopted in Gujarat would need to be modified in order to be applied in Madhya Pradesh, where conditions—such as the irrigation infrastructure, farmers' socioeconomic status, cropping patterns and provisions of the PIM Act—were quite different from those in Gujarat. Thus, DSC adopted a different strategy for involving farmers in PIM and promoting WUAs in the central Indian state.

During its initial years, DSC focused on enhancing the supply of water and access to it in irrigation systems. But the increased supply of water led to some unintended consequences, such as changes in cropping patterns and an increase in the demand for water. Thus, DSC promoted sustainable agriculture practices by reducing the use of chemical inputs and improving soil health. This enhanced productivity, allowed for better access to markets and, most importantly, reduced the demand for water through mulching, drip irrigation and crop varieties that required less water.

While surface water structures and schemes were well-understood and managed by the communities, groundwater management was an enigma. Since there was considerable use of groundwater even in the command areas, DSC needed the help of Arid Communities and Technology, a Kutch-based NGO specializing in groundwater management and capacity building. Together, they mapped the aquifers in the command area, built community capacities in monitoring and managing groundwater, trained bhujal jankars in surface and groundwater management and carried out water-balance exercises with the rural communities. DSC facilitated *sujal samitis* for water governance at the village level, which led to more inclusive planning and implementation and greater sharing of water.

DSC strongly believes in values such as participation, equity, efficiency, cost-effectiveness, sustainability, honesty and transparency. These principles act as a moral compass for the organization to reflect on both its own work as well as the work of the WUAs, and help in building appropriate systems, cultures and leadership within DSC and the WUAs. These policies have helped the WUAs challenge local politicians and not be dependent on their help, instead creating their own revenue sources to meet their costs. An example is when a WUA did not wait for government funds to prevent water logging, instead using their own funds to lay plastic sheets in several stretches of the canals and thereby solving their problem by themselves.

Since public irrigation systems are owned by the government, DSC's strategy has been to work with the WRD to create more space for the communities and NGOs in implementation of PIM. It has not always been easy to work 'with'—rather than 'for'—the government, which led to the development of strategies to effectively engage with it.

In canal irrigation, DSC originally faced resistance from WRD officers when it came to devolving technical tasks to WUAs. DSC was able to demonstrate that with some guidance and training WUAs could effectively carry out canal rehabilitation works. With the help of a few champions in the WRD, DSC developed detailed community-friendly guidelines to carry out the technical work so that quality was not compromised.

Bringing about procedural and policy change could take many years, but DSC persisted in its approach. It facilitated field visits for policymakers, provided evidence through research and identified champions within the government, eventually bringing about the necessary changes. Though the discussions were not always successful, DSC continued its interactions with the bureaucracy as it realized that sometimes even a small change in policy could have a large impact on the participation of communities and NGOs in development work.

External Factors

The 1990s saw states such as Andhra Pradesh and Madhya Pradesh pass PIM Acts to operationalize the programme on a large scale. The Gujarat government issued a series of orders that encouraged and facilitated community participation and the involvement of NGOs in promoting PIM. At the centre, PIM was a priority and the Planning Commission invited NGOs such as DSC to consult on Five-Year Plans.

DSC could emphasize the need for incentivizing WUAs and building capacity of WUAs as well as the WRD. Funds were allotted for developing physical infrastructure—including the rehabilitation of canals—and for creating awareness and building community capacity. Thus, there was a great deal of enthusiasm at the state and national level to demonstrate, learn and reflect and share experiences on participatory approaches in collaboration with NGOs and the community.

When DSC began operations in 1994, the rural communities with which it worked were more cohesive and had more time for meetings. While collective action was a challenge, given some patience one could win the trust of the community. Rural communities were aware that water availability and access were major problems and had largely depended upon the government to solve these problems. However, when an alternative approach was suggested, they were ready to come together and leave aside their political and religious affiliations to repair, maintain and manage their canals.

They had realistic expectations regarding the benefits of PIM and the time required for it to show results. Given their economic condition and the limited opportunities in the non-farm sector, they were keen to enhance their incomes from agriculture and animal husbandry.

One of the major factors that contributed to the success of PIM in north Gujarat was the presence of able community leaders. They were truly altruistic and believed in doing good for their community. Since many of them also had leadership roles in dairy farming at the village and district levels, they shared a good rapport with the farmers. DSC identified these leaders and built their capacity to motivate members to expand their role in the management of their canals and to deal with the irrigation bureaucracy.

As leaders of the WUAs, they believed in good governance and social justice and provided an excellent example to the younger generation. In recognition of their contribution, DSC felicitated many community leaders and community-based organizations by conferring on them the Anil C. Shah Gram Paritoshik award.

Similarly, some government officials at the state and national levels provided able leadership in anchoring PIM. They were proactive about supporting greater community involvement in the management of canals and made field visits to understand the communities' problems and complaints. These officers took new initiatives and corrective action even when they faced resistance within their own department.

They realized that working with the community and reaching the last mile was not easy, but was necessary to implement the programme. Understanding the strengths of other agencies, they collaborated with NGOs and technical and academic institutes. Some of the policy measures would not have been possible had such officers not taken the initiative in convincing political leaders.

Learnings

Water security is becoming a major issue as demand is increasing but the quality of water and soil is deteriorating. Agriculture is becoming increasingly susceptible to climate change, which mostly affects small and marginal and women farmers. Aspirations of the community have changed over the last few years, with tech-savvy youth in rural areas having lesser interest in in-person meetings. They prefer receiving information on their mobile phones and online. They use remote devices to operate their field pumps and irrigate their fields through automated drips and sprinklers. PIM needs to take cognizance of these changes if it is to remain relevant and efficient enough to respond to people's needs in the present-day context.

Based on these realities, DSC needs to modify its strategy to make PIM holistically integrated with water management. PIM is currently practiced through a one-size-fits-all approach, but cropping patterns, agriculture and irrigation practices and the aspirations of the communities have changed considerably over the last two decades. Areas are increasingly being irrigated through underground pipelines rather than open canals. Farmers use the canal water to fill their wells or *khet talavdis* (field ponds) to use when needed.

In addition to canal water, farmers in the command area use groundwater, so there are several wells and tube wells which impact and are impacted by canal irrigation. Thus, there is conjunctive use of canal water and groundwater by default rather than by design. However, there is little integration of the surface irrigation system with the groundwater and hardly any thought is given to catchment-area treatment. A contingency model taking into account groundwater, surface water, agriculture, energy and socioeconomic aspects is needed for each command area.

Water security plans and physical interventions for management of supply and demand need to be promoted in areas where groundwater is depleted as well as in rain-fed areas and in the command areas of water-scarce irrigation systems. The use of GIS informatics tools and drone technologies for smart planning and monitoring would help with water governance and in developing trust between the government and the community. However, care must be taken not to undermine people's capacities and technology must not overpower them.

DSC has piloted technologies for improving water efficiency in canal commands and enhancing groundwater recharge, which can be applied in other areas too. User-friendly technological innovations in canal irrigation would make agriculture more profitable and attract young people to the cause. When face-to-face meetings with the community were not possible during the Covid-19 lockdown, DSC had developed and piloted online modules for creating awareness. In the future, DSC would like to work on water quality, water recycling and farm and off-farm water-use efficiency.

DSC would like to develop appropriate processes and modifications in the policy for greater involvement of women and tenant farmers in PIM. The WUAs in Gujarat and Madhya Pradesh tend to be dominated by men. The PIM Act in Gujarat and many other states—but not Madhya Pradesh—allows WUA membership for women only if they are landowners. While women can participate as nominal members or in the executive committee, they rarely attend or participate in the WUA meetings. Prevailing social norms and household responsibilities further inhibit their participation in these associations. Also, many of the landowners are 'absentee landlords' and their fields are being irrigated by tenant farmers. DSC has made conscious efforts to include women and tenant farmers in WUAs, but there remains considerable scope for enhancing their participation in the decision-making processes.

Elements of Success

The National Water Policy of 1987 advocated the involvement of farmers in the management of irrigation systems, particularly in water distribution and collection of water rates. The enactment of the PIM Act in several states has led to the formation of several thousand WUAs in the country. However, due to various reasons, only a small percentage of these seem to be functioning satisfactorily. This has led to a lot of skepticism about PIM. Yet, several studies show that wherever an enabling policy environment, capacity building and support have been provided to the WUAs by the WRD or NGOs, it has led to better operation and maintenance of canals, higher recovery of water charges, equitable water supply and enhanced incomes of farmers.

DSC's experience in promoting PIM in Gujarat, Madhya Pradesh and Maharashtra shows that PIM requires mutual trust, commitment and accountability from the state and the community. Wherever there have been sensitive officers who believed in farmer's participation, listened to their problems and tried to solve them, the WUAs have taken greater responsibilities in the management of the canals. Similarly, one needs to build a sense of ownership of the irrigation systems among the community so that they realize that PIM is in their interest. The processes DSC adopted for the formation of the WUAs and to bridge the trust deficit in its operational area could be adopted in other geographies as well.

PIM is not about water management alone but also about soil health, groundwater, agriculture, animal husbandry and above all the social dynamics of the community. It is important to have a multidisciplinary team comprising civil and agriculture engineers, agronomists and social scientists—including gender specialists—to understand and address the social, technical, economic, financial and legal aspects of canal irrigation. Given the dynamic nature of agriculture in the command area, water management and distribution practices by the WUAs also have to change with changing times and therefore their capacities need to be built accordingly.

PIM needs be viewed in an integrated and holistic manner as part of the larger ecosystem. There is need to work on the natural as well as anthropogenic factors to develop overall water security in the command area. The sources of water (supply) and uses of water (demand) should not be viewed in silos. Cooperative thinking and collective action are needed for its sustainable management. In addition to physical and technological interventions, it is critical to have behavioural change communication, water governance institutions and water audits in the command area. There is a need to move from PIM to participatory water, land and agriculture management in the command area of irrigation systems.

13

ANANDI: The Long Road to Gender Just Development

SRILATHA BATLIWALA, SEJAL DAND AND
NEETA HARDIKAR

IN 1995, FIVE YOUNG FEMINISTS started the Area Networking and Development Initiatives, popularly known as ANANDI. They had been working together to advance the spaces for co-learning and sharing while also challenging power structures by organizing rural women and girls from marginalized communities in Gujarat. ANANDI was formed with the mission of mobilizing women and young people to work towards transformative change based on social justice, sustainable development and accountable governance. Transformative change celebrates diversity and solidarity, one that is realized through a process of empowerment and claiming rights.

ANANDI works to strengthen women's social, political and economic rights across 274 gram panchayats in four districts of Gujarat where the organization has helped 10,000 rural women and girls from marginalized communities to take leadership in their communities and local self-governments. Civil society organizations, activists and students trained by ANANDI have spread the movement across the country.

The communities that ANANDI works with have repeatedly suffered from droughts, earthquakes, communal riots, floods and epidemics. Relief and reconstruction efforts led by women have served to break customary caste, class, religious and gender barriers. ANANDI's work and research—

combined with intensive engagement with state and national campaigns and state and parastatal organizations—have led to gender-transformative provisions in laws such as National Food Security Act and Mahatma Gandhi National Rural Employment Guarantee Act (MGNREGA) with wider impacts on engendering programmes and policies for rural women's livelihoods, women's resource rights, communization of health services and gender-based violence.

ANANDI's work has impacted many areas of women's lives, and has led to the formation of four women's sangathans (solidarity groups or organizations). These sites of women's empowerment are witness to concrete actions for change and have formed partnerships with development and social justice organizations and platforms. They have the capacity to address a wide range of issues affecting the most marginalized women and their communities. The sangathans have built credibility within the community as well as in the wider public space and normalized a culture that promotes the equal participation of women.

What Has Changed in Key Areas?

There has been a measurable increase in access to social security entitlements for marginalized and vulnerable communities, especially those in informal wage work. The sangathans' activism and vigilance have introduced accountability in provisions under the public distribution system, ensuring that food grains reach the most impoverished people. They have halted malpractices such as distributing lower quality or quantities of grain to the poor.

There is increased access to pensions for widows, disabled people and the elderly, as well as critical government documents such as birth and death certificates, voter ID cards, Aadhaar cards and caste certificates. Employment under MGNREGA is also more accessible. The sangathans have enabled women to claim their land rights and access agriculture schemes and financial credit. In the words of one ANANDI activist, 'Sangathans have brought recognition to rural women as "informed citizens and knowers"; it is great to see how even non-literate women can oversee government officials carrying out the paperwork on behalf of poor women!' There is an overall decrease in the extent and types of corruption faced by marginalized people, though bringing accountability and transparency in state provisioning still has a long way to go.

There has been a visible increase in access to health services for poor women and those in remote settlements. Most childbirths now take place at health centres, resulting in fewer maternal deaths. Timely identification has reduced malnutrition and awareness of the importance of child immunization has increased in villages. Rural health staff are more present and accessible because of the sangathans' vigilance and monitoring. There are now doctors, an adequate supply of basic medicines and a range of health services available at primary health centres in villages.

In an environment where normalization of violence is endemic, women now participate in the hitherto male *'panchs'* (community-level dispute resolution systems) and have formed women led *'nyay samitis'* (justice committees) to address instances of violence against women. Shedding their earlier reluctance, women now openly talk about the violence they face in their lives and actively seek remedies through collective action and the formal legal system. As a woman who came forward to report the rape of her daughter said: 'something wrong has happened to my child today; if I keep quiet, tomorrow it could happen to anybody here.'

Sangathans also actively tackle cases where women have faced violence after being declared 'witches'. There is a perceptible change in awareness and the community and panchayat response to cases of violence against women.

ANANDI's focus on building leadership among young women has resulted in changes in the profiles of sangathan members and leaders. Now younger women make up 35 to 40 per cent of the association. While this shift ensures a strong future for the sangathans, it also inevitably results in differences of opinion on how issues are seen or analysed. This in turn promotes a healthy mix of debate and multigenerational perspectives on issues, with the wisdom and experience of older women blending with the newer viewpoints and energy of the younger ones.

Creation of Forums for Advancing Rights

ANANDI has catalysed the formation of several people's organizations and forums to sustain the struggle for the rights and entitlements of marginalized women and their communities. These include:

The Mahila Sangathans:[1] Devgadh Mahila Sangathan of Devgadh-Baria and Ghoghamba blocks, Panam Mahila Sangathan of Shehera block in the eastern tribal region, Maliya Mahila Shakti Sangathan in Maliya-Miyana and Mahila Swaraj Manch in Shihore in the western region of Gujarat. These sangathans are powerful organizations promoting empowerment of marginalized women.

Panam Women's Savings and Credit Cooperative Society: This is an AA+ rated women's organization with 3,109 members among whom are landless, small and marginal women farmers. It goes beyond credit, also helping to build women's enterprises and assets while protecting them from the usurious interest rates charged by private moneylenders and the exploitative practices of private financial institutions.

Ratanmahal Adivasi Mahila Sajeev Khet Utpadak Mandli/RASKUM FPO: A women's forest and farm producer organization that helps tribal women receive a minimum support price for non-forest timber produce, increases incomes through value addition and promotes chemical-free agriculture for food and nutrition security for small and marginal farmer households.

Azaad Mahila Machhimaari Sahakaari Mandli: A fisherwomen's cooperative society that enables women fish-workers to gain recognition for traditional livelihoods of natural estuarine prawn harvesting. This organization leverages government investments for gender-responsive services and access to fishing sites resulting in increased incomes for the women through expanded markets.

Lok Adhikar Kendra: Community resource centres for gender justice that collect information on rights violations and support claims and remedies to resolve issues. Women leaders from the sangathans run a desk at the block level (which is often the last post for most government departments). These women process over 10,000 claims annually at five such centres. In 2022, this model became part of the gender advisory for the National Rural Livelihood Mission (NRLM) after ANANDI successfully piloted it in Madhya Pradesh.

The Nyaya Samitis: These are justice committees within each sangathan which navigate between the formal legal system and the traditional adjudication system to make justice more accessible for women in distress. They support over 600 survivors of gender-based violence annually and reach over 8,000 people through campaigns to prevent violence against women.

Mazdoor Sangathans: These are workers organizations at village levels. They work with people from Dalit and tribal communities to include their voices in local self-government.

Over time, these forums have gained the ability to manage their issues and processes and their dependency on ANANDI has been reduced. ANANDI's role has gradually shifted towards information and strategic support. These multiple forums have also enhanced women's participation and built their leadership in tackling key issues affecting them and their communities.

Men have started supporting and joining the sangathans in their activism on livelihood issues as they also benefit from it. They increasingly consult women in matters concerning land and cultivation, which in turn has enhanced women's mobility, decision-making power, finances and access to public spaces.

The sangathans have created a public presence with a strong identity and recognition. Elected representatives have begun to appreciate the value of their work and public health staff attitudes have changed from hostility to respect after seeing how these groups help them reach their targets. Those who are not members of sangathans also acknowledge the benefits gained from the work done by these organizations at both the individual and collective levels.

The sangathans have played roles in improving health and nutrition services and receiving infrastructure investments in water and sanitation. They have also supported survivors of sexual assault through years of judicial processes and strengthened the implementation of MGNREGA. Elected women representatives in the panchayats have received support from sangathans in performing their roles as well as in the prevention of violence against women and girls.

The marginalized communities in general understand that their local sangathan is fighting for their rights and resources and against corruption and malpractices. There are benefits for all and there is thus a wide level of support for the sangathans. They have enabled marginalized people to cope with the challenges of their lives with dignity.

ANANDI's View of Transformation

Within ANANDI, transformation is defined as a radical change in both institutions and social relations that is reflected in the material condition of people's daily lives. The concepts of empowerment and rights inform ANANDI's work and shape the organization's strategies. When the most excluded and marginalized people—particularly women—move from invisibility to visibility, that is transformation.

In this context, empowerment is the enhanced control of women over their bodies, labour, time, life choices and resources. It is the growing ability to raise their voices in both private and public institutional spaces—in their homes and communities as well as in the village council or other policymaking arenas. ANANDI believes in linking empowerment with rights, as the mainstream rights approach often transfers agency out of the hands of the claimants to professionals who claim on their behalf through formal mechanisms. As a founder member said, 'When you don't have access to a right, you collectivize to fight for that right. But when the law comes in, it always focuses on the individual. Fighting for your right can be a lonely process. The strategy is to help fight for individual rights through collective struggles.'

ANANDI chooses to translate rights into the language and experiences of grassroots realities and locates empowerment in the ability to claim the rights for oneself. Empowerment is then the ability to bring home rights in real forms, and this social justice is achieved when all people have equal rights, equal benefits and equal opportunities. It is achieved together, through collective effort and action.

Accountable governance is present when government functionaries see themselves as servants of all citizens—without regard of caste, gender, religion or class. It manifests in actions of the state where the needs and interests of the most impoverished and oppressed citizens are prioritized and when corruption in all forms is eradicated. It is also about framing policies based on and responsive to grassroots gender realities. For example, the government's Kisan Samman Nidhi Yojana—which gives small and marginal farmers up to Rs 6,000 per year as minimum income support—fails to recognize that very few women own farmland in their own names and are thus prevented from accessing such schemes.

Sustainable development is equitable and inclusive of the most marginalized people and meets the practical needs of the poorest people. It conserves natural resources and protects the environment for future generations. ANANDI believes strongly in *'bandhutva'*, which is a concept of proactive solidarity that rises from an intersectional approach. It has brought women together across the deep traditional divides of caste, ethnicity and religion. This solidarity is seen as a kind of fellowship and sisterhood that is expressed and acted upon constantly, beyond the moments of crisis or confrontation that typically bring people together.

Core Strategies

Closely intertwined with strategies of its partner collectives/sangathans, ANANDI's core strategies are:

Collectivization: The idea of mobilizing and organizing women into their own platforms or unified structures. This, in essence, is the movement-building strategy adopted by ANANDI since its inception. Using this pivotal strategy, a wide range of grassroots membership structures have been set up and they have supported the creation of para-judicial forums that investigate rights violations. The sangathans ensure that the cooperatives do not make their focus too narrow and that they retain the collective spirit and basic values that define a sangathan.

Empowerment: Building women's consciousness of their rights, voice and capacity to act for change is a big part of ANANDI's mission, but in supporting women in building their own vision, it has to ensure that individual empowerment is not at the cost of the collective. Neither can the collective voice and power neglect the individual's assertion of her rights in her own unique struggle.

Capacity building: This involves equipping women with critical information and widening their strategic repertoire and skills to make informed choices not only about *what* they want to work on, but *how* they can move forward. This is a lateral, shared process of exchanging information and strategic ideas between ANANDI and the various collectives.

Information/awareness building: This is sometimes referred to as the 'feminist popular education' approach.[2] The lack of access to information and awareness of their rights and entitlements are barriers to women's empowerment. The methods used by ANANDI range from basic information-sharing at the group level to campaigns that travel on foot from village to village. There are public hearings that bring people, government and policymakers together for the collective celebration of occasions such as International Women's Day, Women Farmers' Day and Day for Elimination of Violence Against Women. Intensive workshops with women's groups and local self-governments focus on building awareness of the rights of citizens and women.

Leadership building: This is seen as a lateral process; it includes leadership training programmes, support of young leaders, especially women, through the Fellowship Programme to revitalize the leadership of the collectives/sangathans, and bringing new voices, energy and sustainability into the empowerment process.

Advocacy: ANANDI's advocacy work is largely indirect, supporting women in the vanguard of advocacy with government departments and local councils or engaging these bodies alongside sangathan leaders in an effort to bridge the gap between the government and the community. ANANDI also undertakes some direct advocacy around issues affecting women, such as violence and lack of access to basic services. It has also participated in national and international advocacy campaigns and movements around gender-based violence, food security, right to food, right to information, land rights and workers' rights.[3]

Challenges

ANANDI and the sangathans worked in areas of poverty, underdevelopment and political neglect in the most backward areas and faced a number of critical challenges. Basic services were of poor quality and did not reach everybody. There was a lack of access to schemes for the poor, which was made worse by corrupt practices.

When ANANDI began its work, basic health and education services were woefully inadequate or simply not available. In many places, there were either no primary health centres (there should be one per every 30,000 population in tribal areas) or the centres had no doctors, trained nursing staff or essential medicines. Maternal and child health services essential for the prevention of anaemia were non-existent, and monitoring of high-risk pregnancies and post-partum and neonatal care did not reach the poorest women in the greatest need of these services. The issues of access have been tackled quite effectively over the past decades through the efforts of both ANANDI and the sangathans.

Invisibility was a rampant form of exclusion. Claims to traditional habitats and lands by the poor—particularly women—were questioned, and land was often declared to be government property in the absence of official or legal ownership papers. Claims to subsidized food could not be made without a ration card nor could an application for a widow's pension be accepted without a death certificate. Access to rural development programmes could be negated by redesignating a cluster of hamlets with the urban municipal limits. Denotified tribes were excluded from most schemes because they lacked government-issued identification cards. A key achievement of the ANANDI–sangathan partnership has been making the poorest communities and women visible to the bureaucracy.

Global and national trends that deepen poverty: These trends in market forces and policies have greatly intensified poverty, disproportionately impacting poor women. National discourse and policy have moved on from the issues of right to food and food security and the national employment guarantee programmes have been diluted. Along with the corporatization of agriculture, these issues have intensified poverty in the underdeveloped areas where

ANANDI works. Despite its efforts over twenty-five years, the fundamental dimensions of poverty such as hunger and malnutrition have not diminished but the forms and intensity of violence against women and girls have increased in physical and digital spaces.

Transitioning leadership and keeping participatory processes alive: Even as the organization and women's collectives have grown and matured, internal tensions have invariably arisen. ANANDI and the sangathans have repeatedly tried to transition leadership from the founder collectives but faltered.

Pressures on sangathan members and leaders: Despite the undoubted power and influence of the sangathan, its members and leaders are still members of families and communities where social norms and customs hold sway, and there is sometimes a limit to women's capacity to challenge the existing order on many fronts. They are often put under pressure by families, religious leaders or even politicians to uphold traditions that go against their own beliefs and new understanding.

Gaps in processes: Challenges have also arisen when the ANANDI team's expertise and understanding of vital elements of certain processes has been lacking, such as the increasing use & influence of social media for organizing and communication.

Lessons on Advancing Gender Equality

Lessons about how to make change happen in favour of the rights of women and all marginalized people, and gender equality—can be drawn from the ANANDI experience:

Accelerating the pace of change: 'Change is a slow dance', and change in the deeply rooted issues of gender and caste can take time, but ANANDI has been consistently trying to challenge these resilient and deeply embedded structures of social power. It could be said that the sangathans have achieved success sooner than expected in dismantling multiple pillars of patriarchy that have been entrenched for centuries.

They have challenged everyday discrimination and gender-based violence within the community and led the struggle for social and economic rights of their communities, in the process creating protected safe spaces for women to relearn, rethink and strategize for change. The sangathans have fought all forms of violence against women and made the possibility of justice real, persisting in focusing on the issues of the most excluded, marginalized and oppressed without regard to how their own circumstances have (or have not) changed.

The impact of building women's collective power: ANANDI's approach was not about 'doing' development or women's empowerment work, but about mobilizing women to empower themselves. This empowerment would lead to real gains in terms of their access to development resources, citizenship rights, basic services, freedom from violence, control over their bodies and reproduction and a voice and decision-making power at all levels. The sangathans have become a major social and political force for equitable, sustainable development, and have brought about development in the form of roads, schools, childcare, health and access to government schemes. They have managed to do this by building their collective power to challenge and transform the structures of oppression, and in the process, they have also demonstrated the power of women's leadership.

As one ANANDI founder put it, 'None of these 300-odd women leaders have amassed personal wealth or power in the usual sense; they have embraced the idea that they are fighting for truth and justice. It is amazing to see hundreds of women strategize together on a violence issue without shaming, without making judgments (even if it's violence in an extra-marital affair). And till today, they still prioritize the most excluded, always asking, 'who's left out?' They come from a place of love; they show us that transformation is also about what you hold on to, and not just what you let go of or change!' They have the maturity to know that leadership is not so much about who you are, what you know, and what you can do, as it is about your capacity to mobilize others to join the struggle for change and justice.

Shared leadership and building new generations of leaders: ANANDI has navigated the very complex and often fraught process of sharing leadership with these women's collectives it had built and empowered. Now the leadership is more lateral, with sangathans often taking the lead and ANANDI performing a supporting role.

Bridging practical needs and strategic interests[4]: ANANDI's work is also an interesting and unusual demonstration of how these two approaches need not be sequenced or placed in a hierarchy, as they often are. Indeed, they have shown that building gender and political consciousness can be achieved through processes that address very practical, day-to-day problems women face, which in turn can enable them to advance their strategic interests in terms of voice, visibility and decision-making power.

Sustainable change comes from within: What has become clear is that gender equality and social and economic justice are *not* best achieved through outside interventions led by well-meaning 'experts' or through short-term 'results-oriented' women's empowerment or development projects. Such interventions invariably fail to acknowledge or address the deep structures of power that are the root of inequalities.

ANANDI's work demonstrates that it is the communities themselves that have the greatest stake in change. Those most oppressed by the deep structures of power and most excluded by development processes and political interests are the ones who best understand what needs to change. It is these individuals who must be the architects and catalysts of change. Outside expertise can help, but only under the leadership of the communities.

These strong collectives and their highly impactful strategies are still unable to resist the negative impacts of larger forces—whether political or market-driven. ANANDI soon realized that the sangathans are marching just to stay in the same place. The organization and the collectives are powerless against the political and economic tides sweeping over them.

Food production is being corporatized even as the government abandons its role of protecting the poorest from the impacts of the market. Political power is increasingly leveraged to advance narrow, divisive agendas that have few development benefits, least of all for the poor. In the face of all this, it is important to sustain hope for a better future and deepen the commitment of the sangathans to keep working for truth and justice.

14

SELCO: Building Inclusive, Sustainable and Climate-Resilient Solutions

HARISH HANDE AND SURABHI RAJAGOPAL

TWENTY-SIX YEARS AGO, ARVIND RAI, a school teacher in south India, took a leap of faith and installed a solar home lighting system, so that his children and his neighbours' children could study in the evenings under brighter lights. Today, most of those children, if not all, have solar power in their homes as their source of reliable and quality energy supply.

In 1995, access to electricity was a luxury for most rural communities in India. Less than 40 per cent of rural India was electrified.[1] There was a significant challenge in providing energy for basic lighting, water heating and irrigation for households and villages not connected to the grid, perhaps not even close to a grid. Even when they were connected to the grid, electricity supply would be often unreliable and infrequent. As we are well aware today, energy is a critical catalyst for local development—by improving household wellbeing and convenience, by powering healthcare appliances to deliver much-needed last-mile health services, by mechanizing livelihoods, and improving productivity and income-generation opportunities. The absence of energy stalls the process of development.

At the time, households with no reliable electricity supply were forced to depend on a mix of kerosene and candles for basic lighting, and on diesel generators, if they could afford them, to run their larger appliances. Communities were spending a significant amount of their disposable income on energy sources that were unreliable and provided poor-quality electricity.

It was in this context that Solar Electric Light Company (SELCO)[2] was conceived, with the aim of enabling access to energy as a means to stimulate local development. Providing reliable and quality electricity in a country with a mix of rural agrarian communities, remote hamlets, riverine islands and forest-dwellers is a task that requires decentralization. Decentralized solar energy, produced where it is consumed, as opposed to being transmitted from hundreds of kilometres away, could provide an energy source for households when they needed it. However, this was a time when a solar panel—or 'solar plate' as it was colloquially referred to—was a novelty in rural Karnataka, viewed with a mix of curiosity and skepticism. Could this really power a light or a water pump? Would people be willing to pay for it? Who would repair it if something went wrong?

SELCO sought to answer these questions and dispelled three myths in the process. The first two were linked to energy provision itself: that the poor cannot afford decentralized solar energy systems and that it would not be possible to maintain and service these systems in rural communities. The third myth was that a social enterprise could not do this while making profits and being sustainable. Dispelling these three myths has been the guiding principle behind the design of SELCO's core efforts: to enable doorstep implementation and servicing of decentralized solar systems; to facilitate doorstep financing for end-user households, entrepreneurs and farmers; and to do so in a manner that is sustainable. The design and creation of a sustainable social enterprise has been as significant to the SELCO story as was its goal of providing energy to the last mile.

Since then, the organization has grown to identify and understand the varied energy needs of last-mile communities—from government agencies, schools and healthcare facilities to livelihood value chains across agriculture, animal husbandry, textiles, crafts and small business. SELCO's primary stakeholders range from the schoolchild studying at home to the home-based worker running a tailoring unit or small shop; from the individual street vendor to the women's self-help group (SHG) running a flour-processing mill and the local farmer producer organization (FPO) operating a cold storage facility to reduce wastage of their produce and increase their bargaining power.

Individuals and communities have seen the benefit of holistically designed sustainable energy solutions. Here sustainable energy includes three interlinked infrastructure components:

1. Energy-efficient appliances, such as efficient grinding and milling technologies for spices and flour, motors for sewing machines, efficient baby warmers, and vaccine refrigerators for healthcare;
2. Decentralized solar energy systems on rooftops powered by batteries;
3. Efficient, green built environments with natural lighting, ventilation, and thermal comfort, built with local, eco-friendly building material that increase the wellbeing of end-users and reduce their energy needs and costs.

These are deployed in combination with affordable credit, appropriate delivery models, and relevant skills or capacity building to help end-users and communities access, utilize, own and maintain these solutions in the long run. They have improved the quality of life of their users, reducing their drudgery, and raising their productivity and their ability to earn a living. At the very basic level, it has enabled access to a reliable, modern energy source, something that all of us often take for granted.

Application to the Current Context and Today's Crises

Across the world, poor people have been repeatedly thrown into crisis management mode—dealing with one disaster after another. Be it the fallout from the Covid-19 pandemic or climate-related emergencies such as droughts or floods, the poor are the worst affected. Their needs differ across geographies, and social and cultural contexts. For example, a Manipuri weaver needs modernization of loom technology to reduce her drudgery, while a marginal farmer in drought-prone north Karnataka needs access to on-farm appliances to help cultivate crops and better cold storage facilities to preserve the produce. Their needs and their inability to meet these, stem from the income poverty, climate risks and social deprivation they face.

Introducing the SELCO microcosm

These are complex challenges faced by the poor that need customized solutions and committed institutions to address these. Over the last twenty-five or more years, SELCO's efforts have been to turn the idea of 'fortune at the bottom of the pyramid' on its head, and focus instead on 'fortune for the bottom of the pyramid'. To do so, we have created a microcosm of the social sector ecosystem that we believe is needed to set up conditions where poor communities can improve their livelihoods, health, and wellbeing; where society can become more environmentally, socially, and economically sustainable using decentralized clean energy as a catalyst.

Developing an enabling ecosystem is quintessential to the way enterprises and sectors have been created and have evolved. SELCO's efforts for ecosystem development include four independent but inter-linked structures:

- A for-profit social enterprise: SELCO India dispelling the three myths of doorstep financing, doorstep installation and social entrepreneurship;
- A not-for-profit, field-based, research and innovation hub: SELCO Foundation for innovation and ecosystem building (finance, skills, policy, institutional linkages) to integrate energy for improvements in livelihoods, education, and healthcare delivery;
- A local entrepreneurship incubation hub: SELCO Incubation for strengthening local and social entrepreneurship through energy solutions delivery and technology/appliance innovations and supply chains;
- A fund for the infusion of patient and high-risk capital: SELCO Fund investing in local, non-English speaking entrepreneurs enabling them to innovate for the last mile.

SELCO Foundation, the not-for-profit, field research and innovation arm, was established in 2010 to develop holistic solutions that use sustainable energy as a catalyst to address poverty alleviation along with ensuring environmental sustainability. SELCO's interventions led to the sustainable delivery of essential services such as healthcare and education, and enabled improvements in livelihoods productivity; so far more than 50 lakh people have been impacted.

SELCO Incubation was created to inspire local grassroots innovators and enterprises that could design solutions customized to the context in which they work. Finally, the SELCO Fund was set up to break away from mainstream investment practices and re-looking at terms and conditions for shareholder agreements.

Traditionally, investor terms have been developed for English-speaking, middle-class entrepreneurs, including those within the social sector. This cuts off access to patient capital or equity for rural enterprises owned by siblings, for example—something that is an intrinsic element in the context and fabric of our local societies and yet would be considered a 'conflict of interest' in the due diligence processes of impact investing. The Fund focuses on helping these rural entrepreneurs strengthen their organizational structures and access much-needed high-risk and patient funding for their local innovations and solutions.

Having established its energy–health nexus and energy–livelihood nexus models in India, SELCO Foundation is now extending its work to other developing countries, such as Tanzania, Ethiopia, Sierra Leone and the Philippines by providing practitioner-driven technical knowledge to local partners there, such as NGOs, enterprises, financiers, government stakeholders, etc. The Foundation also seeks to learn from solutions developed elsewhere that can be replicated and applied through South-South cooperation. As an example, specific farming solutions in drought-prone Koraput district in Odisha may be relevant to a drought-prone, millet-producing region in Ethiopia. This helps accelerate much of the context learning, so that segments of the solution can be replicated directly, such as setting up millet-grinding and processing units and the financial products for the purchase of these solutions based on the cash flow of millet farmers.

Other parts of the solution may need to be customized for the Ethiopian context. For example, identifying alternate financing sources in the absence of banks, such as informal savings and lending groups, credit through cooperative societies that can lend to individuals to purchase solar energy solutions, and the creation of market-linkage channels for the processed millet within the local community and for sale outside.

Defining Success and Impact, across Levels

SELCO was started as an experiment and continues to be one today. While it is yet to achieve its objectives of eradicating poverty, creating safety nets for all and strengthening the resilience of communities against climate change and future disasters, its work has seen some successes evidenced across three different levels:

At the end-user level, with a direct impact on the wellbeing, income levels and health of households, women, individual entrepreneurs, and farmers through sustainable energy solutions for:

- home lighting and basic household appliances, reducing their need for kerosene and providing reliable, quality energy access;
- agricultural equipment such as water-pumps, sprayers, threshers and other on-farm equipment, and for processing of spices, flour, millets, which increase income and productivity, and reduce some of the drudgery of farming;
- livestock such as vaccine refrigerators to store vaccines essential for the health of cattle, poultry, etc.; and for hydroponics to grow green fodder in dry regions or summer months;
- small businesses to enable a diversification of income sources and reduce the drudgery in local crafts, such as pottery, weaving, etc.;
- healthcare facilities across rural and remote areas, to help identify high-risk pregnancies with maternal kits, undertake safe immunization and vaccination by storing these in refrigerators, provide better maternal, childcare, and provide diagnostic services to people at the primary point of contact with the public health system; this will prevent their having to travel long distances, avoid transportation costs, quite apart from the opportunity cost of visiting a higher-tier facility such as a district hospital for the same services.

At the ecosystem level by developing processes, financing products, skills and technology innovations to help the poor access sustainable energy for their wellbeing, livelihoods, and healthcare. For example, training financiers and bankers to aid formal financial institutions (FIs) extend finance for small-scale, sustainable energy solutions to the poor; determining the kind of risk-mitigation mechanisms that would be available to financiers, determining appropriate monthly repayments based on the cash-flow of the end-user, and leveraging financial innovations such as interest subsidies, risk-guarantees, down-payments on energy loans to help households, entrepreneurs, and farmers access sustainable energy solutions.

These replicable processes and models are available to be adapted and applied in other developing country contexts.

At the community and societal level, with implications for local-level entrepreneurship and job creation; reducing and eliminating carbon emissions by replacing diesel, kerosene and, in some cases, fossil-fuel-dominated grid electricity, thereby furthering climate change mitigation; increasing adaptive capacity of communities to climate disasters and risks; and advances in social inclusion for marginalized communities hitherto left out of the development process.

While SELCO India's work has largely focused on four states, it has been able to impact more than 1.1 crore people, with solar energy systems for 5,57,000 households, 83,000 microbusinesses, and 22,000 community facilities which provide education and healthcare services. Most of the solar home systems and microbusinesses are financed through local banks, regional rural banks, and microcredit institutions.

The focus of SELCO India's work on the other hand has been on inclusive innovation and building ecosystems to replicate and scale up successful processes and solutions for energy to be integrated across livelihoods and healthcare.

The key milestones and impact across the timeline of these institutions are represented in the following schematic:

188   ANCHORING CHANGE

1995
SELCO India established

1996:
First solar home system financed

Till 2010,
Installed more than 100,000 Solar Home energy systems, impacting more than half a million people
Most of these were focused on improved access to lighting

Till 2021
Implementations with more than 500,000 Small households; 83,000 Micro businesses And 22,000 community facilities for education and healthcare

SELCO India has directly and indirectly impact 11 million people since it began in 1995

2010:
SELCO Foundation established

2014
Energy-livelihoods nexus- solutions for small livelihoods- printing, digital services, tailoring, refrigeration in petty shops

2017- 2021
Energy for livelihoods for Agriculture and Animal Husbandry with Farmer Producer groups and cooperatives in addition to small businesses;

90 different Solar energy-driven livelihood solutions implemented across sectors

2022-2025
Scale up of specific tested and well-established solutions
Disaster and climate resilience lens to solution implementation

Explore district level blanketing- decentralized clean energy solutions for all types of livelihoods in the district; unlocking govt funds

Implemented more than 90 energy-livelihood solutions, impacting nearly 1 million people

2016- 2018
Energy-Health nexus efforts underway

30 health centers (proving models and processes with partners, largely implemented in remote and vulnerable areas Testing Models for portability/ mobility

2019-20:
+ District level facility powering
+ 100 Sub Centers solar power + efficient equipment with State Govt (National Health Mission)

2021: Replication in 10 districts across 5 states, in partnership with State Health Depts, District Admin, Blanketing public health facilities with local servicing and financial allocations

2022-2025
22,000 health facilities to be solar powered with efficient equipment across 5 vulnerable state

Ministry of Health and allied depts establish guidelines on procurement and solar powering across India

Impacted more than 2000 nodal points so far, helping 4.8 million people access better healthcare

Ecosystem building: Incubation, Financing and skill development:

- Establishing targets with FIs to finance more than 800 Energy- for- livelihoods solutions;
- Regional programmes to help finance extremely vulnerable communities in tribal areas in Odisha and the north east;
- Training 10,000 bankers from 100 local FIs financial institutions to institutionalise finance for sustainable energy- powered livelihood solutions;
- Incubation efforts to support 50 local energy enterprises located in tier 2 and tier 3 cities impacting over 300,000 individuals.

Factors That Have Impacted Our Success

An end-user-centric design accompanied by the ecosystem approach

In trying to find solutions to a developmental problem, there is often a tendency to look for a single product to tackle the issue: a solar lantern for all energy-access issues, microfinance (albeit at higher interest rates) for all the credit needs, increased supply of medicines and vaccines to solve all health challenges. But they are not based on the nuanced needs of each end-user: the small panel with a solar lantern cannot function without repair infrastructure and availability of spare parts; it would become a dead asset in due course, apart from the fact that the lantern is only the equivalent of a torch, it cannot energize an entire household, nor can it run a sewing machine or power a water pump; multiple microfinance loans to the same person, without considering their current cash flows, usage of the credit, market linkages, or their ability to increase revenues. None of these can bring the transformational change in income generation that communities need—it only drains them of their disposable income.

End-user-centric approach places the end-user at the heart of the problem. In energy, this would include their needs, pattern of using the appliance, ability to pay for the energy, and the structures to own and manage the energy system. These are critical to develop a design that is acceptable to the end-user and creates a real impact.

While a number of social enterprises and practitioners are working to fill the energy access gap through decentralized solutions, replicating or scaling up these solutions can be hindered by the absence of a supportive, enabling environment. Broadly, this could include the limited availability of skilled human resources to install and maintain systems, challenges with technology supply chains because of terrain or transportation costs, high cost of capital for entrepreneurs trying to provide solutions to the poorest, limited access to affordable financing for those poorer end-users, and top-down approaches to policy making that focus on 'one-size-fits-all', making it harder to break the cycle and actually build stronger enabling ecosystems.

Our solutions in northeast India are a reflection of how end-user-centric design and local ecosystem development might look. Weaving is an important supplementary livelihood for women in Manipur and Meghalaya. It is, however, a tedious, manual process. To explore solutions to alleviate the drudgery of weaving, we worked with partners to identify local manufacturers of small-scale looms with the option of mechanisation. We tested the looms for efficiency and on how they are utilized by home-based, small-scale weavers. The local loom manufacturer was supported with seed funding to make iterations to the design before we designed the solar energy system that could power the system. This was then supplemented with linkages to financing through local cooperatives, etc., to support women in procuring the solution.

Micro-Entrepreneurship, Livelihood and Community Development requires an enabling ecosystem

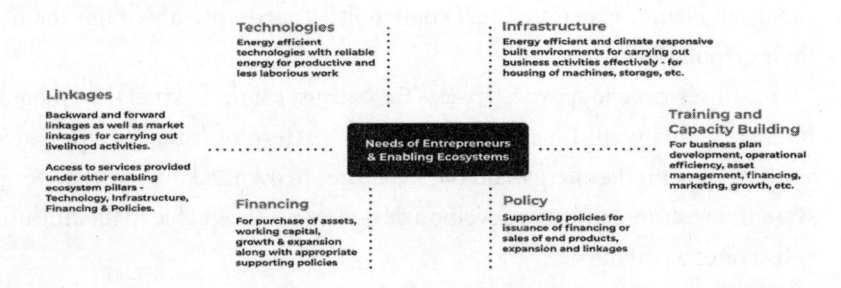

Linkages
Backward and forward linkages as well as market linkages for carrying out livelihood activities.

Access to services provided under other enabling ecosystem pillars - Technology, Infrastructure, Financing & Policies.

Technologies
Energy efficient technologies with reliable energy for productive and less laborious work

Financing
For purchase of assets, working capital, growth & expansion along with appropriate supporting policies

Needs of Entrepreneurs & Enabling Ecosystems

Infrastructure
Energy efficient and climate responsive built environments for carrying out business activities effectively - for housing of machines, storage, etc.

Policy
Supporting policies for issuance of financing or sales of end products, expansion and linkages

Training and Capacity Building
For business plan development, operational efficiency, asset management, financing, marketing, growth, etc.

Bringing diverse perspectives to solution design and implementation

Young people play a significant role within the organization. In a society where youngsters face pressure from parents, schools and peers for taking up stable careers, they are choosing to join the social sector, their skills adding a new perspective to addressing the challenge—be it social work, agricultural economics, electrical design and installation, product design, architecture, mass communication, planning and public policy, or finance and business administration.

The partners and champions that we work with include women and men across the age spectrum; local community leaders from marginalized tribal communities and local agricultural groups; experts from the energy, livelihoods and health sectors; bankers, field officers and investors; and district commissioners and panchayat leaders. They are role models and an inspiration for our own teams to really engage with problems and make a difference. Role models cannot be of one gender, one age-group, or one ethnicity. As a country looking to solve myriad socio-economic and environmental challenges across multiple contexts, building a base of role models and champions which represents the diversity of India is essential to generating ideas, challenging perceptions and thereby moving the needle.

Our teams, champions and partners embody the values of social inclusion and equality of opportunity that power our work. It is not by accident but rather by design that all the key stakeholders of SELCO are passionate and committed to solving challenges faced by the poor. The varied backgrounds of individuals within the team have helped challenge perceptions and move the thinking process forward. More than 80 per cent of SELCO's team represents rural India, often with first-hand experience of the challenges of energy access and a nuanced understanding of the end-users' needs. Their ability to interact with stakeholders across all levels—programme beneficiaries, partners, government agencies and FIs—but represent the end-user in each conversation, has been essential to shaping the organization's internal ideas and potential solutions, enabling us to iterate and develop those most suited to the community needs.

Maturity of the local ecosystem

SELCO's initial success was in large part due to the maturity of the local ecosystem in south Karnataka, in particular the financing ecosystem. This region has been home to nationalized and regional rural banks, such as Canara Bank, the erstwhile Syndicate and Malaprabha Grameen Bank, etc. Formal financial inclusion and banking, particularly among rural and poor communities, was relatively well established here compared to other parts of the country. The cause of energy access was championed by a progressive banker in erstwhile Malaprabha Grameen bank (now renamed Karnataka Vikas Grameen bank) who released the first loans in India for solar home lighting systems to individual rural households in the mid-1990s.

SELCO leveraged the networks of livelihood promotion institutes such as the Rural Self-Employment and Training Institutes, which have courses and credit-linkages for potential entrepreneurs, technicians and plumbers. They provided the foundation for SELCO to build up local human resources for installation, system design and maintenance. NGOs that worked on building women's SHGs to enable credit linkages, livelihood training, and input and market linkages became the channel for identifying potential end-users and early adopters of solar-powered solutions. These organizations continue to be critical for SELCO's operations even today.

Since 2010, SELCO's work through the foundation and incubation centre has included building ecosystems in regions with low incomes and high levels of energy poverty, such as northern Karnataka, southern Odisha and the Northeast. It has extended its reach to other developing nations in areas such as Sub-Saharan Africa. These regions still see a limited number of local mentors and a lack of resources to strengthen financier capacity to lend for sustainable energy technologies or supporting local entrepreneurs.

Background and safety nets

While it may be uncomfortable to admit, the social and economic background of the founding team is one of those factors that definitely aided the success or gains, especially in our initial years. One must ask, were those initial hurdles of being an entrepreneur in the 1990s comparable to those faced by an entrepreneur from a marginalized caste or religion? Would it have been as simple for someone from the tribal Siddi community in north Karnataka with the same qualifications to be sanctioned the loan for the first solar home lighting system in south Karnataka?

Recognizing and acknowledging the privilege that many of us have—be it by religion or caste, safety nets or educational opportunities—is essential. This recognition and acknowledgement can open the doors for us as a society to push for and build greater equality of opportunity, where the small tribal farmer in southern Odisha is able to access a low-interest loan to invest in millet cultivation with the same ease as an Ivy League-educated Indian can for her tech start-up in Bengaluru.

What Would We Have Done Differently?

In the early 2000s, basic lighting was still our main focus, it was the need of the hour. Hence, we concentrated on engaging with stakeholders purely in the energy sector to determine innovations and influence new policies largely through energy departments. There was very little learning or engagement on linkages to other development sectors such as agriculture beyond installing basic solar water pumps and heaters. This was perhaps a missed opportunity to develop a more integrated approach where energy access was part of every development-oriented conversation, policy or solution; where innovation was aimed at looking beyond LED lights to more efficient appliances for healthcare and livelihoods; where partnerships and engagements with government stakeholders could have pushed for a more conducive innovation and incubation ecosystem to enable such innovations for the poor, alongside the growth of the internet and information technology in the 2000s.

Another aspect to consider in retrospect relates to SELCO's journey as a social enterprise. It highlights the need to look inwards at all points in the organization's growth—at its mission, its shareholders, management structure, and control. By the mid-2000s, SELCO had begun to feel the pressure from its investors, who were pushing for profits. It was forced to explore models of dealerships and franchisees that on paper would be more lucrative. But as soon as these structures were set up, the dealers focused on upper-middle class or richer households to meet their targets leaving the poor behind. The rising costs of solar panels during that period, a lack of focus on ensuring maintenance of the systems sold and the relentless pressure from investors all nearly led to the end of the organization.

At this critical juncture, owing to an outstanding loan from International Finance Corporation and its terms of repayment, SELCO was given the opening to look for new investors to avoid defaulting on the loan. It used this opportunity to refocus its mission, ensure control of management in the shareholder agreement, and approach new social investors whose vision was aligned to its own—reaching the poorest and maximizing social returns in the true sense, rather than maximizing financial returns and profits for the benefit of investors. While it would have been easy to accept all types of funding given its needs at the time, SELCO placed its mission above everything. This was critical to ensuring that the organization secured a shareholder agreement that embodied that mission and kept in mind the interests of the poorest people.

Another area in need of a shift is how we strengthen the human resource base for the social sector and sustainable energy provision. As a country, we have spent time and resources creating a large pool of engineers with strong IT skills that can benefit the country's exports and Gross Domestic Product. We have created financial products and instruments that help English-speaking entrepreneurs access venture capital for real estate and IT-enabled solutions. But we have not put that same effort and rigour into creating a resource base or financial and entrepreneurship models needed by the social sector to address the complex challenges in providing basic welfare, particularly to the poor—be it clean water and energy, agricultural appliances for small and marginal farmers, healthcare delivery, or quality education.

The challenge is solvable. It involves working with Industrial Training Institutions to integrate sustainable energy into vocational training and building management skills on social-sector issues within rural and urban entrepreneurship institutions. It is essential to create financial mechanisms for local entrepreneurs who may not be well-versed with technology and English to access capital and low-cost debt for their enterprise. Integrating energy solutions into ongoing development programmes and schemes is also important.

Building these opportunities for social-sector development at the grassroots would mean that small and marginal farmers can earn an income from farming and other supplementary rural livelihoods, without being forced to migrate to an urban centre and take up unskilled, temporary jobs that do not value their primary expertise.

Essence of Success

The real success for SELCO will be when the organization ceases to exist, while its processes and models are mainstreamed through stakeholders working across technology, finance, skill development, entrepreneurship and policy, not just within India but across developing country contexts.

We are building our processes to allow for customization across different contexts and geographies, and at the very heart of everything we do are certain replicable elements:

Technology alone is not enough—build the ecosystem for holistic solutions

We often have to remind ourselves that it is not the solar panel, battery, or LED light that can bring about change in people's lives. It is how that panel and battery are used, how they are financed, the structures for their maintenance and servicing, their supply chain, and their role in reducing the time taken or drudgery involved in a certain task or their ability to increase productivity and delivery of other services that really makes the difference.

Designing holistic solutions is good, but building the ecosystem for those solutions to be efficiently and effectively utilized is what makes them truly sustainable.

Duplication is inefficient—institutionalize and leverage what partners do best

Solving complex problems means that we need to be extremely efficient with the limited resources available. Reinventing the wheel dissipates the work we do with poor communities—it delays the accessibility and availability of solutions for last-mile communities. As such, working with health partners to understand the health-energy gaps helped shorten our learning curve and accelerated the pace at which we could design and test solutions, obtain feedback, and actually implement these. This approach has now resulted in scale-level programmes with the governments of Meghalaya and Manipur that provide solar power and add efficient equipment for all sub-centres, health and wellness centres and primary health centres[3] across entire districts. Resources are being leveraged from the funds that the National Health Mission has allocated for health facility infrastructure.

By capacitating these partners with sustainable energy solutions which reliably power efficient baby warmers, spotlights and portable maternal health kits, along with staff training on equipment usage, building local technician networks for maintenance and health centre-level fund allocation for this maintenance, we are institutionalizing energy within the healthcare sector and supporting partners in their larger efforts to reduce maternal and child mortality, especially in rural and remote communities.

Addressing a crisis in isolation is dangerous

Over the last decade, solar water pumps have been touted as the key solution for the problems of the farming community. The replacement of diesel generators will reduce costs for farmers and reduce carbon emissions. But in isolation, this solution fails to acknowledge that the convenience of switching on the water pump as needed could result in the overuse of precious water resources, particularly in water-stressed and drought-prone areas, exacerbating conditions there.

Rather, the solution lies in sustainable irrigation, which combines the solar pump with water conservation techniques such as farm ponds and borewell recharge interventions.

This can be further aided through efficient irrigation techniques such as drip-and-sprinkler systems, appropriate cropping patterns and soil management. Achieving this requires irrigation pump manufacturers and energy enterprises to work closely with water users' associations, farmer groups, and field-level NGOs to design solutions best suited to their local needs. Investors, governments and NGOs need to be thinking about these interlinked components, ensuring that their interventions aimed at the economic wellbeing of the poor do not hurt the community's ability to deal with climate risks or its access to social inclusion opportunities.

Conclusion

The poor, across the world, are repeatedly thrown into a crisis management mode, dealing with one disaster after another, be it Covid-19 or climate change-induced droughts, cyclones and floods. Civil society organizations and social enterprises are working across geographies and socio-cultural contexts to develop solutions that enhance socio-economic wellbeing and strengthen the poor's resilience to future shocks.

SELCO's efforts, like those of numerous others, illustrate that India's is an example not merely of an emerging economy, but one of inclusive innovation, of sustainability-led development, community resilience and climate action. India at seventy-five has the opportunity to lead the way in creating models and processes that can enable millions out of poverty across developing country contexts.

15

Basix Social Enterprise Group: Innovations in Microfinance to Promote Livelihoods for the Poor

VIJAY MAHAJAN

A New Generation Livelihood Promotion Institution

BASIX[1] IS WIDELY KNOWN AS the pioneer microfinance institution (MFI) in India, yet it is much more than an MFI. It is a group of social enterprises, addressing various aspects of livelihood promotion for lower-income households. It emerged from my experience and work of nearly a decade with two non-governmental organizations (NGOs), first with Association for Sarva Seva Farms (ASSEFA), a Gandhian organization, and then with PRADAN, co-founded with Deep Joshi in 1983. While in both cases the organizations managed to persuade banks to give loans to the poor for livelihood promotion, one could see the problems generally faced by poor rural households in accessing bank loans. Even after loans were disbursed, they faced several other problems: they lacked the technical and business skills, infrastructure, risk coverage and input and output linkages. Moreover, ASSEFA and PRADAN were dependent on grants, so they were able to work with a relatively small number of poor households. Progress was limited.

Looking for a more comprehensive and sustainable way to promote livelihoods for the poor, I left PRADAN in 1991 and formed a group of independent development consultants and researchers. Supported by the Ford Foundation, we studied the functioning of organizations such as the SEWA Bank in Ahmedabad, the Grameen Bank and BRAC in Bangladesh, the Bank Rakyat Indonesia (BRI) and the Shorebank Group in the US. 'Minimalist' MFIs like the Grameen Bank and BRI Unit Desas limited their work to the delivery of microcredit, while SEWA Bank, BRAC and Shorebank went beyond credit and offered a range of support services, like technical assistance and training, often through affiliates. The latter group of organizations seemed to be having a greater impact on the poor, which convinced us that *credit is a necessary but not a sufficient condition to promote livelihoods*.

We set about to design Basix as a 'new generation livelihood promotion institution'—the subtitle of the 150-page feasibility study to establish Basix. Its mission was: 'To promote a large number of sustainable livelihoods, including for the rural poor and women, through the provision of financial services and technical assistance in an integrated manner. Basix will strive to yield a competitive rate of return to its investors so as to be able to access mainstream capital and human resources on a continuous basis.' The first part of the mission was similar to that for ASSEFA and PRADAN, while the second part was the result of my learning that, to scale up, Basix would have to be financially sustainable. Our original goal was to work with at least 10 lakh poor households, but given that there were around 10 crore poor households (in the mid-1990s), we realized that 'it will need a hundred Basix to address the livelihood issue in India'. Thus, one of the aims of Basix was to build a livelihood promotion sector, with a whole supportive ecosystem. This chapter describes the path Basix took to address these ambitious goals, and the extent to which it was successful.

The corporate structure of Basix was adopted from the Shorebank Group, US. Along with Bharti Gupta Ramola, who was with Pricewaterhouse Coopers, and Deep Joshi of PRADAN, I established a holding company with personal contributions of Rs 11 lakh in 1996. The holding company was named Bhartiya Samruddhi Investments and Consulting Services Ltd., which was abbreviated to BASICS Ltd, and its homophone Basix became the name of the group of companies under the holding company. The initial corporate structure in 1996 was as follows:

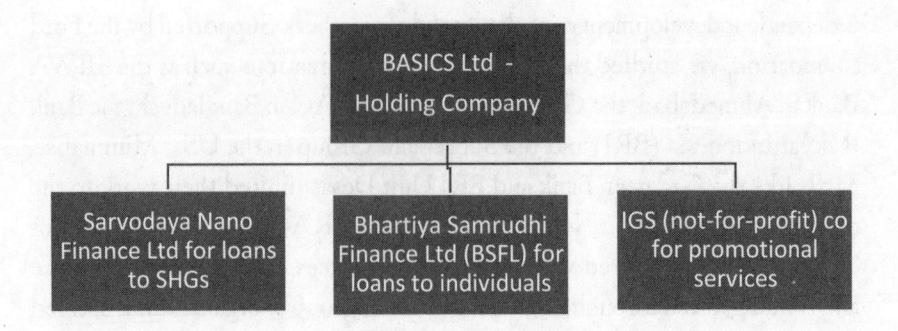

```
                    ┌─────────────────────┐
                    │   BASICS Ltd -      │
                    │   Holding Company   │
                    └──────────┬──────────┘
           ┌───────────────────┼───────────────────┐
┌──────────┴──────────┐ ┌──────┴──────────┐ ┌──────┴──────────────┐
│ Sarvodaya Nano      │ │ Bhartiya Samrudhi│ │ IGS (not-for-profit) co│
│ Finance Ltd for loans│ │ Finance Ltd (BSFL) for│ │ for promotional     │
│ to SHGs             │ │ loans to individuals│ │ services            │
└─────────────────────┘ └─────────────────┘ └─────────────────────┘
```

The holding company had three subsidiaries: Bhartiya Samruddhi Finance Limited (BSFL) a non-bank finance company (NBFC) registered with the Reserve Bank of India (RBI), which extended loans to rural farm and non-farm enterprises; Sarvodaya Nano Finance Ltd (SNFL), another RBI-registered NBFC focused on smaller loans to the landless poor and women though SHGs; and Indian Grameen Services (IGS) a non-profit, Section-25 company, to provide training, technical assistance and support services to borrowers of BSFL and SNFL, and for trialling development innovations that could address livelihood challenges.

In May 1995, the Sir Ratan Tata Trust was persuaded to give IGS a loan of Rs 1 crore to test the microfinance model, even before Basix was registered. With this fund, Basix began its operations in Deodurg (Raichur district of Karnataka), the poorest block in the state. It extended its first loans on 6 June, 1996, to women's self-help groups (SHGs) set up by Prerana, an NGO established by Pramod Kulkarni, a former PRADAN colleague. A field office was established in Raichur town, and we began lending to small farmers, as well as non-farm micro-enterprises.

By the end of the year, IGS had disbursed loans of over Rs 1.7 crore, including funds it managed to borrow from the Small Industries Development Bank of India (SIDBI) for non-farm loans and ITC Agrotech for farmers.

During 1996, further loans of up to Rs 15 crore were secured from Ford Foundation and the Swiss Agency for Development Cooperation (SDC). These were long-term 'external commercial borrowings' in rupee-denominated US dollars and, as the first of their kind, required support from Bharti and V. Nagarajan (a chartered accountant and the auditor of

PRADAN), for explanatory and follow-up work with the finance ministry and the RBI. This loan fund was downstreamed by BASICS Ltd. as equity in BSFL and SNFL, which as NBFCs could leverage it to borrow up to four or five times the amount from banks.

In 1997, IGS's loan portfolio was taken over by BSFL, and IGS used the proceeds to repay its borrowings from the Tata Trust, SIDBI, and ITC Agrotech Ltd. Subsequently, the Tata Trust gave IGS a Rs 1 crore grant to provide technical assistance and support services to BSFL and SNFL borrowers. The management of IGS was also handed over to Sankar Datta, a former PRADAN colleague who then became a faculty member at the Institute for Rural Management, Anand (IRMA).

Basix continued to grow, mostly in the poorer districts of Andhra Pradesh and Karnataka. It extended credit for agriculture (crop cultivation and irrigation facilities), allied activities (dairy, sheep and goats, poultry and fishery), and non-farm enterprises (grocery shops, artisans, tailoring, mobile vendors, etc.). While BSFL's loans ranged from Rs 10,000 to Rs 25,000, SNFL began giving bulk loans for on-lending by SHGs, whose average loans to individual women SHG members were in the range of Rs 3,000 to Rs 10,000. Basix established multiple channels of lending to different segments: joint liability groups of farmers and non-farm micro-entrepreneurs, and direct loans to individual micro-enterprises, all serviced by motorcycle-borne customer service representatives.

By March 1999, Basix's loan portfolio had crossed Rs 10 crore, with an average loan size of Rs 12,000 in over 300 villages in six districts. The repayment rates were in the range of 95–97 per cent, which drew wide attention, and often incredulity, from bankers, themselves struggling with repayment rates of 30–60 per cent in loans to similar borrowers. On analysing its operations, several bankers were convinced that the Basix model was working, but the company still found it difficult to raise loans from banks, as the latter were not clear how to channel loans to the poor through NBFCs.

Thus, to meet our growing need for funds, we tapped international development lenders such as CordAid and Bilance in the Netherlands and the Canadian International Development Agency for funds. It was only in 1999 that BSFL successfully raised its first commercial loans from a bank: Rs 50 lakh from the Global Trust Bank. By the following year, SIDBI, the newly established ICICI Bank, and HDFC Ltd started giving bulk loans to BSFL for on-lending to microcredit borrowers. But the organization also needed capital to grow; two years of global efforts eventually fructified into the first international equity investments in an MFI in India, from the World Bank's private sector arm, the International Finance Corporation, ShoreBank and Triodos Bank, Netherlands.

Mindful of its founding belief that 'credit is a necessary but not a sufficient condition for livelihood promotion', Basix channelled technical assistance and support services to BSFL borrowers through IGS, which also helped it incubate several innovative ideas. For example, application of pesticides through the stem was tried in cotton, to reduce pesticide spraying, which proved to be very successful; and dairy cattle borrowers were linked with local milk societies for milk marketing and to dairy societies for veterinary care. For non-farm borrowers, we organized training in skill upgradation and better business practices like improved items display, stock management, and account keeping. For the SHGs and SHG federations, we provided training in accounting, loan appraisal and fund management. The loans being given to SHGs from SNFL were merged with the work of BSFL by 2001.

Alongside, we continued our policy and sector-strengthening work, keeping in view our goal of building the entire sector. BASICS Ltd, the holding company, provided consulting services to various institutions: to SIDBI to establish the SIDBI Foundation for Micro Credit; Department for International Development, United Kingdom, to establish a SHG capacity-building institution (the Andhra Pradesh Mahila Abhivruddhi Society; and to the World Bank for reform of the regional rural banks (RRBs). In 1998, under the leadership of Elaben Bhatt of SEWA, we established Sa-Dhan, an association of community development financial institutions, and persuaded the RBI Governor, Bimal Jalan, to set up a taskforce on microfinance: its 1999 report has become a framework for the growth of the sector.

Basix was one of the first applicants to set up a local area bank: in 2001 it established the Krishna Bhima Samruddhi (KBS) Local Area Bank. The bank was named after the two rivers that flowed through the three districts the bank worked in—Raichur and Gulbarga in Karnataka and Mahabubnagar in Andhra Pradesh. Deep Joshi became the first chairman of the bank and

D.R.K. Rao, an IRMA alumnus, became its first managing director. Through the bank, Basix was able to offer banking services to several unbanked customers. By 2001, the corporate structure of Basix looked as follows:

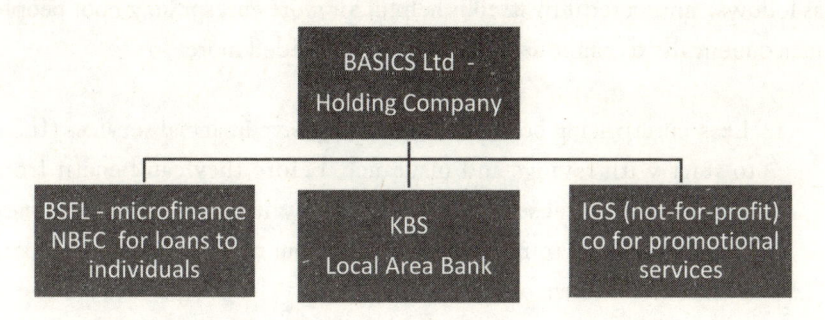

```
                    BASICS Ltd -
                   Holding Company
        ┌───────────────┼───────────────┐
  BSFL - microfinance        KBS         IGS (not-for-profit)
  NBFC for loans to     Local Area Bank   co for promotional
     individuals                              services
```

Mid-Course Correction: The Livelihood Triad

In 2002, Basix embarked on a review exercise, OLÉ, Organizational Learning and Evolution, to evaluate the work done in the first five years and to build a roadmap for the future. It was a 360-degree review across various stakeholders, including customers, staff, collaborators, investors, bankers, board members and competitors. One of the components of the review was a survey of Basix borrowers of five years standing. To the surprise of many, especially Basix founders and the board, only 52 per cent of the microcredit clients reported an increase in income; 23 per cent reported no change; while a staggering 25 per cent reported a decline in incomes, compared to a control group of non-borrowers.

Upon analysis, the Basix team identified three main reasons why microcredit alone was not enough to raise incomes. It was because most microcredit borrowers:

- were impacted by low productivity in the economic activity they pursued;
- faced many unmanaged risks to their lives and livelihoods; and
- had to buy inputs at higher prices while receiving low prices for their produce.

This formed the basis for a major overhaul in our business strategy. After extensive deliberations and consultations, we came up with a new strategy—the Livelihood Triad. The rationale behind the Livelihood Triad strategy was as follows: microcredit by itself is helpful for more enterprising poor people in economically dynamic areas; but they also needed more:

1. Less-enterprising households need inclusive financial services (IFS), to start with savings and insurance, before they can benefit from microcredit, because they need to cope with risk; and also, money transfer services to receive payments from migrant family members and the government.
2. In less-developed regions, poor people would also require a whole range of agricultural, livestock and enterprise development (AGLED) services, such as input supply, training, technical assistance, and market linkages. These services could not be supplied cost-effectively to individual poor households; they would need to be organized into informal or formal groups.
3. The formation of such groups and ensuring their effective functioning required institutional development services (IDS).

The three sets of services, inclusive financial services, agricultural, livestock and enterprise development services and institutional development services, formed the Livelihood Triad. The SDC gave Basix a grant of Rs 10 crore to develop and test the Livelihood Triad strategy. From 2003, Basix began to strengthen the three vertices of the Livelihood Triad.

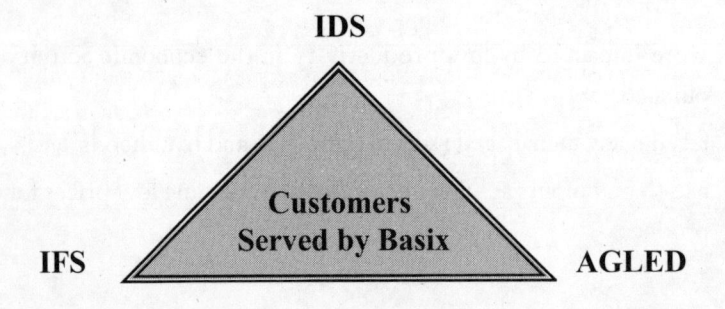

IDS

Customers Served by Basix

IFS   **AGLED**

Services in the Basix Livelihood Triad

IFS	AGLED	IDS
Savings: directly only in areas where Basix had a banking license and later all over as the bank business correspondent model.	Productivity enhancement: increase in yields through adoption of packages of practices recommended by experts	Individual-level awareness, skill and entrepreneurship development
Credit: agricultural, allied and non-farm, short and long term	Productivity enhancement: reduction in costs through adoption of packages of practices recommended by experts	Formation of groups, federations, cooperatives, mutual benefits, etc., of producers
Insurance: for lives and health; for crops, livestock and micro-enterprise assets	Risk mitigation (other than insurance): by selecting drought-proof varieties, soil and water conservation, livestock vaccination, etc.	Accounting and management information systems using information technology
Money transfers: to receive migrant remittances and government payments	Local value addition: sorting, grading, washing, drying and packing of fruits and vegetables before selling	Building collaborations to deliver a wide range of services
Financial orchestration: arranging funds from various sources	Alternate market linkages: input supply, output sales	Sector and policy work, analysis and advocacy for changes/reforms

Inclusive financial services

For inclusive financial services, a savings bank account is perhaps the most important for poor and under-privileged people, as it enables them to receive funds from their family members in distant areas, and from various government schemes like MGNREGA and old-age pensions. These were possible even before the accounts became digitally accessible.

We had learned from SEWA Bank, that when poor people have the opportunity to deposit funds in a financial institution instead of freezing them in unproductive assets, they often use them to finance productive investments when needed. Thus, the KBS Bank became a testing ground for Basix to experiment with savings services. It began collecting daily deposits of amounts as small as Rs 20 directly from homes and workplaces. Later, it established non-branch fixed outlets for collection and withdrawal, which were connected to the nearest branches by computer cables. This became the precursor for the business correspondent (BC) model.

One successful outcome of Sa-Dhan's policy advocacy work was that RBI supported the need for a 'financial inclusion' agenda and deployed the BC model for last-mile delivery of banking services. Basix began experiments using Axis Bank technology to facilitate remittances from migrant labour working in Delhi to Muzaffarpur in Bihar.

By December 2007, Basix had enrolled over 4,000 customers with no-frills saving bank accounts, opened inside slums and villages based on very basic Know Your Customer (KYC) documents. The customers were issued biometric authentication-based smart cards, which gave them access to savings and withdrawal services, and other financial services at their doorstep. The transactions were done with a kit comprising a mobile phone, a fingerprint scanner, and a printer. Transactions could be done either online (instant server updating) or offline in remote areas which had no signal. The field operator (BC agents) carrying the transaction-kit was the human equivalent of an ATM machine, with mobility; technology allowed for risk-management and fraud control.

In acknowledgment of our work, I was appointed member of the Rangarajan Committee on Financial Inclusion. Among the Committee's recommendations were: to open a bank account for every adult, and set up a

Rs 500-crore financial inclusion fund and a Rs 500-crore financial inclusion technology fund. Subsequently, we visited various states to persuade chief ministers to provide these services. In response, Smt. Vasundhara Raje Scindia, Chief Minister of Rajasthan, launched a major financial inclusion programme—the Bhamashah Yojana—and asked Basix to implement it. Under the programme, bank accounts were opened for nearly 30 lakh women, who along with their family members, were also enrolled for health insurance.

Recognizing the risks in the livelihoods of borrowers, in 1999 Basix experimented with providing insurance for its microcredit borrowers. My colleague Sattaiah and I shared our experience with the newly established Insurance Regulatory and Development Authority of India (IRDAI), impressing on it the need to offer micro-insurance through various products and channels. In 2003, IRDAI became the world's first insurance regulator to formally recognize micro-insurance products and channels. I served as part-time member of the IRDAI for five years from 2005.

AGLED services

Here, Basix focused on specific crops—paddy, soybean, groundnut, cotton, pulses and vegetables, particularly potatoes and onions—for intensive interventions to improve productivity by increasing yields and reducing input costs per acre. Most of the interventions were based on work done by the agricultural research institutions based in the respective regions. For livestock activities, we chose the dairy, poultry and fishery sub-sectors, once again picking up techniques developed by livestock research institutions from the respective regions.

By 2005, Basix began to offer fee-based services to producers, usually in clusters, charging Rs 450 per annum for training, demonstrations and exchange visits to expert outlets. Other more-specific services, such as soil and seed testing and vaccination and artificial insemination of livestock, were priced separately. For non-farm activities, we focused on a few that were practiced by a large number of microcredit borrowers, such as weaving on handlooms, tailoring and ready-to-wear garment making, cottage and microlevel food processing, wood and metal working, and grocery stores.

By 2010, Basix had over 6,00,000 fee-paying customers for AGLED services and earned over Rs 25 crore from this vertical.

Institutional development services

Basix began to organize producers into informal or formal groups, registered variously as associations, cooperatives and, after 2010, producer companies. Over 500 such producers' organizations were set up across the country, with memberships varying from 200 to 15,000. Many of these are SHG federations with their own funds running into several crore rupees; others are cooperatives and producer companies also with a turnover of several crores. As the institutions being formed or strengthened were not fully able to pay for the capacity building services, some of the institutional development services work was supported by funding agencies such as SDC and SIDBI.

An Overextension of Microfinance Institutions

Despite its success in developing an integrated livelihood promotion model and demonstrating its sustainability, BSFL was finding it difficult to raise capital to fuel its growth. This was because between 2003 and 2008, it had yielded its place as the top MFI to several newcomers focused solely on microcredit. Investors on BSFL's board felt that the organization was too narrowly focused on promoting livelihoods and had not taken into consideration the company's financial results; it decided to induct a professional banker to head the organization. In 2009, a former Citibank employee was hired as the CEO of BSFL, to lead the company through its next phase; he was instrumental in growing the portfolio rapidly, attracting two rounds of equity totalling Rs 160 crore from various impact and private equity investors. This paved the way for BSFL's rapid growth: by September 2010, it had had over 10,000 employees across twenty states and 300 district offices; and it had 18 lakh customers, with microcredit worth Rs 1,808 crore and less than 1.5 per cent non-performing assets.

By 2009, with the rapid growth of the microfinance sector, concerns around fair lending practices started cropping up. Focusing on growth, many newer MFIs began to cut corners, as well as poach customers from BSFL and offer multiple loans. For customers who could not repay their loans, these

MFIs engaged in coercive collection practices, in order to maintain a good repayment track record. These practices sometimes had most unfortunate outcomes: borrowers ran away from their homes and, in a few dire instances, even committing suicide. MFIs had already become a target for political leaders, public sector bankers, and social workers, for charging what they felt were usurious interest rates; when news of coercive collections and borrower suicides spread, this fuelled further widespread animosity.

To take corrective action on this downward drift in the microfinance scenario, we established Microfinance Institutions Network (MFIN) as a self-regulation organization of all NBFCs and MFIs in India. I was elected its first president in 2009. MFIN acted quickly and rolled out a code of conduct to prevent an MFI from giving a loan to a borrower who already had two loans or an outstanding loan of over Rs 50,000. A credit bureau was established to ensure that multiple loans could not be given to a borrower; and to identify institutions that violated the code. MFIN also set up a coordination committee of MFIs with the Andhra Pradesh government, which was concerned over MFIs giving loans to women from SHGs who already had loans from public sector banks.

In October 2010, the Andhra Pradesh government passed an ordinance in response to the alleged involvement of MFIs in farmer suicides in the state; while nothing was proven, the ordinance which soon became AP Microfinance Institutions (Regulation and Moneylending) Act 2010, virtually spelled the death knell of MFIs in the state. The Act instituted various restrictions on MFI activities, making it virtually impossible for them to continue business. As a result, portfolio quality started deteriorating for all Andhra Pradesh-based MFIs, and loans to them from banks dried up overnight. Basix was one of the worst-affected organizations, as more than 30 per cent of its loan portfolio was in Andhra Pradesh; it lost nearly Rs 70 crore.

Within a few months of the crisis, the CEO of BSFL left and I was called back into harness. In 2012, we negotiated a Corporate Debt Restructuring deal with banks. BSFL repaid Rs 1,200 crore to banks over the next two years, by collecting loans outstanding in states other than Andhra Pradesh, but it had to shut down most of its branch offices. When the company was on the verge of closure, the banks agreed to undertake a one-time settlement of the outstanding amount, taking all the assets the company still owned. As a result, BSFL, once considered one of the world's top ten MFIs, was left with no significant assets, borrowers, or employees by September 2016, when I retired. But the story does not end here; we have to go back to 2010.

Rebirth: New Shoots from the Root Stock

The business correspondent model which Basix pioneered in 2007, marked the beginning of a new era of digital financial services. Amit Mehta of Tata Consultancy Services and a few colleagues joined Basix, and built a mobile technology platform that could integrate with the core systems of banks for real-time transactions. Basix then established a separate business correspondent company, Sub-K i-Transactions Ltd in August 2010. Sub-K means 'for all' in Hindi; its English meaning of 'sub-thousand' indicated micro-transactions of less than Rs 1,000, access points less than 1,000 metres way, and at a cost less than 1,000 paise.

Sub-K established partnerships with KBS Bank, Syndicate Bank, Axis Bank, ING Vysya Bank and RBL Bank and built a nationwide business correspondent network. It raised equity capital from the Michael and Susan Dell Foundation in 2012. By mid-2014, it had served over 10 lakh customers through its business correspondent model. By 2021, under the leadership of T.N. Sasidhar, a Basix colleague since 1998, Sub-K served more than 20 lakh customers through twelve bank partnerships and over 7,000 business correspondent outlets across the country. It managed a loan portfolio of over Rs 1,200 crore with 5,50,000 customers and also extended credit to over 25,000 small enterprises in partnership with State Bank of India, UCO Bank and Punjab National Bank.

The work on the AGLED services under the Livelihood triad was also hived off from BSFL and re-launched into a separate company, Basix Krishi Samruddhi Ltd. The company works with hundreds of farmers' producer companies in several states on various agricultural commodities. The work on skill development for non-farm activities was also hived off into a company called Basix Academy for Building Lifelong Employability (B-ABLE) Ltd. The functioning corporate structure of Basix Group by 2012 looked as follows:

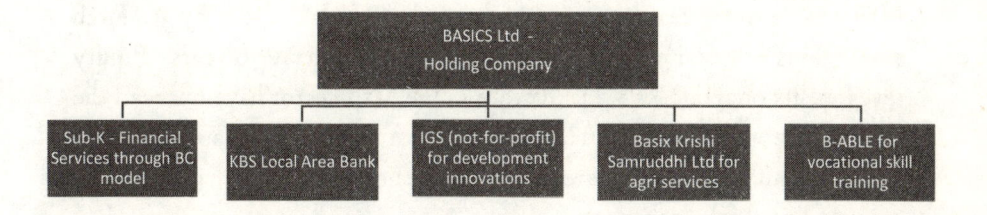

```
                    ┌─────────────────────┐
                    │    BASICS Ltd –     │
                    │   Holding Company   │
                    └──────────┬──────────┘
    ┌──────────┬───────────┬───┴────────────┬──────────────┐
┌────────┐ ┌────────┐ ┌──────────┐ ┌─────────────┐ ┌────────────┐
│Sub-K - │ │  KBS   │ │IGS (not- │ │ Basix Krishi│ │ B-ABLE for │
│Financial│ │ Local  │ │for-profit)│ │Samruddhi Ltd│ │vocational  │
│Services │ │ Area   │ │for devel-│ │  for agri   │ │skill       │
│through  │ │ Bank   │ │opment    │ │  services   │ │training    │
│BC model │ │        │ │innovations│ │             │ │            │
└────────┘ └────────┘ └──────────┘ └─────────────┘ └────────────┘
```

Conclusion: Taking Stock

Basix's journey is replete with accomplishments, as well as serious setbacks. In terms of its founding mission, it has successfully managed to address the goal of 'promoting a large number of sustainable livelihoods, including for the rural poor and women'. Despite the severe shock from the Microfinance Institutions (Regulation and Moneylending) Act, 2010, that led to the closure of BSFL, its flagship company, Basix continues to fulfil its founding mission through Sub-K, providing inclusive financial services to poor people in rural areas, small towns and lower-income urban areas. Sub-K provides access to comprehensive financial services including microcredit, savings, insurance, pensions, remittances, government services and utility payments, as well as financial counselling.

The second part of the mission was to offer technical assistance and support services in an integrated manner to financial services customers, which was initially done through a combination of IGS and BSFL and later done through specialized companies like Basix Krishi, providing agricultural and livestock services, and B-ABLE for vocational training and employability skills. Each of these is a growing profitable company with its own board, CEO, and investors. Integrating the work of the livelihood services companies with the financial services provided by Sub-K in the same region is an ongoing challenge, being constantly addressed.

The third part of the mission, to harness mainstream financial resources for the poor, was achieved by getting banks to lend to Basix and then to all MFIs, and by attracting equity investments in Basix and the rest of the sector. As described earlier, Basix itself was not as successful in attracting capital as the rest of the sector. Suffice it to say that starting from the first Rs 50 lakh loan to Basix in 1999, the banking system financed nearly 80 per cent of the

MFI's loans to the poor, amounting to nearly Rs 6 lakh crore by 31 March 2021. This is a nearly million-fold increase in twenty-two years. Equity investments of about Rs 1.2 lakh crore in the MFI sector have financed the remaining 20 per cent of Rs 6 lakh crore. Investments in MFIs and those that became small finance banks are now mainstream; several have had IPOs and are listed on stock exchanges.

In terms of attracting mainstream human resources to the sector, Basix played a major role. Hundreds of young professionals who joined Basix rose to higher positions in the organization, other MFIs, banks and insurance companies. The founders of several MFIs have acknowledged how much they learned about microfinance while visiting Basix during its quarterly reviews, when it welcomed all types of visitors to study its field operation for three days. Samit Ghosh, the founder of Ujjivan Financial Services Ltd, said, 'Basix is not an MFI, it is a university for microfinance and livelihood promotion.'

Basix's mission to build a sector with a supportive ecosystem has also been fairly successful. Apart from working with the finance ministry, RBI, National Bank for Agriculture and Rural Development, IRDAI and Rangarajan Committee on Financial Inclusion, we were also able to seed the idea of small finance banks as a member of the Raghuram Rajan Committee on Financial Sector Reforms (2008–09). This recommendation eventually became a reality in 2014, when nine of the major MFIs were given licenses to become small finance banks.

Internationally, first as a board member and later as Chair of the World Bank's Executive Board of the Consultative Group for the Poor (CGAP), I advocated for moving from microcredit to financial services, and for deepening financial inclusion. During my six years on the CGAP Board, we led global advocacy efforts to enhance financial inclusion with the Bank for International Settlements, Basel, which is a norm-setting body for all the world's banks, and the International Association of Insurance Supervisors, Basel, to work on micro-insurance for risk coverage to the poor. G-8 also established a permanent working group on financial inclusion.

Yet, I feel that the mission of promoting a large number of sustainable livelihoods for the poor, has not been adequately addressed by Basix or by the sector. Growth in the MFI sector, though impressive, has not translated into widespread integrated efforts for livelihood promotion. In 2021, there are still as many poor households in India, as there were when Basix began in 1996. Though this was largely a result of the Covid-19 pandemic, the fact is that the financial system did not rise to the occasion and provide the much-needed support for either subsistence livelihoods or for the continuation or restart of the micro-enterprises of the poor which had to be shut down: all this while the banking system is flush with liquidity of trillions of rupees. Neither pilots, nor scale-ups, nor policy work seems enough—the ultimate answer seems to be in sorting out our political economy, to make it pro-people and pro-environment

16

Kudumbashree: Where Women Climb the Ladder of Empowerment

S.M. VIJAYANAND AND SAJITH SUKUMARAN

'KUDUMBASHREE',[1] THE PROGRAMME TO ELIMINATE poverty in all its dimensions through community action in the form of network of self-help groups (SHGs), called neighbourhood groups (NHGs) in Kerala, started as an initiative of the state government in 1998, immediately after the launch of the People's Plan Campaign, which transferred nearly a third of the development budget or 'plan funds' to local governments[2], practically in an untied form for participatory local planning. 'Kudumbashree' is coined from two Malayalam words, 'Kudumbam' meaning family and 'Shree' meaning prosperity. It was really evidence-based and its roots can be traced to the Urban Basic Services Programme in Alappuzha Municipality in the early 1990s, followed by the Community Based Nutrition Programme in the rural areas of Malappuram District, both of which were supported by United Nations International Children's Emergency Fund (UNICEF). In Alappuzha, the focus was on the organization of the poor to access services; in Malappuram special efforts were taken to enable the women to effectively use reproductive and child health services as also education. In both cases, through organization and collective understanding, the women groups achieved high visibility which demanded a positive response from the authorities.

The key innovations of the early initiative were a normative identification of the poor using a nine-point index drawn from the multiple deprivations and manifestations of poverty, rather than based on income, focus on reaching out to the families through women, and reaching out to the community through the families. An organizational structure with a strong bearing on the grassroots of the community was created by organizing the families represented by women in a given locality into a three-tier structure of NHGs of fifteen to forty families at the local level, networked into Area Development Societies (ADS) at the level of electoral constituencies or wards of the local governments, and federated into Community Development Societies (CDS) at the level of the gram panchayat/municipality/corporation. The NHGs were conceptually a larger entity than SHGs and placed equal emphasis on human development and other entitlements as on thrift and credit. The organizational structure of NHGs was different from SHGs. It had a president and secretary and a volunteer each for three domains: health and education, infrastructure and income generation. These volunteers were trained in their respective fields to become community resource persons (CRP) or 'barefoot' specialists. This structure was adopted when the programme was rolled out.

The following diagram gives a snapshot of the present Kudumbashree system:

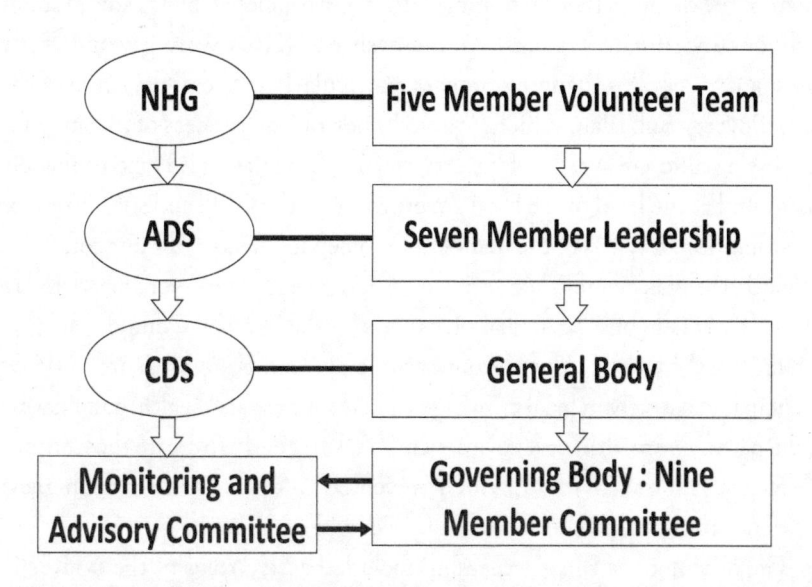

NHG	Five Member Volunteer Team
ADS	Seven Member Leadership
CDS	General Body
Monitoring and Advisory Committee	Governing Body : Nine Member Committee

The early initiatives benefitted from the total literacy campaign that had achieved remarkable success in the state. Though the initial support came from UNICEF, Kudumbashree was developed by the local governments and owned and supported by the state government. This was different from the SHG movement in the rest of India that were either nurtured by non-government organizations (NGOs) or brought in as part of large donor-driven projects for poverty reduction, such as that of the World Bank.

The Kudumbashree model went beyond thrift and credit to address the multiple dimensions of poverty such as health, nutrition and education. To enhance social capital, the NHGs were networked into a formal organization, which gave them collective power. The neighbourhood element strengthened the identities of women.

Strengthening Development Outcomes

A significant policy decision taken by the state government in 1997 was to mandate a strong synergy between local governments and the Kudumbashree system through an equal partnership safeguarding the autonomy and integrity of both the institutions while ensuring an active functional two-way relationship. This conscious harmonization in a way ensured that the community-based organization of women functioned as community wings to enhance the democratic functioning of local governments, but as sub-systems and not subordinate systems. Kudumbashree NHGs were given definite roles in the People's Planning process, particularly in the preparation of the Anti-Poverty Sub Plan, which involved a bottom-up process of planning for addressing different aspects of poverty, starting from the NHGs and ultimately integrated at the level of the local government by the CDS and submitted for consideration. In view of the number of women involved and their collective strength, the plans were taken seriously. Local governments were mandated to spend 10 per cent of their annual plan funds for the Women Component Plan, which mostly went to the Kudumbashree system. Kudumbashree NHGs participated actively in local campaigns for cleanliness and health, culminating in the partnership with local governments, most recently to create the frontline of defence against Covid-19, which prevented Kerala, in spite of the highest incidence of the epidemic, from being overwhelmed.

The outcomes of this partnership included active roles of the NHGs in the gram sabhas or ward sabhas (village assemblies, which are the electoral constituency at the local level), particularly in the selection of beneficiaries of local government schemes leading to high pro-poor expenditure under the People's Plan.

This has enabled poor families to better access the facilities of anganwadis[1], schools and hospitals, which have been transferred to local governments as part of decentralization. Over time NHGs have been assisting local governments in providing civic services, of course levying reasonable charges, enabling the poorest of the poor to earn decent wages. As of now, 977 groups employing 28,604 women are involved in carrying out activities like door-to-door collection of inorganic solid waste, managing 1,110 material collection centres and 291 resource recovery centres across 1,034 local governments in Kerala; besides they are running 142 vermicompost and other waste manure plants. This outsourcing to the NHG network has been a win-win situation not only for the poor women and the local governments but also for the citizens.

Balancing Power

This relationship with local governments has endowed the NHGs with additional 'capitals' over and above the five 'capitals' usually associated with the SHG system in the context of livelihoods, i.e., physical, financial, human, natural and social. The Kudumbashree women have acquired 'civic capital' in terms of accessing citizen rights and, more importantly, 'political capital' in terms of power through organization, capable of effectively influencing decisions on local resource allocation. Interestingly, 36 per cent of the elected women representatives in local governments are from the Kudumbashree stream cutting across types of local government and political parties. The presence of so many elected members in local governments with Kudumbashree background has given a new dimension to the empowerment of the poor—from the feminization of poverty to the feminization of local governance.

In a larger sense, through regular interaction with the local governments, the poor have developed a good understanding of 'power' and how its levers get pulled at the local levels enabling them to negotiate and at times challenge the way it works. A kind of mutual respect has developed between the women groups and the local governments. This has helped the women to access public facilities, programmes and funds relatively better. They have also been able to create an effective demand for public services that have translated into better performances. The best example is in respect of health; when the People's Plan Campaign started, only 28 per cent of the public used government health facilities; this increased to 33.5 per cent in 2014 (NSSO 71st Round) and further 47.5 per cent in 2018 (NSSO 76th Round). Similarly, the share of students in government schools has increased by more than half a million in the last ten years or so. By attending gram sabhas and participating in several inter-active fora, the women have acquired the capacity of carrying out what could be called a silent concurrent social audit which has contributed to improving transparency and accountability.

Effective Delivery

Kudumbashree has been given the central role in the implementation of the employment guarantee scheme under Mahatma Gandhi National Rural Employment Guarantee Act (MGNREGA), right from the preparation of the labour budget, to organizing of work and ensuring payment. This has resulted in Kerala being the highest spender in this programme in relation to the population below poverty line (BPL) across the states. Kerala absorbs 3.47 per cent of MGNREGA funds with just 1.57 per cent of BPL families. In 2020–21, 90.49 per cent of expenditure under MGNREGA went as wages to women, almost all of them from the Kudumbashree family, totalling a substantial amount of Rs. 2,727.61 crore. This experience has enhanced the organizational capacity of the poor women and instilled an understanding of pro-poor development besides providing social and financial security. The central role of Kudumbashree has willy-nilly engendered the programme.

This has led to a pivotal role for Kudumbashree in other centrally sponsored schemes, including livelihoods and skills programmes both in rural and urban areas, and the housing schemes and a nodal role in the implementation of programme for slum development in urban areas. This has ensured better targeting and gender-sensitive implementation of these programmes.

Building Local Livelihoods

Kudumbashree has promoted over 45,000 micro-enterprises, which go beyond individual NHGs, stretching out even over a district. Most of them are given professional support services and are provided with a recognizable brand. Many of these are social enterprises, such as the 241 enterprises under the Amrutham Nutrimix brand. They employ 1,680 women to produce packaged food for anganwadi centres to be distributed to children between six months and three years of age. Having a regular, assured market for their products, they generate an annual turnover of Rs 120 crore. Another area is food service enterprises called 'Café Kudumbashree' with 1,064 units functional as of now, employing around 8,000 women, offering food at affordable prices.

Over 70,000 joint-liability groups comprising the landless poor (including 3,36,207 women) took around 33,000 hectares of land on informal lease, (as leasing of land is illegal in Kerala), mostly for growing commercial crops like fruits and vegetables. Closely related to this is the conversion of ordinary unskilled agricultural labour into skilled workers. Groups of women were trained and organized (called the Green Army when it was innovated by the Wadakkancherry block panchayat fifteen years ago) to deliver turnkey services to farmers covering the whole gamut of farm-level services using appropriate machines. It has replicable elements for the whole country and has the rare advantage of the farmers benefitting from skilled labour and improving their productivity and the farm labour getting proportionately higher wages.

Addressing Welfare and Social Security Needs

Kudumbashree realized that participatory planning often bypasses the poorest of the poor, and started the 'Asraya' scheme in 2002 to provide basic entitlements to poor families. The past two decades have seen over 1,50,000 such families receiving over Rs 2,000 crore in aid. It then started the 'BUDS' school for children with learning disabilities. The school now has 5,126 students and is directly managed by Kudumbashree. This period also saw the establishment of 165 rehabilitation centres for mentally disabled adults. The NHGs are involved in providing community support to over 1,50,000 patients under palliative care, of which nearly 60,000 are bedridden, as well as the provision of home-based healthcare under the brand 'Santhwanam'.

These programmes have inculcated a palpable element of care and compassion in public programmes and moved on from welfare to entitlements accepting a right to life approach. For nurturing social capital among children and preventing poverty being passed down generations, Kudumbashree has started *bal sabhas and bal panchayats*, which are children's versions of the village administrative organizations. Nearly 4,00,000 children have joined these organizations.

Gender Self-Learning

To further gender empowerment, Kudumbashree has a gender self-learning programme developed using real-life experiences of women. Help desks were set up in all fourteen districts of Kerela, where over 350 trained female counsellors are available to aid women and children affected by violence and trafficking. There are 'gender corners' in all local government offices as also over 700 gender resource centres, through which the CDS map crimes against women and children and devise joint action to combat them at the local level. Gender status studies linked to the People's Plan have been initiated by at least 140 CDSs. These have provided a deep understanding of the status of women and paved the way for analysing the causes behind the present situation and in moving forward to address them with the help of the community and the local governments very much on the lines of the Freirian concept of analysis, reflection and action.

Building Internal Capacities

Community resource persons run a significant share of Kudumbashree's activities. Of special mention are the training groups which are organized as nineteen micro-enterprises with 163 members delivering quality training to the NHGs. There is also a Kudumbashree Accounts and Audit Services, conducting internal audits through 46 groups having 355 community auditors. An initiative, which is now being attempted to be replicated across the country is Micro Enterprises Consultants (MECs) from among the community who have been organized into thirty-three units with 360 members providing regular services to the micro enterprises set up by women, so that problems are identified early and remedial action initiated. The MECs have developed a rule of thumb which has been validated by the best experts in the country, that the micro-enterprises face an initial crisis around the end of the first year, essentially relating to internal management and insufficiency of working capital, and later the second crisis after another year or so more to do with marketing. If these are properly attended to in time, the enterprises have a greater chance of survival. With the support of professionals, Kudumbashree has developed a business education programme for the poor that takes the best learnings from conventional management theory and merges it with the real experiences of micro-entrepreneurs and the NGOs supporting them.

Kudumbashree has maintained a unique approach to its core staffing. Most of its officers at the district and state levels are drawn from among government servants, cutting across departments, identified through a process of application and selection. At a time, there were officers drawn from nineteen departments including police, prisons and correctional services. In a sense, Kudumbashree is supra-departmental. A pool of professionals recruited from the market for specific projects and programmes works in tandem with these government servants. Perhaps, the most significant feature is the tenure of the mission director. After the State Poverty Eradication Mission, as Kudumbashree is formally called, became fully functional, it had only four mission directors over twenty-two years and the fifth mission director has just assumed office and all of them were selected solely on the basis of their capacity and attitude. This has, more than anything else, enabled it to function as an activist mission focusing on interesting development experiments which take time to show results.

Challenges

An early challenge was to overcome the bureaucratic and political opposition arising from those who saw Kudumbashree as an endeavour to operate outside the web of control of government. This challenge was overcome by the members not through protests or agitations, but literary creativity. Testimonies and stories, oral and written, conveying the angst of women in a male-dominated system were collected and narrated *suo motu* and *sui generis*.

This triggered such a spontaneous outpouring of support that the detractors had no option but to back off.

The persistent challenges are societal and structural. In spite of being the leader in the country, there are serious concerns as well, of which the biggest one is the relatively lesser flow of benefits to marginalized groups like scheduled tribes and traditional fisherfolk. This appears true in most parts of the country and calls for a new approach focusing on rights-based entitlements. In tribal areas, there is a scenario of powerlessness with all the strings being pulled by outsiders, many of whom could be poorer than the tribes. It is a sad spectacle of poor exploiting the poor and local politics favouring the dominant non-tribal sections even while the tribes are in numerical majority. This reality needs to be addressed sooner than later to prevent alienation, a real challenge to development professionals and activists. This calls for stronger interventions from higher levels of political leadership.

Though the women have gained in visibility and confidence, their intra family status needs to be strengthened further, to give them decisive roles in taking important decisions and resisting deeply entrenched negative social practices like dowry, physical and sexual harassment of women and children, and unhealthy consumerism.

Another challenge is the upscaling and upgradation of micro-enterprises combining the strengths of self-help groups and cooperatives, a kind of combination of Kudumbashree and Amul—difficult to achieve in the current times but worth striving for. As an incisive observer remarked, it is very difficult to come across another Varghese Kurian; but to get a visionary people's leader like Tribhuvandas Patel seems to be practically impossible, when unifying forces seem to be weakening in the phase of divisive agenda all over.

Localizing Sustainable Development Goals (SDGs), with SHGs working towards 'communitization' of SDGs, offers interesting possibilities and this is on Kudumbashree's agenda.

Learning from Kudumbashree's Experience[2]

The most important factor in Kudumbashree's success is the networked inclusive organization of the poor with clear norms for active democratic functions. The focus on capacity building, nurturing of leaders from within the community and giving them a formal role made it an active organization. This, along with the formal functional partnership with local governments, which keeps changing every five years, has enabled the institutions of the poor to acquire dynamism warding off stagnation and decay. This was complemented by the approach of state and local governments cutting across political lines to support Kudumbashree. The reasons behind the support are anybody's guess. On the positive side, Kudumbashree could function as the community front line of government both in delivering services and giving feedback enabling effective citizen interface with governance at the cutting-edge level. And over time, political parties recruited Kudumbashree women as their candidates in local government elections and their high success rate has given them political visibility leading to some sort of political support. Also, the high brand equity of Kudumbashree among the public cannot be ignored by the political leadership. Of course, politicians who thought beyond votes and had some sense of the importance of pro-poor governance, cutting across political identities strongly supported it. The fact that these politicians held critical positions of authority at the beginning made this support even more beneficial. On the downside, politicians have used the women as their foot soldiers in electoral campaigning and agitations; the existence of organization enabling them to communicate easily through the networked system.

It is also to be noted that political support can be a double-edged weapon especially in a highly politicized society throwing up interesting insights into the very concept of democracy. The regular elections to Kudumbashree which have been fair, have revealed unfortunately, a negative side too. Political parties openly sponsor panels and through this, effective process of deciding leadership is transferred to hopelessly male-dominated party leaderships. The more vibrant elections are, the more triumphant the victor is. And there are many instances probably increasing in number which prove that electoral democracy can divide the poor into winners and losers. The losers instinctively withdraw into a shell and bide their time or skulk. Majoritarianism can deplete social capital. So, it is time to think of developing democratic instruments which strengthen unity of poor and promote communicative democracy.

At a broader level, the Kudumbashree system brings into positive relief the following:

- The importance of recognizing the multi-dimensional nature of poverty and deprivation, especially elements related to human development and focusing on building capabilities as the foundation of poverty reduction.
- Organizing the poor and linking them to the local governments to bring in social democracy to balance political democracy.
- Conscious promotion of micro-enterprises and nurturing the community to mentor and manage so that there is a graduation from thrift and credit to entrepreneurship, and slowly finding space in the formal economy.
- Multi-focused capacity building ranging from awareness building to skills and management capabilities, and from accessing basic entitlements to empowerment.
- Developing a proactive approach to include the poorest of the poor and other marginalized and vulnerable groups like the tribal communities and traditional fisher folk who remained outside the net.
- Using the SHG system for creating social enterprises particularly for delivering good quality services at affordable costs to citizens, especially in health.
- The SHG network can be an instrument for public action to enhance responsiveness of public service delivery institutions and also, by itself, function as the delivery mechanism for services especially in times of need as in the case of disasters like floods or pandemics.
- The human resources of the Kudumbashree Mission should be a healthy mix of staff drawn from different departments on the basis of competence and commitment and from outside government through a process of rigorous and fair selection.
- The brand equity of the programme is very critical. Though it may take at least five years to develop it, it can serve as a guarantee of continued governmental support and as a motivating factor for

responsible behaviour on the part of the SHG network to live up to the public image.
- The Kerala experience has equal relevance for both rural and urban areas.

As participant observers for nearly a quarter of a century, it is possible to envisage a ladder of empowerment starting from rudimentary 'financial capital' through thrift and credit quickly moving on to 'social capital' and gaining confidence to access 'physical capital' particularly from public programmes like sanitation, water supply, and housing. Simultaneously 'human capital' develops through a realization of importance of health, nutrition and education and a capacity to access the related services. Then comes what can be called the 'green capital' relating to sustainable livelihoods, with growing diversification and/or intensification. At this stage the acquisition of 'civic capital' becomes visible when the women start asserting their rights as citizens in public fora like gram/ward sabhas and other local platforms. This confidence enables them to achieve 'political capital', meaning the capacity to influence local decisions relating to allocation of resources and benefits with a growing ability to confidently and successfully negotiate power relations. The movement up the ladder is not automatic and the stages could vary across groups and localities. And the pace of the climb up is also not uniform. These features call for appropriate enabling environment which is best provided by a progressive government preferably in partnership with the civil society.

To conclude, the Kudumbashree system has contributed to democratizing local development and making it more gender sensitive, opening up new spaces for women. There is a silent understanding of development and power. As the journey from livelihood to public action is on, there are expectations of transformation of the poor women from objects to subjects, from individuals to collectives, and from beneficiaries to actors in pushing rights-based inclusive development.

17

Goonj: Reviving the Barter Economy and Changing the Lens with Dignity at the Centre

ANSHU GUPTA

GOONJ[1] WAS INITIATED IN 1999 with the unconventional idea of highlighting 'clothing' as a basic but unmet need in the country. Along its twenty-three-year journey, with the realization that there were many similar neglected and unmet needs, Goonj has come to shake the world gently, waking it up to the notion of human dignity, a most vital—and often forgotten—human need. Goonj's story contains many deep insights for the development sector, as it questions the broken system of charity and aid-centric development that robs people of their dignity and agency, by highlighting the bifurcation of donor versus beneficiary, giver versus receiver. Goonj's work with a vast majority of people, usually made to believe they are unworthy of dignity and respect, places human dignity at the centre of its societal system. It reminds people of their inherent value, and brings us back to fundamentals, to the fact that each of us, as an 'equal stakeholder' in the world, must do our bit.

Small Beginnings

Goonj began from a young couple's home; two people starting life in India's capital. At the time, in the late 1990s, the sight of people sleeping on the roads was still new for me, coming as I did from the beautiful small town of Dehradun. Habib Bhai's story from my journalism days revealed another dimension to this situation, especially in winter. I met him on a pavement outside the Lok Nayak Jai Prakash hospital in Delhi, where he worked picking up abandoned corpses for the local police. After spending a fair bit of time with him, I learnt one of my first lessons about clothing: during winters, he picked up many more dead bodies, as financially poor people who slept on the roads often had too few layers of clothing to withstand the city's freezing winter nights. And then came his little daughter who said: 'when I feel cold, I hug the dead body and sleep'.

We decided to take stock of the surplus items of clothing and utility material, which we had not used in three years of marriage. The pile of things we did not need (sixty-seven items) gave us some idea of how much other people could be hoarding. The idea of Goonj was born with that first insight: to connect the dots between urban India's vast stocks of surplus necessities, from clothes to utensils, with rural India's everyday struggle for basics; to create a link between these two unconnected worlds, tackling the problem of excess in one part of society and using it to address the problem of scarcity in another. While exchanging surplus clothes for new utensils was, and still is, a common practice in small towns, Goonj started working on this material systematically, on scale, throughout the year, across diverse populations and geographies.

This also set us off on a journey to understand the role clothes play in our lives. On a deeply personal level, it brought up childhood memories of my mother ensuring that my siblings and I always left our home dressed in neatly ironed clothes, no matter what our personal circumstances were for some period. While talking to women across rural India, another story brought home women's deep connection with cloths. In Firozabad, Uttar Pradesh, I met a woman who shared, how her sister died of tetanus: in the absence of clean cloth to use as a sanitary pad, she had used an old blouse which had a rusted hook.

In the initial days of Goonj, we were taken aback when, on a visit to a small village in Bihar, people started touching our feet in gratitude. We later found that they had coincidentally received clothes from Goonj just before Chhath, Bihar's biggest festival, a time when even the financially poor buy clothes for their family, often having to take high-interest loans from a local moneylender to do so; unable to pay it back, many were forced into a vicious cycle of bonded labour. Getting Goonj's family pack of good-quality clothes freed them from the need to take loans. This startling story highlighted the connection between disparate things such as festivals, clothes, debt and bonded labour. Shocking as they are, these stories are not aberrations but glimpses into lives with many neglected and ignored needs, and the vast majority's daily struggle for the bare basics.

Habib's story has inspired Goonj for over two decades, and highlights winters as an annual, predictable issue for the financially poor, that can be tackled. Well in time, we try to connect the woollens we usually stuff back into our trunks at the end of north India's winter with people who do not have enough warm clothes. The story of the woman who died of a rusted hook brought home two sombre realizations: one, the urgency of this deeply personal, yet highly taboo, need of millions of women across India and worldwide; and two, a deep awareness of our own lopsided lens which prevents us from recognizing issues which we have either not experienced or not been exposed to. To imagine a woman's struggle for a piece of cloth during menstruation, I had to let go of my own assumptions and experiences. Only then could I see the enormity and urgency of her need, and the complexity of the socio-economic, infrastructural and cultural challenges to her dignity that she faces every month. Over the last two decades, as we spoke to thousands of women in urban and rural India, we broadened our understanding of the issue, going beyond the cloth pad to focus on mainstreaming menstruation as a human issue. Interestingly, even though clothing is one of the three universal basics among 'food, clothing and shelter', it still does not find mention on any development agenda.

Creating a Barter System between Two New Currencies

In the early years of Goonj, an incident in a flood-hit village in Assam led to a new initiative being born. While driving down a broken muddy road in a vehicle filled with relief material, the person accompanying me complained about how difficult it was to travel on this road daily. My question as an outsider, 'why don't people fix this road?' sparked an idea. We took a break and sat down for a chat with the locals, asking if they would like to solve the problem themselves, i.e., repair the road and then take the relief material with pride as a reward for their efforts, instead of taking the material as charity. To our surprise, people immediately agreed; within days, they got together and repaired the road, making us realize that we had hit on a unique and valuable model of barter. The flagship initiative was named 'Cloth for Work' (CFW), also known as Dignity for Work.

In another flood-hit village in Bihar, a local community living by a riverbank lacked a bridge that their children could cross to attend school, narrated how their children risked their lives every day to swim across the river to get to school. Thirteen precious young lives had already been lost by drowning. We asked if they could build a bridge across the river for their children—and heard a loud 'yes'! They got together, every family bringing bamboo from their land or collecting money for that, and in the span of a few days, these courageous people had built a bridge for themselves. All we did was arrange some rope and nails to pull together the structure. After the bridge was built, every family received kits with assorted material that would be of daily use, as a token of their efforts for their community. Today, there is a large cement bridge in place of the bamboo bridge that served them for many years. The people of the area, having done the base work of making a bamboo bridge, had gone on to demand a cement bridge from the local government.

On a visit to Salidhana village in Khandwa district of Madhya Pradesh, we found that fetching water was a daily struggle for the village women: they frequently injured themselves on the climb up and down a slippery hill slope, to reach the only hand pump in the village. We initiated CFW, with the village inhabitants getting together to build steps across the slope. The seed of change had been sown—they then wanted to dig a well to tackle their water problems. Ramkuvar Bai, a daily wager, offered her land for the well after a village elder had identified a suitable spot, using *padiyar*, a traditional method of rolling a coconut to identify a suitable location. On the first day of work, only seven people arrived, but work began and continued, and soon the entire village got involved in building the well. In 2009, we struck water in the first-ever well dug under the CFW. Government had earlier spent around Rs 1,50,000 on machines to dig deep but had found no water. Thus, in a district declared 'dry', a precedence was set, inspiring neighbouring villages to follow their path. The villagers of Salidhana later made their well pukka under the Mahatma Gandhi National Rural Employment Guarantee Act (MGNREGA). It was an exciting moment for all of us and the beginning of our extensive work under CFW on other water bodies in the country.

These and many other initial experiments in tackling the diverse issues identified by people have led to the development of a sector-agnostic model that can be customized to local issues, resources and solutions. Goonj's teams and partners work deep in the interiors of India, mobilizing and motivating civic participation among communities. Over the past two decades, people have taken up thousands of activities such as digging wells and building bamboo bridges and retaining walls, small irrigation canals, drainage systems and village schools. They have undertaken more complex projects such as the building and repairing of long stretches of roads, and have developed water-harvesting systems to clean up ponds. This has been accomplished through helping people understand the power of their own community and through carefully chosen material as a reward for their efforts. In the process, we have found that a simple solution around water has an impact on migration; positive work on sanitation saves people travelling miles for basic treatment; a repaired mud road increases business; while a piece of second-hand cloth used as a sanitary pad improves women's reproductive health. Over twenty years, we have created a model based on a whole-system approach that addresses not only the issue of surplus material in urban homes and material poverty in millions of other homes, but also two other systemic, unmapped problems: the neglected dignity of people and the lack of resources for small development problems.

Repositioning India's surplus material as a new resource to tackle vast material poverty could also be a powerful sector-agnostic tool to fix ignored issues. Instead of the traditional charity/aid model we created a barter between two new alternate currencies—surplus urban material and the knowledge and labour of communities. This allowed Goonj to achieve development and impact at scale while keeping the dignity of the villagers at the centre of the process.

Goonj Material Kits—A Complex Matching of Needs with Material

Goonj processing centres serve as the key link connecting its urban and rural work. At these centres, the material collected from cities is matched with the specific needs of diverse communities, which depend on climate, age, gender and social and cultural norms—to create customized kits for distribution. There are a wide range of kits to meet different needs: regular family kits, school kits, wedding kits and dignity kits for women, among others. Receiving these kits allows people to use their meagre resources for other urgent needs. In return, the recipients of these kits agree to work on improving specific local issues that they have identified.

It brings to mind the handful of salt stored in an eggshell in a hut in Andhra Pradesh. The family clearly had very little salt, but they also did not have a utensil to hold the little they had. It drew our attention to the other deprivations people face during a natural disaster, such as household utensils; most relief operations include water tankers or dry rations, but no utensils or cookware in which to store or cook. As a result, utensils have been an essential part of our relief kits for years. Another essential are shoes: I have fond memories of meeting an old granny in a drought-hit village of Chattisgarh. She danced with joy wearing the slippers she got in the kit, saying: 'Today for the first time I am experiencing slippers on my feet. My soles will not burn now on the scorching hot floor in summer. I will have to learn how to walk in these since I have never worn slippers before'.

While working in the hilly terrain of Uttarakhand our team noticed that the children in Silgaon primary school had to walk long distances every day to school, some with slippers but most barefoot, over pebbled, rough roads. When the children got shoes with their school kits from Goonj, they were ecstatic. In one stroke, a new pair of shoes took away the disparity between the 'haves' and 'have-nots' in the school. One child refused to put on his new pair of shoes. His reason? 'If I wear them every day, they'll get damaged quickly. I have kept them safely for bigger (special) occasions.' The word dignity means different things to different people but for a child, wearing shiny black shoes to school is a recognizable metaphor for happiness too. In many villages and slums, people do not have anything for their feet, something we may never notice or call it a habit or tradition instead of understanding the affordability.

Another lesser-known kit is our 'pandal kit' (tent kit). Despite all their hardships, the India of the villages revels and lives for its festivities and religious rites; it can also run into high debt marking occasions under social compulsions. Goonj's pandal kit is created keeping in mind a village's needs for organizing big community events. Typically, people rent the materials at high rates; Goonj hands over these kits to village committees on the condition that those using them do *shramdaan* or community work. Also, the family using the kit often adds a few items while returning them, which is how the kit becomes like a tent bank. We have reached hundreds of pandal kits across rural India. Each kit usually contains large cooking vessels, buckets, tea containers, utensils, bedding, etc. This has now become a huge asset for villagers, helping them save a lot on the expense of rentals apart from giving easy and timely access.

General-use clothes, winter wear and other household material are distributed throughout the year. The school kits are prepared as part of the school-to-school programme, which takes materials from urban schools to resource-starved small village schools. They include schoolbags, stationery, uniforms and even computers and other school building infrastructure. Cloth sanitary napkins called 'My Pad' are distributed specifically to women. Raw materials to promote cottage industry are also sent, which generates employment and income for the villagers. This distribution network is effectively used during natural disasters in any part of the country to quickly reach specific relief material to the affected areas.

The table below illustrates Goonj's work during the Covid-19 pandemic in India:

RAHAT: Goonj's Covid-19 Response (April 2020 to December 2021)	
States and Union Territories reached	30
Families receiving a comprehensive kit	10,51,768
Cooked food or meals provided	4,96,200
Vegetables and fruits procured directly from farmers	4,31,000 kg
Ration and other essentials channelized	2.3 crore kg
CFW activities on water, sanitation and infrastructure	29,651
Pond-related activities	919
Canal-related activities	1,791
Community and individual kitchen gardens made	5,009

Private spaces or bathrooms made or repaired	2,071
Masks made	22.4 lakh
Sanitary pads made	27 lakh
Organizations supported	700
Family medicine kits	1,05,000
Health worker kits	39,000
Not Alone (Caregiving centres)	20

A People-to-People Connection

Goonj works with both urban and rural people, involving and engaging them in acting for change. In the cities, it works with corporates, schools, colleges, NGOs, small businesses and resident welfare associations; and on an individual level, it works with homemakers, professionals, retired people and schoolchildren, most of whom are isolated from rural realities. Goonj tries to make them aware of the challenges and issues in villages and slums of India, and solutions that can be achieved simply by passing on their so-called discards. Individuals and organizations play a vital role in its processes, whether it is in spreading awareness, collecting material or sorting, packing and distributing items. Goonj has now developed a vast grid interlinking transporters, suppliers, urban contributors, retail chains and educational institutions.

The backbone of the Goonj model is the strong network of over 500 grassroots partner organizations—including units of the Indian Army, NGOs, community-based organizations (CBOs), panchayats as well as social activists and reformers, providing crucial last-mile reach. These partner organizations are the hands, ears and eyes on the ground. The entire operation becomes sustainable, involves everybody, remains transparent, and gives every stakeholder a chance to serve, without a high financial burden. In this linking of urban people donating their surplus items with rural people in need, Goonj's role has been to frame the relationships between cities and villages in an integrated way. The Goonj model offers a shift from fragmented systems to an integrated model of mutually beneficial relationships between cities, villages and the environment that regenerates the wellbeing of all.

Efforts made by Goonj during major disasters such as earthquakes, floods and cyclones have spawned three innovations that connected urban surplus material, human dignity and disaster response in a new way. The first of these are the '*sujni* centres' in Bihar. The state has been one of Goonj's laboratories for experimentation and innovation ever since the massive Kosi floods of 2008. A remote village called Tamot Parsa became the hub for making sujnis—traditional rural quilts layered with tattered and shredded pieces of clothes stitched together, which serve as a multipurpose quilt-cum-mattress in village homes—after a chance meeting with a farm worker by the name of Hansa.

Hansa was the sole earner in her family as her husband was unwell. She would be paid only Rs 25 to 30 for eight to ten hours of arduous daily work at the farm. She needed to take loans just to be able to feed her family. Many like Hansa live in extreme poverty, often falling deep into debt. Goonj decided to make Hansa's home village of Tamot Parsa the hub of their sujni initiative. Hansa was among the first to join, learning the craft quickly and producing many high-quality sujnis. Her income soon grew and she was able to repay her debts. 'It feels good to see everyone in my family enjoying better food,' she said to the Goonj team. Today Goonj has sujni centres across the country, employing hundreds of women like Hansa making thousands of sujnis every year.

After the Kosi floods, Goonj created kits for people who had lost their occupations. About thirty types of local skills were identified and workers were provided with appropriate kits. In return, people contributed voluntary labour for their own community. This became the second innovation, named *Vaapsi*. A local hairdresser called Mahavir recieved a Vaapsi kit and was able to start his ruined business afresh. He set up shop again with renewed vigour and within six months, he was earning Rs 80 per day, so he expanded his shop, bought large mirrors and new benches and chairs.

Recalling the conditions right after the disaster, Mahavir says, 'It was a tough time, as I didn't have any money. But thanks to Vaapsi, I was able to start again. People don't understand the importance of small gestures. But they make a big difference.' During the Covid-19 pandemic, Goonj has given thousands of Vaapsi kits to people returning to their villages to restart their lives as part of the country's biggest wave of reverse migration.

The third innovation is linked to the second. Vaapsi Haat is a type of village market set up by Goonj across India. They bring together people who had received Vaapsi kits to sell their wares at a central location. Some of these village markets have gradually become a popular and regular feature of the local economy.

Over seven years since 2015, Goonj has delivered 4 crore kg of donated material to over 26,000 villages across the country. Over 1.17 crore rural lives have been enhanced by Goonj's work.

Activities from 2015 to 2022	
Water resource management: Cleaning, making and repairing of ponds, wells and canals	9,388
Hygiene and sanitation: Large-scale cleaning and hygiene-specific work of open and closed spaces	15,569
Local infrastructure and community spaces: Bridges, bandstands and bus shelters, among others	16,244
Agriculture and environment: Land bunding, kitchen gardens and plantations	12,227
Miscellaneous activities	441
Jobs created by repurposing surplus cloth to make daily utility items	3,00,000
Crossover livelihood created by communities in other geographical areas	6,00,000
MyPads: Clean cloth sanitary pads made of repurposing cotton material delivered to adolescent girls or women	69,00,000
Sujnis made	18,00,000
Total cloth used to make these products	1,46,00,000 square metres
Cloth repurposed into daily-use items	5,113 tonnes

Learning about Dignity and Material Poverty

In the creation of this model, India's villages have been our first university and our biggest learning ground about people and their needs, and the issues at the root of development. In my initial years of work in the villages, I was intrigued by the absence of beggars in some of the poorest villages, in complete contrast to the sight of them in many metros. Wherever I went in rural India, I also experienced a warmth towards outsiders and a strong sense of community among the people.

The biggest learning, I would like to share from our journey is the need for dignity to replace charity. This one insight changed the direction of our thinking and work, away from what could easily have been a traditional model based on charity. It came from understanding the value that people in villages place on their self-respect and dignity and made me pause to reflect on how Goonj should manifest itself among these proud, warm and courageous people. This is how human dignity emerged as the core value of our work.

The other insight is related to the giving and receiving of material. People commonly use the word 'donation' for such giving, but can we honestly term the giving of second-hand clothes or used household material, a donation? Are we not really 'discarding' what we do not need or use anymore. It also underlined the deeply flawed language of development, which refers to people who receive materials as 'beneficiaries', whereas they help us extend the lifespan of our material, prevent it from clogging our landfills and water bodies or polluting the air; indeed, we should actually be grateful to them.

Charity worldwide creates a divide between givers and recipients, with an inherent power dynamic that goes against the grain of development. It acknowledges and legitimizes only some kinds of giving and givers—of money, material, expertise and solutions, but fails to recognize and value the giving of the poor, instilling instead a narrative of their being the resource-less recipients of 'help' from the world. After a disaster, we all need a helping hand to get back on our feet, therefore post-disaster aid or charity is needed for some time, but development that is built on an unequal paradigm of charity cannot lead to successful outcomes. Every one of us is an equal stakeholder in the world and when we are active participants and feel valued, heard and respected, we can make the impossible possible. I equate it to the havan, the holy fire ritual common in India. In a havan everyone makes an offering, someone puts in the wood, another lights the fire, people pour havan material into the fire to strengthen it, and so on. The havan is successfully concluded with everyone's contribution. If the match that lights the havan fire believes that the havan happened only because of it, that could be described as misplaced arrogance.

People experience poverty in different ways, which underscores the need for customized, localized solutions. Working across the country, Goonj's core design principle of 'Let's improve the world before we change it,' focuses on acknowledging these different contexts, valuing what people already know and have in these diverse settings, and transitioning from the traditional model of trying to introduce something from outside in the shape of assistance, new skills, or materials. Our work has been around mobilizing and motivating individuals and families to take their own decisions and actions, through their own creative thinking and effort, for their own empowerment and improvements in their quality of life.

Nudging People Towards a Shift in Mindset

At the core, Goonj is nudging for a shift in people's mindsets about themselves; around their own dignity, agency, poverty, capacities and knowledge. As a community we mobilize and collectivize people to try and bring about a visible, measurable change in their own ecosystems, helping them with two key questions: Is it worth it? Can I do it? Initially the Goonj family kit becomes the motivation and nudge for people to apply their skills and local resources; their freedom to decide which issue they will tackle with a local workable solution makes it worth doing. In many instances, people have gone on to doing similarly self-mobilized work on other (non-Goonj-led) issues, learning from their earlier experiences.

When we ask people in cities to give their surplus for a good cause, it embeds the habit of continuously looking through their possessions with the thought of helping another person; in the process, it builds an attitude and culture of continuous mindful giving. Such an attitude and culture among our volunteers and contributors has, in turn, over the past decades ensured a continuous supply of material for sustained rural development work. Our partner grassroots organizations in the rural areas work on diverse issues like land rights, health, education, nature conservation, etc., where the material inputs from Goonj nudges them to examine the needs of their communities in a broader way, helping to bring them closer to their communities. On a systemic level, we have firmly established that material (earlier considered fit only for charity) is a powerful tool and resource for social change and development.

Goonj's work has been about recognizing the many 'taken-for-granted non-issues and people', and the viable solutions around us. In an era of machines, Goonj is about valuing the role of the needle: we see cloth as a needle in the overall human development process, and a piece of cloth in the form of a sanitary pad as a needle in the larger struggle of millions of women for dignity. I see the power of ordinary people as a needle to improve our own world. Despite our huge investment in intellect, resources, good intentions and hard work to improve our societies, we have not been able to solve the problem of poverty and other troubling issues. Perhaps it is time to change our vocabulary and the narrative around problems and solutions, the givers, takers and doers. I often say that half the world does not need a disaster, as poverty is the biggest ongoing disaster. That is why we must listen to and work with people who are most impacted by the development and disaster agendas and policies. That I believe calls for a humble re-look at our own lens and how we define knowledge, intellect and what is valuable. I wonder what we need to do for that.

18

Society for Elimination of Rural Poverty: A Paradigm Shift in How Government Tackles Poverty

K. RAJU

IN 2000, THE SOCIETY FOR Elimination of Rural Poverty (SERP) was established by the government of the undivided state of Andhra Pradesh as an independent organization with the objective of eliminating rural poverty. After the bifurcation of Andhra Pradesh in 2014, SERP-Andhra Pradesh[1] and SERP-Telangana[2] continue to work on this mission. Over the last two decades, SERP has implemented many successful interventions in the battle against poverty. It has helped poor village communities build their own organizations, in which they participate to take decisions for improving their lives.

Self-help groups (SHGs) comprising poor women have taken a lead role in the mission, operating at the village, mandal[3] and district levels through village organizations (VO), mandal samakyas and zilla samakyas, respectively. SERP has brought 1 crore rural women into the fold of 10 lakh SHGs, 45,000 VOs, 1,100 mandal samakyas and twenty-two zilla samakyas in the undivided state of Andhra Pradesh. Commercial banks in the state have provided credit to these organizations under the SHG–bank linkage programme. In 2020–21, SHGs in Andhra Pradesh and Telangana received Rs 27,800 crore of bank credit, a quantum jump from Rs 100 crore in 2000. This is testimony to the confidence banks have in SHGs in those states. Given their impressive repayment rates and the negligible levels of non-performing assets, SHGs can be one of the safest investments for banks.

By investing in income-generating activities, many of the extremely poor communities have managed to pull themselves out of debilitating poverty. Small and marginal farmers have raised productivity by investing in their land and venturing into dairying, horticulture and marketing. Livelihoods opportunities for the poor have expanded and become more diversified, leading to enhanced incomes. This is particularly true for the unemployed youth who benefitted from SERP's skill development and placement initiatives. Children who were being pressed into labour are now enrolled in schools; the health and nutrition status of pregnant and lactating women has improved; and social security support to poor and vulnerable groups has expanded.

SERP's policy advocacy with the state governments has helped shape many of their pro-poor policies and programmes. For example, banks used to charge interest rates of 7 to 9.5 per cent on loans to SHGs, but the Andhra Pradesh government's policy of providing budgetary support for interest subvention for these loans has enabled SHGs to avail zero-interest loans. SHG representatives and SERP staff are members of banking committees at the district and state levels.

The efforts by SERP to eliminate child labour resulted in the state government establishing eighty-eight residential schools for girls who were working but are now enrolled in schools. In 2009, the government of Andhra Pradesh enacted legislation on a co-contributory pension scheme for SHG members. SERP has also done pioneering work on skill development and placement, which has created job opportunities in private enterprises for rural youth.

SERP's strategy has been to incubate an initiative in a few villages in each district, and then expand the successful initiatives systematically to all villages. The process of expansion has been through community-to-community learning led by community resource persons (CRPs). They are usually women who have, through their own efforts, managed to emerge from poverty. Thus, they are best equipped to communicate their experiences and learnings to others in their community. SERP has helped train over 2,000 CRPs in social mobilization, registration, audits, governance, bank linkages, livelihood enhancement action plans (LEAP), insurance, health and nutrition, gender, agriculture and livestock, among others.

CRPs support SERP in training various stakeholders on a large scale in Andhra Pradesh and other states. When Bihar launched JEEViKA, its poverty elimination initiative, CRPs from Andhra Pradesh visited Bihar and spent several weeks working closely with local teams and helping mobilize poor villagers to form SHGs. Within a couple of years, Bihar had developed competent local CRPs. Further learning was organized through systematic exchange visits, training, orientation and exposure to the Andhra Pradesh model.

In 2011, the central government launched the National Rural Livelihood Mission (NRLM), to intensify the efforts towards elimination of rural poverty. SERP's CEO was transferred to the government to take key responsibility for the implementation of the mission. The NRLM was based on learnings from the social mobilization and community empowerment models from Andhra Pradesh, Bihar and Kerala. Replication of the Andhra Pradesh model in other states was facilitated by hundreds of CRPs from Andhra Pradesh.

Best practices promoted by SERP in Andhra Pradesh are now fully internalized and emulated in other states and contribute significantly to the empowerment of the poor. These include promotion of CRPs to enable community-to-community learning, formation of SHGs and their federations at the village and block levels, participatory identification of the poor, organization-building for specific vulnerable groups, SHG–bank linkage initiatives, community auditing systems and recovery mechanisms, LEAP, skill development for unemployed youth and health and nutrition initiatives for children and pregnant women.

The most important learning from the Andhra Pradesh model is the need for ownership of the programme at the highest political level, along with professionalization of the implementation architecture, continuity of bureaucratic leadership in the programme and ensuring the programme is truly led and managed by the community.

Factors in Success

The poor have tremendous potential to help themselves, so SERP puts them at the centre of its anti-poverty programmes and values their experience and ability to find solutions. This represents a radical shift from the dominant mindset among the political executive and bureaucracy that views poor people as passive subjects in need of help. What paved the way for this change in how poor communities are perceived?

It began in the 1990s, when poor women in Andhra Pradesh collectively accomplished inspiring achievements that demonstrated their indomitable spirit. No one in the state could ignore their small voices, but big victories. Four such victories contributed significantly to shaping the paradigm shift in the state's approach to dealing with the poor. When literacy campaigns were introduced under the government's Total Literacy Mission, they appealed most to women: both potential students as well as teachers. Many literate women enlisted as volunteers to teach, and the ones attending the classes were mostly poor women. These newly literate women clearly perceived possibilities for change in their lives through this new ability. Literacy classes and literacy centres also gave rural women an opportunity to come together and discuss their lives and challenges.

Another incident was the violent destruction of alcohol shops by women in Dubagunta village of Nellore district. The attackers had been deeply moved by a story they read in their literacy class. In the story—called 'Seeta Katha' (the story of Seeta)—the wife of an alcoholic commits suicide after failing in her efforts to reform her husband. The story invoked intense discussions among the women, as many were themselves victims of domestic violence inflicted by alcoholic husbands. The women decided to stop the sale of arrack in their village by demolishing the local liquor shop. Nearly a hundred village women ransacked the shop and prevented further sale of alcohol in the village. This show of aggression won the praise of local authorities, who were impressed by the women's courageous stance.

The Dubagunta incident eventually also made its way, as a story titled 'Adavallu Ekamaite' ('If Women Unite') into a book supplied to village reading rooms that had been set up to promote reading among neo-literates. Other women in the district, who visited the reading rooms, were in turn inspired by the success of the Dubagunta women, and also began forcibly closing down village arrack shops. Despite a backlash from contractors, including the use of violence, the women did not relent. Within a few weeks, all alcohol shops across the entire Nellore district had been destroyed. The anti-arrack movement spread to other districts, forcing the state to officially ban all alcohol in October 1993. For a state heavily dependent on revenue from the sale of alcohol, forcing the government to introduce prohibition was no small achievement.

For the first time in their lives, these women were able to make a collective decision to bring about change. They understood the power of organizing themselves to tackle collective problems, and decided to form SHGs. The SHG movement of Nellore district was called 'Podupulakshmi'. The groups met once a fortnight and pooled their savings to lend funds to members in need. This promoted thrift and credit activity among poor women. Their activities were covered extensively in the press, and these news reports of successes inspired women in other districts to form and join SHGs. Encouraged by the women's willingness to form SHGs, district collectors of other districts started largescale promotion of these groups.

Soon, vibrant VOs and mandal samakyas appeared as federations of SHGs in about 500 backward villages in Mahabubnagar, Kurnool and Anantapur. Their growth was facilitated by a pilot project supported by the UNDP called the South Asia Poverty Alleviation Programme (SAPAP). The objective of SAPAP was to demonstrate a replicable model for poverty eradication through social mobilization and community empowerment. The state soon witnessed self-managed, self-reliant organization among the poor at the village and mandal levels. Poor people were taking control of their own lives and defining their own way out of poverty. Within a matter of years, the poor people's socio-economic empowerment became so visible that the World Bank and the Ministry of Rural Development offered the state government support to replicate the model in all villages around the state.

These achievements eventually resulted in the state government recognizing the poor communities' desire for self-organization. They also identified activists who could lead these processes and took the step of establishing a formal, independent organization to implement them. That organization was SERP. The former Collector of Nellore during the Total Literacy Campaign and the anti-arrack movement, who later steered the SAPAP project successfully, was seconded to SERP as its first CEO.

Evolution as a sensitive support organization

SERP endeavours to only hire people who believe in the potential of the poor. Its unique HR policy has encouraged the induction of young postgraduates passionate about working with the rural poor as well as professionals from the government, banking, NGO and private sectors. The primary duty of the staff is to listen to the voices of the SHGs and VOs and help them to improve their lives. Every member of SERP undergoes a village immersion programme, which requires them to stay in a village for two weeks and interact with the poor communities to understand their lives and aspirations. Apart from facilitating the formation and development of SHGs, SERP staff impart training to SHG members on management, bookkeeping, internal lending and SHG–bank linkages.

SERP's district units cover institution building, training, social inclusion, SHG–bank linkages, financial management, farm and non-farm livelihoods, food processing, gender equity, social security, insurance, health, food and nutrition and convergence with panchayati raj institutions. SERP has partnered with several civil society organizations, drawing on their expertise to support the CBOs, including MV Foundation for child labour elimination, Basix for microfinance and livelihoods, Andhra Pradesh Mahila Abhivrudhi Society for capacity-building of SHGs, Action Aid for participatory identification of the poor, Akshara for livelihood enhancement action plans, Jattu for organic farming, and Shodhana for learning among pre-school children. It has always engaged in conversation with SHGs and their federations before initiating an intervention. The ideas and plans emanating from such conversations are vetted by professionals to make sure the intervention is technically sound. When an intervention is introduced and its strategy formulated, SHG leaders are given specialized training to ensure its correct implementation.

Ownership of the programme at the highest political level has helped SERP navigate its way without serious obstacles. Its Executive Council (EC) is chaired by the chief minister, with the members including ministers, bureaucrats heading relevant departments, eminent members of civil society and subject-matter experts. It meets periodically to discuss and approve SERP's strategies, plans and programmes. The EC has also helped SERP forge a convergence with ongoing programmes in other departments targeting the poor. Prior to the establishment of SERP, local officials and non-officials used to exercise enormous discretion in the selection of anti-poverty programmes and their beneficiaries. But SERP has empowered CBOs take all the decisions, and in this they have been aided by the ownership of the programme at the top political level.

Institution Building

Between 2000 and 2010, SERP worked on institution-building by the poor, a process that affected every poor rural family in the state. It is in these institutions that discussions and decisions on how to improve their lives take place and leaders emerge to help the poor interface with the external world and demand their rights and entitlements from the government. For instance, SERP helps SHGs hold monthly meetings with all their members, expand their capital with members' savings, disburse loans to members from the group's capital, recover the loans with interest, maintain books of accounts, subject accounts to audit and secure bank credit to enable members to engage in income-generating activities.

In villages where SHGs have become self-reliant and self-managed, a VO is formed to act as a federation of SHGs at the village level. The VO evolved as a forum for SHGs to learn from each other's experiences. The president and secretary of each SHG is a member of the VO. In monthly meetings, members apprise the VO about their respective group's activities. Other services provided by VOs include training to SHG bookkeepers, auditing of SHG accounts, liaising with banks for credit for SHGs and monitoring repayment.

The VOs support SHGs in their campaigns against child marriage, child labour and social and gender inequities. They also help poor communities access their rights and entitlements from the state. Their representatives make the concerns of the poor known to the gram panchayats and government departments for grievance redressal. VOs in a mandal are federated into mandal samakyas. Each VO is represented by its president and secretary in the mandal samakya.

The mandal samakyas hold meetings every month and have evolved as a platform for VOs to exchange ideas. Most government departments are present at the mandal level. Mandal samakyas therefore have a meaningful interface with these institutions to represent issues concerning the poor in the mandal. The mandal samakyas in all twenty-two districts of undivided Andhra Pradesh have been federated into zilla samakyas, which interact with the district officers of various departments to ensure the poor benefit from ongoing government programmes. Zilla samakyas are implementing agencies of insurance schemes targeting poor families and for the co-contributory pension scheme for women.

SERP has created awareness about the importance of registration, members' rights and entitlements and the need to fulfil compliances. All the 45,000 village organizations, 1,100 mandal samakyas and 22 zilla samakyas are registered with the Cooperative Department of the state government. Since 2013, CBOs have been fulfilling legal compliances such as holding general body meetings and elections, conducting statutory audits, and submitting annual returns.

SERP has also adopted community-to-community learning for institution-building through having its staff nurture SHGs and VOs in one or two villages in each mandal through regular visits, meetings and training for members. This enabled the SHGs and VOs to manage their own activities. Villages where SHGs and VOs meet all these requirements are selected as 'resource villages'. SHG members from other villages visit resource villages to study their methods, which they then share with other SHGs and VOs.

Members of SHGs and VOs who have been identified as best practitioners and who have experienced a transformation in their own lives are designated as CRPs. They are trained by SERP staff to visit villages and stay for a week or two to help the poor there set up SHGs and VOs. The concept of the CRP has been leveraged by SERP not just for social mobilization and training of SHGs and their federations but also for financial inclusion, enhancing agriculture and livestock productivity and driving behavioural change on health, nutrition and sanitation.

For example, one of the key reasons SHG women can access regular credit from commercial banks is the presence of a bank mitra—a CRP trained in financial inclusion at rural bank branches in the state. CRPs also help with auditing of accounts, securing land rights, accessing markets and gaining remunerative prices for their produce. CRPs trained in disabled welfare work towards ensuring the inclusion of disabled persons, and health and nutrition CRPs promote nutrition-cum-day care centres which also serve as focal points for health education and behavioural change among poor rural communities.

Financial Inclusion

SERP has adopted a focused approach in expanding the capital base and livelihoods of poor families. It is the first organization in the country to work extensively on linking SHGs with banks. It has ensured that SHGs maintain books of accounts and that these accounts are audited regularly. SHGs have been trained to prepare credit plans and to manage transactions-based digital accounting systems that capture financial transactions on a real-time basis. SERP has facilitated visits to SHGs for bank managers to build their confidence about the creditworthiness of the SHGs.

Its work on SHG–bank linkages has secured dependable lines of credit to most SHGs in the states of Andhra Pradesh and Telangana. Today, these states together account for 30 per cent of the country's SHG–bank linkages. Bank managers in the two states hold monthly meetings attended by SHG and VO leaders to discuss the SHGs' credit requirements, their eligibility, utilization of loans for asset creation and recovery performance. These meetings have ensured a smooth flow of credit to SHGs and a prompt repayment culture among them.

SERP has helped VOs develop a broad view of the livelihoods that can be promoted in their villages. It introduced LEAP as a participatory planning process to help create comprehensive village-level plans for interventions that can enhance livelihoods. SERP has trained active leaders in VOs in the use of LEAP tools such as social mapping, resource mapping, livelihoods mapping and the analyses of income and expenditure. They were also taught about value chains, seasonality and migration, credit, vulnerability and institutional issues. These analyses bring to light gaps and opportunities in the locality, based on which suitable and viable action plans can be prepared to plug the gaps, harness opportunities and enhance livelihoods. The implementation of LEAP is with financial support from government and banks.

SHGs in Andhra Pradesh practice 'zero-budget natural farming' in about 5 lakh acres. This practice has been nationally acclaimed as the country's largest climate-resilient farming initiative. The VOs in Telangana operate in about 4,000 paddy procurement centres across the state, enabling farmers to easily sell their paddy crop and receive immediate payment without having to travel long distances. To expand job opportunities for rural youth, SERP has partnered with private enterprises and zilla samakyas to establish skill development centres across the state.

Most villagers who completed a short-duration course titled 'English, Work Readiness and Computers' found jobs in retail, security and private banks. Enthused by the response from the private sector, the government of Andhra Pradesh now has a mission for employment generation and marketing to help young people in rural areas upgrade their skills and get private sector jobs.

In summary, SERP has facilitated the formation of partnerships among the poor communities, and between them and the government, NGOs, banks, experts in various fields and private organizations to help them out of poverty. It continues to stand by its commitment to the poor: 'nothing about you, without you.'

Conclusion

SERP was able to transcend limitations inherent in a government agency mainly because it forged partnerships with organizations managed by poor communities. Two decades of SERP's work has seen the poor taking ownership of decision-making processes of their own organizations. But the most profound change was the movement's ability to strengthen women's autonomy in decision-making. In a society that often curtails women's rights, the SHG movement not only augmented their avenues for livelihood creation but also empowered them to exercise their autonomy in the public and private spheres. It has paved the way for rural women to have more meaningful participation in society.

19

ITC e-Choupal: A Lighthouse for Truly Inclusive Value Chains

SIVAKUMAR SURAMPUDI

OVER THE LAST TWO DECADES, a quiet transformation has been gaining ground among a section of farmers across India—a wave of change borne forward by collaboration, knowledge, skills and technology that is helping them break free from traditional hurdles and equipping them for a rapidly changing world. These farmers are learning contemporary techniques, and using better varieties and diversifying their crops. They are joining together to buy high-quality inputs and hire equipment at prices they cannot afford individually, and collaborating to regenerate and manage local water, soil, and biodiversity resources. With access to real-time weather information, expert advice, and daily prices offered by nearby mandis and private buyers, they are taking informed decisions on when to sow, irrigate, harvest and sell. Allowing for variations across different geographies, crops and adoption levels, on average these farmers experience increases in incomes of up to 50 per cent as a result of 6 to 10 per cent savings on costs and 10 to 25 per cent improvements in yields.

Despite most of these farmers being small and marginal landholders with less than two hectares of farmland, their long-precarious livelihoods have now become more robust, sustainable and climate-resilient. This is because of the multiplicity of changes they have embraced, all of which emanate from a single focal point. These focal points are 'e-Choupals'.[1] They are meeting places where farmers from nearby villages can access a personal computer with an internet connection. There is no charge to use the facility.

This computer has a customized portal that brings them real-time information on crop prices, weather, best practices and much more, all in their local language. With over 6,100 e-Choupals reaching over 35,000 villages, observers might tend to assume that they have been installed as part of a large-scale government programme, perhaps in collaboration with NGOs. But e-Choupals were conceived and established by ITC Ltd, one of India's leading business conglomerates with a long history of close relationships with agricultural communities.

Launched by ITC in 2000, just over twenty years ago, the e-Choupal project was intended to digitally empower farmers and make Indian farming more competitive, profitable and sustainable. Conceived at a time when electricity supply in most villages was erratic and few farmers had ever seen a computer, let alone used one to connect to the internet, it was a visionary notion, a business innovation designed to generate broad-based value across the agro-chain. The information and services offered by the portal have only grown in impact over time as rural infrastructure improved. ITC's e-Choupal network is currently used by over 40 lakh farmers across nine Indian states.

As e-Choupal farmers have become more competitive and resilient, extensive collaboration through the platform has helped ITC's agribusiness division to sustain its position as one of India's largest exporters of agriproducts and to become one of the country's largest integrated agribusiness enterprises, with significant operations across every node of the agri-chain. ITC Foods is among India's fastest-growing food businesses, its agri-procurement capability sharpened considerably through e-Choupal. ITC's strategic focus on sustainable and inclusive growth and its aim to develop innovative business models extend to e-Choupal, in supporting vibrant value chains that penetrate deep into rural India and generate economic, environmental and social capital.

Delivering outstanding value on all three dimensions of the 'triple bottom line' (profit, people and the planet), the e-Choupal platform has grown into a multi-infrastructure, multiservice ecosystem. The e-Choupal kiosks provide relevant information through ITC's farm portal, which is conveyed to farmers through an educated local farmer called a *sanchalak*, in whose house the computer is usually located. The sanchalak also facilitates other services supported by the portal, such as helping farmers purchase agri-inputs in bulk or connecting them to finance and crop insurance schemes.

If farmers decide to sell their product to ITC, they are helped by Choupal Saagars, which are integrated rural hubs that serve as ITC procurement centres, warehouses and retail outlets. At Choupal Saagars, scientific quality assessment and digital weighing usually garner farmers an additional 4 to 5 per cent in the selling price, and immediate cash payments allow farmers to avoid moneylenders. ITC procurement centres provide these services in areas where there is no Choupal Saagar nearby. The retail facilities at Choupal Saagars present an ambience and product range comparable to the urban centres, catering to the changing tastes of rural consumers. There are also Choupal Haats, which are markets that bring multiple companies and brands to rural families through events organized on the lines of village fairs.

Choupal Pradarshan Khets have demonstration plots, classroom teaching, audio-visual demos and customized expert advice that give farmers the knowledge and skills to raise productivity, save costs and branch into new high-value crops. Other models such as *Baareh Mahine Hariyali* (BMH)—'Greenery All through the Year'—a 360-degree initiative with solutions ranging from improved varieties and increased cropping intensity to climate-smart techniques and appropriate mechanization. Of the 2,00,000 farmers covered so far by BMH, about 35,000 who adopted all the recommended practices reported a doubling of incomes, while those who adopted a selection of the practices reported 35–75 per cent increases.

The newest version of e-Choupal (version 4.0) is being designed as a crop-agnostic integrated solution framework that will aggregate new technologies such as remote sensing, precision farming and drone-based services to bring participating farmers highly personalized services and recommendations. Version 4.0 will also serve as a channel for agricultural entrepreneurs to start farmers' services such as climate-smart farm techniques and equipment. They could also offer custom hiring and output market-related services such as warehousing, quality testing and access to commodity futures and options. Additionally, the new version will provide support for global certifications such as Organic, Rainforest Alliance, Forest Stewardship and Fairtrade.

On the environmental front, e-Choupal is the primary vehicle for ITC's programmes for water stewardship, climate-smart agriculture and biodiversity conservation. Anchored in community participation, these initiatives have increased water availability for agriculture, enhanced water resources through a combination of supply- and demand-side interventions. They have also enabled farmers to adopt climate-smart practices complemented by measures to restore and maintain common resources and local ecosystems on which agriculture depends. An animal husbandry initiative supports cattle owners in crossbreeding their cattle to boost milk yields and creates opportunities for them to enter dairying and add another income stream through surplus milk sales. In all these programmes, ITC links up with government schemes and programmes wherever possible to amplify its reach.

For farm households, e-Choupal's most important impact is no doubt the growth in their incomes. But for these rural families, the proliferation of farmer-centric services has also helped to foster a sense of optimism and connectedness to the urban world. The structure and services that constitute the e-Choupal ecosystem have largely evolved based on farmer feedback, with farmers reciprocating by treating e-Choupal as a trusted partner, enabling the platform to act as an agent of change.

On the business front, e-Choupal is the cornerstone of ITC's agri-procurement capability. Its agribusiness division is one of India's largest procurers and exporters of agri-commodities, sourcing over 30 lakh tons of agriproducts from twenty crop value-chain clusters across twenty-two states. Two-thirds of its total procurement is sourced through e-Choupal. ITC is also the country's second-largest procurer of wheat after the government's Food Corporation of India, and its wheat procurement is almost exclusively through e-Choupal.

The depth, range and reach of ITC's agribusiness provide strategic support to its foods business, enabling it to source high-quality raw materials with the accuracy of value-added services such as identity preservation, traceability and certification. As ITC focuses on high-demand, value-added products, close engagement with farmers through e-Choupal strengthens its ability to source preferred-quality, attribute-specific agriproducts. A rapidly expanding list of such products already includes food-safe chillies, organic mango pulp traceable to farms and speciality coffee certified for Fairtrade, end-use specific wheat flour, and frozen snacks. These are taking agricultural value chains to greater growth and enhancing profits for both farmers as well as ITC's businesses.

Resting on the foundation of ITC's close partnership with farmers, the e-Choupal ecosystem continues to drive change, reorganizing the value chain to support efficient transmission of services, knowledge, technology and consumer signals. Through co-creating platforms and services with farmers and evolving with a changing world to create opportunities for them, e-Choupal has demonstrated how inclusive value chains can transform the agricultural scenario and create a more demand-responsive and sustainable production system.

Building Blocks for Success

ITC's unique insights into the macro and micro aspects of agricultural value chains gave it an informed perspective when conceptualizing the e-Choupal model. From its close relationships with farmers through its agribusiness activities for over a century, ITC also had a deep knowledge of their challenges, weaknesses and strengths. It knew that it was important to break the vicious cycle that farmers get into when buying and selling without any knowledge of prevailing prices. This compelled them to sell at whatever mandi prices were offered on the day as they had already incurred the cost of transporting their produce there.

By making price discovery possible in advance within the village, e-Choupal changed the game by enabling farmers to time their sales and get better prices. ITC was also able to design its procurement facilities to counter the problem points in the conventional channel, offering electronic weighing, quality testing, premiums for better quality and immediate cash payments to farmers who choose to sell to them.

Although there were various institutions along the value chain that attempted to free the farmer from the exploitative cycle of dependency on moneylenders, the farmers still had to expend money and time trying to access the services of these varied institutions. With ITC's insight and experience, e-Choupal was designed to offer a single integrated platform for these services, saving time, cost and effort for farmers. Moreover, e-Choupal services are free, equipping farmers with information but allowing them the freedom to make their own choices on how to use it. As more and more farmers began to use e-Choupal to step away from moneylenders and break free of their vicious cycle, ITC worked closely with participating farmers to develop crop-specific models that increased their incomes while creating greater economic value for the company.

Another vital element in designing the e-Choupal model was to ensure that even small farmers could use the services and benefit from the virtual aggregation supported by e-Choupal, enabling them to gain from the scale economies. ITC came up with the idea of the sanchalak, an educated villager who is trained to use a computer and familiar with ITC's site, who can help others avail of the information and services provided. ITC realized that the role of the sanchalak was critical to the success of e-Choupal, and he would have to be someone the farmers considered one of their own; only then would e-Choupal attract widespread participation. Therefore, the choice of sanchalak was crucial to the success of the process.

ITC needed to determine the most appropriate type of person to play this role as well as to define a profile template that could be applied across various e-Choupal locations.

To achieve this, it used an implementation model called 'Roll Out–Fix It–Scale Up', which is a modular expansion approach that limits risk and makes it possible to achieve substantial scale and wide scope in a relatively short span of time. The intervention is rolled out on a small scale at first to determine the best ways to make the idea workable. Ground operations are treated as a process to identify weaknesses and problems, allowing for mistakes to be made for solutions to be found. During the process, ITC relies on a portfolio of experiments to determine the right solution, especially when introducing new methods, roles or institutions.

ITC tried different types of individuals in the village to play the role of sanchalak—including schoolteachers, headmasters, postmen, local cooperative leaders and panchayat presidents—before finally deciding that a farmer would fit the role best. Through these iterative trials, ITC was also able to develop a carefully designed selection process that could be applied across geographies. The process involves extensive consultations with local farmers before shortlisting a few candidates and conducting interviews, and is similar to an election but avoids the pitfalls of actual elections. While ITC is closely involved in every step of choosing a sanchalak, the resulting choice is a farmer whose fellow farmers are confident will represent their interests and accommodate their individual choices, while also enabling them to gain from the benefits of acting as a group, which is the very foundation that constitutes the strength of e-Choupal.

While ITC crafted a new village institution in the form of the sanchalak, it sought to create new roles for traditional players who would lose out through the transparency engendered by e-Choupal and could present a roadblock if they were eliminated from the chain altogether. Different roles and safeguard options were tried for the informal intermediaries in the conventional system to find a new place for them through iterative on-ground experimentation. The outcome was the creation of the role of *samyojak*, to co-opt conventional intermediaries and to provide services within the e-Choupal platform, thus leveraging the traditional middlemen's considerable capabilities in logistics, storage, cash disbursement, etc., but bypassing them when it comes to transmitting information and market signals.

When e-Choupal was rolled out, the inadequate physical infrastructure of the time was a significant potential roadblock. ITC worked closely with various companies to find solutions before arriving at a best fit, and then collaborated on research and development to fine-tune the final components. Thus, it worked with companies manufacturing solar panels to develop panels that were effective even in cloudy weather, and with battery companies to ensure back-up power would be affordable. The decision to invest in high-bandwidth VSAT receivers to ensure internet access in remote villages, in turn pushed ITC to innovate and develop more revenue models to offset the higher cost.

Once the basic model is in place after Roll Out and Fix It, MECE (Mutually Exclusive Collectively Exhaustive) experiments are employed to decide the right approach to Scale Up and to fine-tune the design. MECE frameworks help to develop a toolkit of possible solutions rather than a rigid standard operating procedure (SOP); they provide a menu of options with the flexibility to fit diverse local conditions rather than a one-size-fits-all approach. Prior to actual scale-up, pilots are implemented to test scalability, and to iron out inconsistencies and account for the various factors that will come into play in the larger, scaled-up environment. This approach has allowed ITC to develop tailored business models for different crops across different geographies using the same basic e-Choupal model. ITC designed e-Choupal to evolve continuously, to keep it contemporary and responsive to changing times and changing needs.

Evolutions of e-Choupal

2000 (1.x series): Reorganizing commodity supply chains into crop value chains for greater efficiency in buying commodities in rural markets.

2003 (2.x series): Leveraging the reengineered value chains as platforms for the reverse flow into rural markets of goods and services such as farm inputs and agri-related services, natural resource management and other community-development initiatives, as well as for organized retail sales through Choupal Saagars.

2009 (3.x series): Creating a new ecosystem of services by building linkages with multiple partners co-opted in the 2.x series and offering the ecosystem to other companies to access rural markets. These services include farm mechanization and custom hiring, employment portals, healthcare, consumer goods and brand promotion through Choupal Haats.

2017 (4.x series): Offering more personalized services and plug-and-play systems supported by technology advances.

The e-Choupal is launching a super app, called ITC-MAARS (Metamarket for Advanced Agriculture and Rural Services) with the aim of creating a robust 'phygital' ecosystem that combines physical and digital interventions to deliver seamless, customized solutions to farmers. It will focus on microservices by offering a full complement of agricultural solutions, including hyperlocal services, AI-based personalized advisories and online marketplaces. ITC-MAARS will offer a high level of personalization across various farm profiles for the health, nutrition, irrigation and mechanization of different soils. Farmer profiles and real-time conditions such as hyperlocal weather forecasts, pest predictions and crop stage and conditions can also be personalized.

Each e-Choupal series continues to run concurrently, expanding in scope and scale. For example, e-Choupal 1.0 started with a model for reorganizing the soybean value chain, called the e-Choupal 1.1. ITC then went on to develop

1.2 for wheat, 1.3 for coffee and 1.4 for shrimps, using MECE experiments to map the various dynamics and create different versions that could be delivered through the same e-Choupal model. Since then, these series have been used in different combinations for an expanding basket of crops. If the existing series cannot be applied for a specific value chain, then ITC develops a new series, as it did recently when it needed a model to enter the dairy sector. This saves on time as it can borrow from previous learnings from earlier series, and the process of Roll Out-Fix It-Scale Up is virtually the same. Change is a constant, and ITC uses the building blocks that have made e-Choupal a success to keep it in tune with the times. Leveraging its own unique insights and experience, it develops design principles that are then defined and tested through extensive iterative experimentation that functions as the core execution process.

Now that farmer producer organizations (FPOs) are being given a significant impetus by the government, ITC is considering how e-Choupal will work with these organizations. They are likely to develop collectively owned local infrastructure such as warehouses, nurseries and small food processing centres with incentives or seed money from the government. Recognizing that FPOs have a tremendous potential to augment farm livelihoods when linked to the markets effectively, ITC has proposed to support nearly 4,000 FPOs for the next decade.

While this would benefit 1 crore farmers across multiple crop clusters, it may lead to a substantial directional shift for e-Choupal, moving from only virtual aggregation of farmers to physical integration through FPOs. As this dimension strengthens, ITC may re-evaluate the roles of the sanchalak and samyojak.

Factors in Success

A changing external environment can make or break a good idea. Three factors have been critical to e-Choupal's development and success:

Without *reforms in the APMC (Agricultural Produce Market Committee) Act*, e-Choupal could not have established itself after its launch, as the reforms allowed farm produce to be sold outside the mandi. The willingness of state governments to partner with private players, including ITC, to strengthen agriculture was also a robust driver. Public–private partnerships ranged from trials to testing the efficacy and calibrating reforms, to coordinating investments to improve value chains; an example is the government investing in infrastructure and ITC in production and processing facilities. Several of the government's recent initiatives are intended to support a shift from production-driven supply chains led by the government, to demand-responsive value chains anchored by consumer-oriented market players to raise farmer incomes. This has been ITC e-Choupal's objective from the beginning and the ecosystem will benefit from and complement government initiatives like the proposed digital Agri-Stack and Value Chain Cluster approach.

Without *developments in digital technology*, the e-Choupal concept could not have been translated into reality. Technological advances have driven its evolution, from taking computers to villages where none had been seen before and connecting farmers to the internet for real-time information, to the rapid and extensive smartphone penetration prevailing today on the back of steadily advancing mobile network generations.

Without *expanding infrastructure to improve rural connectivity*—primarily roads, telecom, and electricity—e-Choupal could not have put in place its hub-and-spoke model in which a single e-Choupal and procurement centre serves a number of villages within a specific radius.

Looking Back

The process of conceptualizing, launching and continuing e-Choupal operations has benefited from ITC's Roll Out–Fix It–Scale Up approach. This approach plus MECE and other iterative experiments provided the flexibility to make mistakes, identify problems and find solutions in a small universe, therefore minimizing the risk of failure while scaling up. The mistakes made and learnings acquired through the process of rectification have expanded ITC's Roll Out-Fix It-Scale Up approach, creating a richer and more effective template that ITC continues to use to implement virtually all its interventions.

With hindsight, one of the major differences that ITC would have charted in e-Choupal's journey would have been to embark much earlier on its 3.0

version. The assumption at that time was that the government's reform agenda was irreversible and that e-Choupal 1.0 and 2.0 models would continue to be expanded. When reforms were halted and reversed in response to inflation in food prices during 2006–07, it was a major setback for the way versions 1.0 and 2.0 operated. Only then did ITC consider turning e-Choupal into a broader-scope platform by launching 3.0. And the learning from this experience gave an impetus to ITC taking an even broader view of the macro-environment and adding more dimensions to turn e-Choupal into a robust all-weather platform.

Learnings for Others

The e-Choupal was designed as a value capture model that would capitalize on ITC's unique enterprise strengths: a diversified company with a triple bottom line focus, a robust and rapidly growing business footprint in foods, hotels and packaging, with strong trade marketing and distribution infrastructure. e-Choupal was crafted as a strategy to enhance business competitiveness, growth, and profitability while creating broad-based value for all players in the chain, which is in keeping with ITC's strategic commitment to triple bottom-line performance. In similar fashion, organizations looking to implement large-scale, high-impact initiatives like e-Choupal should carefully examine how their own individual internal synergies could be best harnessed and reinforced through external collaborations to effectively achieve significant impact.

In fact, the majority of processes used by ITC in developing the e-Choupal model—e.g., Roll Out–Fix It–Scale Up, MECE experiments, re-engineering the value chain, using digital technology— could be successfully used by any organization if adapted to their particular objectives. More importantly, the fact that e-Choupal synergizes the greater good for farmers and the natural environment, and builds the competitiveness of value chains thereby making ITC more competitive too, is perhaps a learning about the potential of synergistic sustainable business models.

20

the ant:[1] Stepping Away from the Trees to Notice the Forest

SUNIL KAUL AND JENNIFER LIANG

Setting Up the Anthill

AS A SYMBOL OF MUCH of what we believed in and how we wanted to work, we fell upon 'the ant' as our name and talisman. Known to work in unison, not give up easily, and be hugely industrious and capable of performing size-defying tasks, the humble ant with its not-so-humble qualities suited us. At that time, as founders we probably did not dare dream gi-ant or eleph-ant-like dreams. We were still healing from the trauma of a recent loss.

A few years prior (1996–97), we were a part of an enthusiastic bunch of young professionals working and living together in the largest inhabited river island in the world, Majuli, in the Brahmaputra river. Just fifteen months into our development work, the leader of our group, Sanjoy, was kidnapped by the militant organization: United Liberation Front of Assam.[2] As ransom for his release, our team was asked to shut shop and leave Assam, which we did, but we never saw our colleague again.

Our return to Assam a few years later was probably part of our healing. We needed to continue the work that had been cut short. If only to ourselves, we had to prove that *ahimsa* or non-violence will win over the violence we had been subjected to. That was easier said than done. After visiting various parts of Assam, we chose to base ourselves in Bongaigaon in the western part of Assam, to work in some of the least developed areas of the state. This region is also close to the Indo-Bhutan border, which had seen some of the worst violence unleashed by armed militants of the Bodo tribe. Bongaigaon at the time was synonymous with bomb-throwing and bridge-blowing by armed militants. Obviously, our families and friends did not warm up to our choice!

In September 2000, we moved to Bongaigaon. A tall, distinctly Kashmiri man cycling with a young Chinese-Indian woman, and sending emails by plugging his telephone into a laptop from a PCO in a little town, raised many curious eyebrows and set tongues wagging. And if we thought we could just walk into remote villages on the Bhutan border and begin our mission of 'developing' them, well, we had to seriously think again! For one, no village was ready to house us for the night as they were concerned about the armed militants. Taking a train at dawn, followed by a four-hour bus ride and an hour by buffalo-cart to reach the village by noon, only to be hurried out after two hours, was not the most effective way to 'do' development work. On the few days in the week when there was no *bandh* (civil strike) and government offices actually functioned, we collected secondary data on various issues. We had a few external training assignments and some part-time work to keep us somewhat occupied—and to help us earn money to run the show too—but we were at a loss on how to work in our 'chosen' far-flung villages.

In a few months, we had our first colleague, Meghali, who was a fresh graduate in social work from Tata Institute of Social Sciences. We were excited to have a co-traveller and hoped that the newly acquired cycles would make our development journey smoother. Her classmate came from a village not far from Bongaigaon, and his father, a farmer, became our advisor and ally in the years that followed. He suggested that we begin working in his area instead of waiting to work in the distant border villages. That may have been against our sense of equity, but made sense. One introduction led to another and soon we were making cycling forays to villages 5 km north of our office.

Never having heard of a non-governmental organization (NGO) or what voluntary organizations do, it was a wonder how patiently the tribal villagers heard us 'aliens' (in look, speech, ideas), out. Sitting with the women on the ground—instead of sitting on chairs with the men—talking about wanting to 'work *with* them and not *for* them' etc., we wonder what they made of us back then. Our exotic, entertainment value may have been more of a draw than understanding our mission! From then it has been a long, albeit most interesting, journey.

Over the years we have learnt to negotiate power centres, both state and non-state, youthful and not-so-youthful, armed and unarmed, political and non-political, and through all this to keep our head, heart and independent spirit intact. Even as we designed programmes in health, women's rights, and livelihoods to respond to the development needs of the community, we learnt to build a team (of largely local youth) who believed in and worked towards the mission. As a team, we have dealt with floods, droughts, waves of ethnic violence, being feted and being slandered, from being on a high moral ground to being demoralized, even as we celebrated many welcomes and farewells of colleagues.

Our action spans two districts of Assam, directly benefiting 21,000 persons and indirectly 61,000 persons in 982 village hamlets. The work spans child development, child protection, gender violence, education, sports for development, livelihoods and emergency relief. We also work through collaboration and networks with seventeen NGOs in four states across twenty-two districts.

The Anthill: Two Decades Later

Twenty-one years down the line, two ants have grown to 220 at last count (though some of us swore when we started that we should not go beyond twenty!). The organogram has become far more complex and our work has spread beyond the contours of our district to partnering with organizations in other northeastern states. While some programmes were non-starters, others have matured and continue to grow and do what they are meant to do. There are challenges galore as we cross the threshold into maturity, but we can pause to celebrate the wins even as we look forward to the future, when we will be in the prime of our life as an institution.

Real Success to Us

Lighthouse to the community

Recently, some young colleagues told us that in the community, the ant is seen as 'people who can do no wrong', which we are guessing means we are seen as being incorruptible and doing only what is just and right. Interestingly, even our detractors (probably grudgingly) grant us this. In a space where weak law and order, poor governance, corruption and the denial of rights to the least are easy bedfellows, it is indeed a badge of honour to have earned that reputation in the community. When asked to compare the ant with a metaphor, Sunil once drew a light house. Lighthouses are sturdy bits of architecture, dour in appearance, needing very little maintenance and, most importantly, dependable. No ship directs itself to a lighthouse, but needs it for invaluable direction, especially when the waves are rough. We are happy to be that lighthouse.

Value for money!

On the programmes front, the ant is known to most people through our work with weavers. Their beautiful weaves and crisp tailoring provides income to hundreds of resource-poor women weavers in our villages, and also helps promote a positive image of the Bodo people in India's metropolitan cities and abroad where they are marketed. Until the pandemic hit, Aagor, the weaving brand we set up, sold products worth over Rs 1 crore each year and transferred about half of this back into the area as wages and salaries. Deep down, we knew that while customers would initially be drawn in by the 'tugging-at-the-heartstrings' story of the weavers, what would sustain Aagor would be the quality and reliability of the brand.

We also trained fifty semi-literate village women as 'barefoot' doctors—before the National Rural Health Mission transformed the health landscape in Assam from 2007—and through their efforts ensured no one died of malaria in their villages, unlike the past when malaria would kill more than 500 people each year. When there appeared to be a need for 'barefoot' laboratory, technicians to confirm their diagnoses of malaria, we trained eleven local men and women to handle a microscope, which in a year's time yielded results we are proud of. The hundred randomly selected slides we sent to the Malaria Research Centre (now the National Institute of Malaria Research) came back with 96 per cent correct identification of the malarial parasite, down to the species identified; this prompted the deputy director of the centre and their ex-director—then a WHO consultant—to travel to the hinterland to witness the month-long training that brought about such results! This was possible because we have always believed in the capabilities of the rural and tribal people: it just requires an opportunity, a modified pedagogy and a strong belief in delivering great quality. The talent of these intelligent people, who have to negotiate a highly inequitable and institutionally prejudiced system, remains untapped even today.

Tough 'troublemakers'

The badge of 'troublemakers' is one we wear with pride; especially when accused by government officials of 'instigating people' to file for information under the Right to Information Act or while organizing the poor to fight for their rightful entitlements. We are also fine with being seen as troublemakers by some men in the community, who rue the fact that because of our interventions, they are unable to beat their wives as easily! Or by rich and powerful people in the community who now go to jail, while earlier they got away with a light fine when they sexually abused girls from poor families, simply because people will now call them out and others will back them up and the poor families will dare to uphold the law.

Wide partnership network

Scaling up happens through our forging strategic partnerships with small NGOs across the region and supporting their growth. This means we can quickly access and mobilize eager, committed and honest NGOs, not just in Assam but in other northeast states too if we want to scale up or start an initiative. For example, the ant's camp-based mental illness treatment model moved beyond our own district of Chirang to fourteen other districts in Assam through partner NGOs. This financially sustainable model now helps quality treatment reach over 2,200 patients in twenty-three locations every month with no external project funds (except for expansion to new areas). The partnership model has created a win-win-win situation for all: for patients needing dependable, reliable care they can afford; for the small NGO whose increased credibility in the community gives them a good reason to continue; and for the ant which has scaled up its work in a sustainable manner.

An eleph-ant?

We are seen today as one of the few NGOs in Assam that works in education at scale—working with teachers and students in around 200 government schools in Chirang district, and running forty learning centres in forest-fringe areas. the ant has worked to 'develop' more than 4,000 children through the use of sports like the Ultimate Disk, bringing together children across divides of gender, religion and language. Whether it is the Stop Domestic Violence Project covering all the police stations in the district or a project on livelihoods development, we have realized that we need to work on a larger scale than before if we are to change violent cultures or build supply chains; that successful work in a few villages is not enough to tackle the challenges in the country.

What Makes Us Tick?

Moving from a founder-owned organization to an accountable, public institution has not been easy. Externally, while there were barriers, there was also a lot which helped us do what we could do. Internally, we had to dictate, coax, force, facilitate and enable at different times and in different measure to ensure that systems and processes were set up for programmatic and organizational success and, when things fail, have ways to detect and course-correct.

Our theory of change

We learnt about the Theory of Change some fifteen years after we established ourselves; we still struggle to articulate an organizational theory of change which will capture our mission and our diverse change programmes. What has guided us are certain principles and values that we have built into our practice. For instance, as far as possible, we do not give charity, as we feel this disempowers people. So, our programmes are built for community contribution (in cash, kind, time, etc.). They are also designed to have the potential to continue—at least in some form—beyond the project period, and not cease operating with the end of project funding. These principles have been built into some key processes in the organization, which have kept it growing.

Evaluation to make sure we walk our talk

To make sure we were walking our talk and that our programmes were doing what they are supposed to do, in our third year of functioning, we introduced our own system of project and programme evaluation. Small teams, comprising junior and senior members from different projects and departments, get together and evaluate and score every project against parameters jointly set by everyone. The initial 'Big 5' parameters were: *Effectivity* (are objectives being met?), *Efficiency* (based not just on material costs but also emotional costs), *Community Participation* (at every stage and not just in attending meetings!), *Gandhiji's Talisman* (are we benefiting the last and the least?), and *Sustainability* (will it be sustained if we stop working?). Over the years, *Gender Equality* and *Fostering Inter-Community Relationships* have been added to this list.

To ensure a fair score, there has to be debate. Important conversations are thus set up and every member is forced to engage with projects and work they do not usually have much to do with, based on which critical programmes have been initiated or changed. For example, we set up a Maid Servant Rehabilitation Centre for our weaving project, because in the *Gandhiji's Talisman* parameter, it was pointed out that though the project works with some of the poorest women in the village, these women do not live in the village. Girls from the poorest families are compelled to work for a pittance as maidservants in other people's homes.

Similarly, the mental illness treatment camps run on project funding always received a low score on the *Sustainability* parameter. In 2015–16, the discussion triggered the decision to charge user fees to offset essential monthly expenses, which made the programme financially sustainable, and enabled its expansion to fourteen more districts, benefiting thousands of patients with mental illness.

Auto-money for autonomy

While money is important for our work, we did not want to be dictated by it. We did not accept funds for the first three years, till we could understand what the community needed, chose the things we could deliver on and to the best of our ability. We funded ourselves by writing and selling handbooks on malaria in different languages, selling health diaries in four Indian languages, conducting training sessions, and carrying out studies for other NGOs. We also kept our running costs low: for example, for the first seven years, we cycled everywhere, so travel cost almost nothing. Cycles also clearly signalled that we were not wealthy, so the armed groups did not make demands of us. Having individual donors, many of them through a platform called Caring Friends, who trust us and donate regularly and significantly to our cause gives us the confidence to independently respond to urgent issues and needs and not be dictated by the goals of powerful institutional funders.

The internal audit committee—our compass

What the statutory auditor reported about our financial transactions was one thing, but for us internally, honesty in financial matters needed to be cultivated, and transparency practised. Being in a conflict area where a mere allegation of corruption could potentially turn dangerous, the team had to completely trust the financial dealings of the organization. The system of monthly internal audits instituted almost from the start, helped build internal trust and the confidence to answer external questions. Led by a senior member (with experience in performing such audits), anyone (even if the person is a day-old in the organization) can volunteer to be part of the three or four-member internal audit committee for the month. The committee goes through the receipts and payment vouchers of the previous month, seeing all the bills, including those of the senior staff. The committee has to report their observations and objections to the accounts team, who in turn discuss these in the staff meeting. This system has generated some excellent conversations about organizational values, and also facilitated policy changes. The staff are encouraged to invite anyone with questions about our finances to inspect vouchers they would like to see, without notice. This has also ensured the accounts team keep their accounts regularly updated.

Appraisal for accountability

As a funded institution working for the public good, we believe that, whether an external funder or an agency demands it or not, we need to be accountable, not just for the work we do but how we do it. So, for the longest time, we have had a 360-degree performance appraisal system. Every staff member evaluated others according to twenty-five qualities that had been generated through consultative discussions with the staff. Each person anonymously assigned a score out of six to the other, on each of the qualities. As organizational elders, this gave us accurate feedback on what our staff members wanted us to improve upon. Based on their average percentile score in the year, members were differentially rewarded with a performance bonus. As the team has grown in numbers and across geographies, a more formal, output-oriented appraisal system has been introduced, something still not very common in grassroots NGOs in India.

Breaking rank to break hierarchy

As a team grows in size, hierarchies based on seniority, skills, roles and positions start to emerge. In the first few years, all of us who lived in the office premises would share daily duties of sweeping, cooking and washing dishes. But as we grew in size, we formalized the system to a *shramdaan* (contribution of voluntary labour) during our monthly (and more recently our three-monthly) meeting. One of the lowest-earning members of the staff assigns people to different task teams and is prepped to ensure that new recruits, especially if they are from high-ranked universities, are on the toilet-cleaning team. This rank-breaking exercise builds team camaraderie, but more importantly, it effectively demonstrates that though roles differ in the organization, all work is equally important, and to be respected and done in humility.

Stepping away from the trees to notice the forest

We introduced a system of annual retreats away from the organization from our first anniversary onwards. At the first retreat we formulated our vision and mission statement; there were just six or seven of us, but we debated each clause and word extensively. In the second year, when we had more members, we listed the core values of the organization. At every annual meeting since, and also at the team meetings, we discuss the implications of each core value, elucidating them with case studies. The team debates which values are being followed and which are being stretched, and then decides the course of action. Providing the team a chance to step back—along with some celebration—annual meetings are spaces for holding some tough but honest conversations about the organization.

Factors That Helped Us

Apart from internal processes, a number of external factors have aided the ant in its successes along the way.

Deep trust of our donors

Implicit trust in the ant's integrity from our donors has given us the confidence to respond to community issues and in emergencies, thus keeping us responsive and relevant. For instance, in 2013, there was a sudden outbreak of ethnic violence in neighbouring Goalpara district. The district administration learnt about us from friends and sent us an SOS for help: entire villages had been burnt, forcing people to flee to relief camps in the bitter cold of January; with no warm clothes, they were falling sick. On hearing of this, an individual from Mumbai immediately sent us Rs 10 lakh, and by evening we had sent a truckload of 5,000 new children's sweaters and 3,000 woollen blouses for women to the Goalpara administration, which were distributed with help from friends in a partner NGO.

This deep trust of our donors has also given us the strength to innovate and, importantly, the honesty to admit to our failures and address them, instead of attempting to hide them. The confidence of knowing that our donors trust our efforts gives us the courage to speak up if things are not going as planned, and have the flexibility for change.

The community watching our backs

When we have been in trouble—with push-back from the government and run-ins with powerful politicians or armed groups—people from the community have stepped forward in support. We have almost never had to defend ourselves.

Once, strong rumours started circulating that the government was going to stop the ant from working, which after a while began to demoralize our staff. But we learnt from a friend that the students union had unilaterally called a special meeting and resolved to 'show the government its place if it tried to banish the ant.' At yet another time, at a public hearing, we exposed the large-scale diversion of funds from the job guarantee scheme to benefit an armed group which was in a cease-fire camp. Despite gunmen blocking their path, women from our self-help groups fought their way through to reach the public hearing to give their testimony supporting us. In retaliation, the armed group burnt one of our motorcycles and threatened to burn our field office; instead of helping, the police chief of the district admonished us for taking on things we could not handle and interfering in local affairs. In response, the students unions of the various ethnic communities converged and hurried to protect our office. It is with reasonable satisfaction we saw our relationship with the All Bodo Students Union strengthen, to the extent that their top leadership asked us for help in following the creed of non-violence. Later, with help from Initiatives of Change, many of them imbibed their core values of purity, honesty, unselfishness, and love, which are very similar to the ant's core values. Their long-time president who drove the move has since been elected chief of the Bodoland (Autonomous) Territorial Administration.

It is to the credit of the community that various wild allegations against us over the years have not stuck, whether labelling us as government intelligence agents, foreign spies, missionaries out to convert people, or Maoists fomenting trouble by organizing the poor against the state. Not only have people from the area had faith in us, but they believed enough to stick their necks out, even at grave risk to themselves.

If We Had to Walk the Same Road ...

Build people to build organizations

While focusing on the tasks to be done, we probably did not invest sufficiently on building up individuals within the organization. While we carried out trainings to build their work skills, we could have definitely done more for the self-awareness, learning, growth and leadership development of the staff at different levels. We might have then created a team that is even more resilient, emotionally intelligent, value-centred, and transformative in its approach. It could have helped build a stronger learning culture in the organization and enabled every individual and team to reach its full potential. This is an area we will be focusing on in the near future.

Investing in synergistic partnerships

For a long time, we did it alone, struggling and stumbling along the way. We could have invested more time, energy, and resources in forging synergistic partnerships with organizations even outside the region. We started doing this much later with our larger projects, such as the education or adolescent girls' leadership programme. Had we done this for the earlier projects, we might have achieved even more transformative results.

No to husband–wife founders

In hindsight, starting an organization as a husband-wife team was not a good idea. Though as professionals we complemented each other's skills, over time the power dynamics was unhealthy for the organization. Both of us having strong personalities, stifled the emergence of other leadership. Then, as very different individuals with distinct leadership styles, it was natural for the staff to exploit the situation, which affected a relationship already strained by the 24x7 intense, energy-sapping venture of starting and running an NGO in a challenging ecosystem. Being in a remote area, meeting the same people, dealing with the same issues, struggling the same struggles, tended to shrink our horizons and also our personal and professional networks.

Lessons We Can Share

As a public institution working for the public good and receiving funds in the name of people, we are primarily answerable to the people and community we work with. While our value-based work earns us the respect of peers, communities and even bureaucrats and politicians, it is good management principles that improve our effectiveness and delivery. Thus, an organizational culture that is based on strong values has to be backed by a supportive management structure prepared to do the right thing—even though it may not seem the 'smartest' thing to do—when it comes to taking the side of truth, justice, the poorest and the voiceless.

Professionalism for us is not about money or qualifications, but of delivering results to the best of our ability. Voluntarism is also a profession, and needs to be planned and executed effectively and with efficiency, but rooted in the values of the individual and of the organization. To remain relevant and in sync with our constituents, as leaders we need to continuously listen to the wind and ride the wave. But that calls for an open and courageous listening heart. Institutions will survive and thrive when the people therein (especially those with decades of experience, who believe they have seen and done it all) are able to retain some humility and be open to listening and learning. One of the prime tasks as organizational leaders is to carefully nurture and cultivate that culture in every individual and team, and also in the systems and processes of the organization.

In the increasingly complex external environment in which the voluntary sector operates, organizations that will ultimately thrive are those that can understand these complexities and build strategies around it. Hence, constantly designing and executing sustainable and transformative solutions to challenges has to become part of the organization's cultural DNA. We have found that creating space for regular reflection and not shying away from tough conversations are small but vital steps towards building that culture. But this also means setting aside money, time and energy, which can work if we see it as a critical investment in organization building.

21

The Brewing of Araku Coffee: Regenerating the Economy and Ecology

MANOJ KUMAR

'Wealth is ... having a forest around you, a forest that is biodiverse. For such a forest nurtures good soil and that is real wealth, sustained wealth.'[1]

NAANDI FOUNDATION[2] WAS ESTABLISHED IN 1998 with the objective of attracting professionals from diverse fields to design and deliver large scale programmes under the guidance of a board of trustees representing captains of Indian industry. In its first decade, Naandi went from being a one-state (in its operations), one-crore (its annual budget) non-governmental organization (NGO) to a multi-state, multi-crore, multi-sectoral development organization, working in partnership with state governments, municipal corporations, investors, and philanthropists worldwide. Today, two decades later, Naandi Foundation works in twenty-two states, has over 300 full-time employees and 6,500 part-timers, with an annual budget of Rs 150 crores. Naandi has impacted over 75 lakh people through channelizing over Rs 100 crore to underserved communities across India.

The second decade of Naandi's work focused on improving young lives by setting up 2,200 skilling and employment centres for youth and 6,300 education and empowerment centres for girls. The skills centres have helped youth transform from day-long loiterers to smart young professionals, with official vehicles transporting them to work and back, within a few months.

The centres for girls reached out to the most unreached children in low-income families—from rural hamlets in Shravasti, Uttar Pradesh, on the Nepal border, to the salt flats of the gulf of Khambhat in Bharuch, Gujarat; from tribal settlements perched on the Araku hills on the Andhra–Odisha border to the mustard fields of Moga, Punjab.

This period also saw pioneering entrepreneurial work in reversing climate change in the mountainous Araku region in southeastern India. Over 3 lakh Adivasi farmers in this region have emerged from poverty through coffee farming. The produce from this area is marketed as 'world-class gourmet coffee' in India and in France under the brand name 'Araku Coffee'.[3] This once eco-fragile region is becoming the world's largest regenerative agriculture hub, now stretching across 2,000 square kilometres with the planting of over 3 crore fruit trees and forest. Coffee, shade trees and pepper was followed by fruit and timber plantations and then cereals and food crops. This led to the creation of a new economic framework called 'Arakunomics'.

Why Araku?

The Araku region is nestled in the Eastern Ghats on the border of Andhra Pradesh and Odisha. The lush hill forests of the region used to be inhabited by over 5 lakh indigenous people living in harmony with nature. However, by 2001 Araku had become an eco-fragile region characterized by the loss of biodiversity, rapid erosion of soil and deforestation. There was also the growing influence of armed insurgents called the Naxals. The forest-dwelling people had been pushed out of their habitat and 'mainstreamed' into acute poverty.

In addition, the growing threat of carbon depletion from the soil had made this region increasingly vulnerable to climate change. Decades of indiscriminate mining and tree-felling by traders and corporations from other regions had 'desertified' their habitat, with the hillsides denuded and the soil depleted. Basic amenities to which the rest of the country had increasingly received access—such as health services, schools, motorable roads and phone connectivity—had not reached the people here, resulting in abject poverty.

Naandi's Intervention in Araku

Naandi's efforts to reverse the poverty of the indigenous people of Araku started with a deep dive into understanding their lives, psyche and aspirations by living with them. The next steps were setting up small village schools with labour contributed by the villagers, and bringing in trained nurses. This latter step was particularly important for the care of pregnant women as there was a high prevalence of maternal mortality in the community. As a relationship of trust with the villagers developed, the Naandi team began to have conversations with community members, village meetings and brainstorming sessions to discuss how the people in the Araku region could build a pathway out of poverty. The team worked systematically through social, economic, cultural and environmental challenges and other complexities of the region to establish livelihood models that—through regenerative agriculture and high-quality produce—would enrich the ecology and increase biodiversity, help lift the community out of poverty and bring back acres of functional forests. The impact of Naandi's work in the Araku region can be measured not just by the increased annual income of the indigenous farmers but also by the improving agricultural yield, the number of trees planted and the volume of carbon sequestered.

Now, produce from this region is sold in niche markets across the world. Impoverished gun-toting peasants have become dynamic, enterprising estate owners. The journey of reversing climate change has begun. Various state governments have been showing an interest in replicating this template of poverty eradication.

A quantitative summary of the impact of Naandi's work in the Araku region would list 3 crore trees of nineteen different species planted (with a survival rate of close to 90 per cent) as well as 3 lakh people lifted out of poverty. In addition, soil organic carbon percentages improved from 0.4 to 1.4 per cent (in some cases as high as 2.1 per cent), which is a powerful way of mitigating climate change. For perspective, the national average soil carbon percentage for arable land in the plains is less than 0.3 per cent. In many conventionally and intensively cultivated areas such as the Moga district of Punjab, it is as low as 0.1 per cent.

This model of having a positive impact on both the economy and the ecology of a region simultaneously has been named 'Arakunomics'. In 2020, the Rockefeller Foundation of the US recognized Arakunomics as one of the world's top ten strategies for a better food system for the future.

Naandi Foundation's work in the region has led to the provision of safe maternal care to tackle maternal mortality, and has also guaranteed ten years of basic schooling for nearly 10,000 girls from tribal families. Small landholdings across 900 villages have been made agriculturally viable through knowledge transfer on scientific, organic and regenerative agriculture practices, with additional help provided on tree planting and monitoring of tree growth. Peer training in these scientific and organic cultivation practices are provided for farmers and their families at 'farmer field schools'.

Nearly 50,000 acres of land has been brought under organic regenerative agriculture over the last decade. This has prevented and reversed environmental damage and strengthened crops to withstand extreme weather conditions while enriching soil quality. The planting of functional forests has revived the tradition of a vibrant, biodiverse environment that provides sustenance to indigenous farming families in the form of food, nutrition, fodder, fuelwood and cash. These families have been given support to build coffee estates and fruit orchards and transform them into profit-making family enterprises.

The organization's work has also led to the formation of the world's largest organic farmers' cooperative. The 12,000 members of the cooperative not only bring the community closer but also empowers it. Half of the cooperative's board, selected unanimously, based on members' service, are women. In addition, a local grassroots sports movement has been started, which has seen 500 volleyball teams being formed. Thirty-five of these are all-girls teams. They actively practise throughout the year and participate in a local league. These sporting activities have kept the local youth—about 5,000 in number—active, keenly engaged and connected to their homeland.

In the process of bringing about these changes, semi-wasteland was converted to nutrient-dense, carbon-rich topsoil, and denuded forests were transformed into functional ones. Apart from coffee, half a dozen varieties of spices, cereals and fruit flourish in thousands of estates and orchards owned by small and marginal farmers. The region has become a haven for millions of beneficial microbes and insects as part of an ecosystem that is now climate-change resilient. Araku now serves as an example for showcasing the prowess and potential of regenerative agriculture.

Understanding Arakunomics

Arakunomics is unique in a world of economic models that are either built around trade-offs or perpetuate inequalities. India requires a new system for producing food, one that regenerates the environment and assures sustained profits to farmers while providing nutritious food to all. Arakunomics can serve as this system, as it places food at the centre around which challenges of poverty, disease and environmental degradation are addressed. The innovation sees farmers negotiating profits rather than prices with buyers. All their costs are borne by Naandi, which serves as the buyer. The price fixed for the produce reflects actual profits. This way every farmer is assured of sustained profits and is insured against declines in global market prices. It allows them to focus on quality. This is enabled by some key process elements:

Deep listening and trust-building

In its initial years of operation, Naandi Foundation had to spend most of its time learning about life in the Araku valley, a place that seemed to have fallen off the map and been written off by the rest of the world. The volunteers took every opportunity to join in discussions with villagers and farmers to understand how their travails were exacerbated during certain seasons and how their families coped with poverty-stricken conditions. They observed what the locals ate, how they celebrated and how closely bonded they were with their land and trees.

The president of the tribal farmers' cooperative, Kondal Rao, said that Naandi had restored his faith in the idea of trust. According to him, once the organization had made a promise, it went to great lengths to keep it. He was referring in particular to the price assured by Naandi to the Small and Marginal Tribal Farmers Mutually Aided Cooperative Society for coffee each year. Irrespective of whether Naandi can locate buyers at that price later in the year, it always paid the promised amount upfront to the farmers. For the farmers, this served as a sign of Naandi's moral courage and its commitment to the area and its development.

Leveraging the caring and sharing culture to build a successful cooperative

The Araku tribes used to be forest-dwelling people who hunted for food. However, they were forced to adapt to settled agriculture from the 1950s due to increasing pressure on forest land. Culturally, they are a people with strong values of sharing and caring. These values meant that they never built boundary walls or sent out invitations for family events—simply because everyone was invited, no one was shut out. There were over thirty-five different tribes in the area sharing a common value system of living in harmony with nature. These indigenous communities are custodians of a rich collective memory of forest produce being a source of sustenance.

Coffee has been cultivated here since the 1920s, when the British found the climate and terrain suitable for the enterprise and introduced it to the region. However, the locals had never tasted coffee and most still do not drink it. This meant that they were unaware of the importance of ensuring the correct ripeness of the cherries at the time of harvest. Neither did they have any idea of the best drying and processing practices. As a result, they were able to get only very poor returns for their produce.

Naandi saw an opportunity here, especially as the Adivasi farmers had never used chemicals in their coffee plots. Work began on building capacities on best practices of organic regenerative agriculture with the aim of improving the quality and yield of the coffee that the farmers were growing. Work also began on getting land parcels of the farmers organic certified. Fair Trade certification followed. Soon, the idea of forming a cooperative came into being.

By definition, a cooperative is an autonomous association of persons united voluntarily to meet their common economic, social and cultural needs and aspirations through a jointly owned enterprise. This seemed the best way forward to ensure the growth of farmers' livelihoods in a way that was sustainable and self-determined. This led to the formation of the Small and Marginal Tribal Farmers Mutually Aided Cooperative Society in 2007. The caring and sharing culture of the people lent itself seamlessly to the working style of a cooperative, in which it was not the individual farmer but the entire village that was rewarded for success. It was a quest for excellence and not a sense of competition that drove their efforts.

The cooperative that started with 1,000 members in 2007 has today grown to a membership of 12,000 because of its effectiveness in helping farmers get better prices for their produce. Membership gives the farmers access to high-quality training organized by Naandi as well as organic inputs such as compost, bioinoculants, seeds and saplings. Very importantly, it enables small farmers to avoid exploitative local moneylenders. The cooperative is run as per state laws, with free and fair elections every five years.

Discovering sustainable solutions for addressing poverty

Naandi wanted to find other employment opportunities for the locals that would leverage the traditional skills and knowledge of the community without requiring them to leave their homes and go to distant cities. Such solutions could not only lift their families out of poverty but also reverse the environmental degradation in the region. Populist welfare economic models proposed in the Five-Year Plans and other government initiatives not only provided education and health services but also attempted to promote livelihoods—however, these schemes did not initially reach regions like Araku.

Even when they began to reach the Adivasis, they found that the initiatives were jeopardizing their connection with the forest. The indigenous people in Araku were closely linked to their forest ecosystem—they lived off it, with it and in it. The new poverty alleviation programmes took them away from the forest and nudged them to align with a rootless, mono-diet, mono-behaviour, monoculture that was being labelled or even celebrated as being 'modern' and 'global'.

The Naandi theory of change was to find local solutions that would not involve imposing a mainstream development model. The forest dwellers were still using barter practices and did not understand concepts such as surplus and profits. The organization wanted to base its solution on the native wisdom of the tribal societies to ensuring self-reliance instead of reducing them to passive receivers of largesse, whether in the form of subsidies and freebies or loan waivers.

A 'shade' of self-interest

Fighting climate change and bringing back biodiversity are lofty goals and they take a lot of selfless hard work with no immediate tangible gain. There had to be some additional motivation if the inhabitants of Araku were going to join the fight and stay in it. This led to the creation of the template for 'one-acre models', which would bring in sizable cash incomes regularly. The Naandi team became 'portfolio managers', helping to decide what to plant in the small landholdings.

It was best to grow a judicious mix of crops such as millet, paddy and fruits for food, along with coffee, pepper and timber for cash income. This would be done using regenerative agriculture practices and optimal market linkages would be established for increasing cash incomes. Winemaking's 'terroir' approach—usually associated with the fine wines of Bourgogne—was adopted in Araku to enable customized crop and cultivation planning. It guaranteed higher quality products and increased yields.

Most Araku farmers were in the clutches of traders and middlemen from whom they would borrow money at high interest. This was because making a livelihood from agriculture meant receiving payments only once or twice a year. The farmers had to turn to these middlemen to meet their recurring, immediate needs for food and healthcare. They would commit shares of their harvest to the moneylenders in return for an immediate cash loan. This often meant that Naandi would not receive the harvest at competitive prices for processing and sale.

The organization decided to make part payments at regular intervals of two months to the farmers in anticipation of the expected harvest. The assured source of cash at fixed intervals allowed the farmer to meet their urgent cash flow requirements and helped them to escape the clutches of the middlemen. It was a leap of faith by Naandi that stands vindicated because of the relationship of trust and respect that grew from it. Today, every farmer makes a profit as their input costs are met by Naandi and they make sizeable earnings from the coffee produced by them and sold to niche global markets through the cooperative. The farmers also grow black pepper as an inter-crop, from which they make further profits.

Various innovative methods have been adopted for ensuring sustained, high-quality agri-produce that would fetch good prices. In the case of coffee, unless the produce was in the top 1 per cent of the global quality benchmark, the Araku farmers would not get a premium. To achieve this high standard, each coffee farm, bush and cherry had to be carefully kept under the most optimal conditions. At harvest time, only those coffee cherries that had attained a deep crimson red colour would be harvested. It was a challenge to ensure that every farmer in Araku across 900 villages did this labour-intensive work correctly.

Even on the same bush, coffee cherries ripen at different times. So, the farmer has to make repeated visits to one coffee bush to pluck the cherries at their ripest. Naandi applied principles of behavioural economics to 'nudge' farmers into doing the right thing. A red truck would come by each farm and procure the cherries only if the farmer had his entire harvest for the day in the optimal shade of red. If he did, he got a premium that was four times the market price and twice the price offered by the blue truck, which procured all other shades of coffee cherries.

Deep investment in building local capacity as a means to self-reliance

Building the capacities of tribal farmers to adopt and own the different practices in organic regenerative agriculture has been one of the key components of Naandi's work in the Araku region. A regular feature is the input of knowledge specific to the current stage in the cycle of a particular crop that happens throughout the year. Every village nominates a farmer as the village trainer.

Every month, this trainer attends a two-day workshop conducted by Naandi. He uses this knowledge not only to tend to his own plot of land but also shares it with all the other farmers in his village. Trainings comprise group instruction sessions held on an agricultural plot. Different types of documentation are given to the farmers for reference. They have simple text in the local language as well as exhaustive illustrations for easier comprehension.

Naandi Foundation's experience and learnings over the years have been documented and collated in an agriculture almanac. It draws from key aspects of permaculture, regenerative agriculture and even ancient agri systems, such as traditional wisdom about the impact of the moon's waxing and waning on growing plants. This diffusion of know-how contributes towards a higher sapling survival rate. The almanac is like a standard operating manual that provides guidance on the correct time for sowing and appropriate level of moisture. Care has been taken to ensure that most of the information in the almanac is accompanied by illustrations so that non-literate farmers and their families can also benefit from it. The almanac is updated by Naandi every year. It can be seen displayed in every farmer's home and serves as a ready reference for him.

Naandi has also worked to promote micro-nursery entrepreneurs to prepare fruit and forestry sapling nurseries locally at the village level. This generates additional income for farmers and encourages local entrepreneurship. It also ensures permanence of technical skills in raising saplings among the farmer community, makes the project budget and operations cost-effective and prevents the logistical nightmare of transporting planting materials to field sites dispersed over a wide area with poor motorable roads.

External Factors

The last two decades have seen several factors external to Naandi's systems, strategies and activities that helped it implement Arakunomics.

India's agrarian crisis

The plight of the small and marginal farmers in India lay at the heart of the acute agrarian crisis in the country. It was an important external stimulus for Naandi's work in agriculture. These small farmers comprise 70 per cent of India's population and despite growing food for the whole country, they are struggling to make ends meet. Reasons for this struggle include excessive dependence on cash crops, increasingly depleted soil, volatile markets, indebtedness and uncertain monsoons with almost no form of irrigation. For

Naandi, this situation meant that it was imperative for it to come up with a solution that would see small and marginal farmers make profits.

Climate change

Over the past two decades, the climate crisis has become an increasingly bigger global issue. With an ever-growing number of countries ratifying the United Nations Framework Convention on Climate Change and Kyoto Protocol, commitments to reduce carbon emissions and increase carbon sequestration are increasing. In this context, multinational manufacturing companies have started to look for opportunities to invest in the developing world in exchange for carbon credits. This new funding mechanism ensures livelihoods for the poor and a rejuvenated ecosystem on the one hand, and carbon sequestration and related carbon-target realization for big companies on the other.

This seemingly win-win model is gaining in popularity and Naandi has been able to take advantage of it to fund its work in the Araku region. This carbon-financing model is advantageous to organizations like Naandi because it represents a long-term commitment, and the size of its grants is far larger than those from traditional donors and funding agencies.

India's changing economy

The economic liberalization that took place in India in 1991–92 could be seen as another major external factor that aided the success of Naandi's work in the Araku region. The globalization processes that followed have enabled Adivasi farmers from remote places to reach global markets and make large profits.

Success Was Not a Given …

The impact/successes enumerated above, needless to say, did not happen overnight. The early years were slow, sometimes frustrating, as we tried to find our way through the complexities of age-old cultural traditions of the forest dwellers and their way of life, current market trends, attempts to reach remote villages, short-term interests of small traders and businessmen, visibly deteriorating natural resources, and the constant underlying menace of armed insurgency. Identifying effective levers, understanding what 'drives' an Adivasi farmer family in a remote village—all these gradually unfolded over time, and our interpretations were not always correct or useful; we returned to the drawing board many times, the learning curve is still rising.

Lessons from Hindsight

Looking back at the past two decades of Naandi's work in Araku provides some satisfaction and perhaps even a sense of achievement to the organization, but that soon gives way to thoughts of 'what-if'. Thoughts about what we could have done differently, about things we should have done but did not.

Looking back, it would have been better to involve the village youth right from the beginning. The younger villagers would participate in all the discussions and night-long meetings Naandi held in the villages in its efforts to work out action plans to tackle poverty in the region. They would volunteer to lead the livelihoods initiatives and the cooperative, and would train to become experts in different aspects of the value chains for coffee and pepper.

Seeing the abject poverty amidst which Araku's Adivasi people survived compelled the Naandi team to explore opportunities for generating cash income for these farmers from their small land holdings. Coffee was the obvious first choice for a crop, followed by pepper. The farmers worked with the Naandi team to keep improving the quality of these crops in order to get higher prices. After a couple of years, the planting of fruit trees was begun. They became a reliable source of food for the farmers.

In recent years, consumption of processed and packaged fast food started to increase in the area. In response, Naandi further diversified the crop portfolio to include different kinds of pulses and millets. If we could start over again, we would invest our efforts and resources in a highly diverse crop portfolio right from the beginning, as it would have ensured a sustained source of nutritious food while leading to cash income sooner. That was another lesson from hindsight.

Araku as a Template for Development

Naandi's work in Araku has demonstrated that it is possible to positively transform a marginalized and geographically isolated region riven with conflict. People from around the world now visit Araku to study how climate change can be combated and biodiversity preserved. Apart from the soil and microbial activity in the region, indigenous varieties of trees and plants have also been revived, contributing to a sustainable and healthy ecosystem. The Araku model can be replicated in all similar terrains in India.

Across the country, there are pockets of land inhabited by indigenous people struggling to eke out a living from a rapidly degrading ecosystem. Actions like the ones taken by the tribal farmers' cooperative in the Araku region will help farmers to emerge from poverty while restoring the forests and transforming the soil. Rejuvenating the soil through organic regenerative agriculture would reduce costs and bring back nutritious food crops in combination with cash crops. Another strategy is to create market linkages with minimal involvement by middlemen.

These are all strategies that can be applied in other places and lead to nutritional and income security, disposable incomes, informed choices, savings for the future, investment in children's health and education and overall improvement in quality of life.

It was necessary to innovate anthropological iconography to convert a group of hunters and food gatherers into gourmet agriculturalists producing high-quality produce by investing time, patience and hard work. It was made possible by combining their values of sharing and caring with a rewarding individual enterprise. Essentially, the spirit of Araku, while it recognized the need for economic self-reliance, never allowed it to happen at the cost of ecology and culture.

Perhaps the body of work by Naandi Foundation in the Araku region could be thought of as a new paradigm in the agriculture narrative that created a whole new economic model with innovative financing mechanisms. The basis for this new paradigm is the equal and balanced focus on economic security on the one hand and ecological security on the other.

22

Seeding and Shaping the Labour Migration Agenda: Aajeevika Bureau's Journey

RAJIV KHANDELWAL AND DIVYA VARMA

AAJEEVIKA BUREAU[1] IS A SPECIALIZED public service initiative whose aim is to achieve an equitable and dignified world of work for labouring communities. Our work spans across rural, resource-poor migrant-sending regions, as well as sprawling urban labour markets that receive millions of workers from across the country. We work mainly in the western migration corridor of Rajasthan–Gujarat–Maharashtra. Focusing on rapidly expanding, labour-intensive work sectors, we help worker communities assert their right to a fair livelihood, dignity, and justice. We do this through providing legal education and aid, social protection, security and safety at work, and skilling and employability to help advance livelihoods. We have also helped incubate institutions, notably Shram Sarathi and Basic HealthCare Services, that provide financial services and low-cost primary healthcare to communities in high-migration regions. Aajeevika Bureau has also nurtured a knowledge body—the Centre for Migration and Labour Solutions (CMLS)—that concentrates on research, policy, teaching and training for state, industry and other stakeholders in the labour ecosystem.

Aajeevika Bureau was established in 2004–05 by a group of development practitioners and professionals with extensive experience of working with tribal communities in Rajasthan. While carrying out a comprehensive study of livelihoods in tribal communities in the early 2000s, we became aware of the growing importance of income from migrant work and the harsh realities confronting migrant workers, and the need to help them tackle some of these hardships.

We began our work by providing photo identity cards for migrant workers and vocational training for rural youth, and rapidly added interventions in response to what we identified as the problems and needs of workers. We began legal aid work in 2009, and in 2012 set up a toll-free helpline—Labour Line—for workers in distress. As we became aware of the effects of male migration on their vulnerable families, especially the women, we began organizing solidarity groups, and successfully collectivized over 14,000 women. Our work in urban centres expanded from North Gujarat and Ahmedabad to Surat, Mumbai and, more recently, Pune.

Aajeevika Bureau enabled the setting up of Shram Sarathi in 2009 and Basic HealthCare Services in 2012, the latter being led by Drs Sanjana and Pavitra Mohan. As allies working in the same communities, the combined efforts of the three organizations have managed to effectively impact a large geographical area and population.

The impact of Aajeevika Bureau's work in diverse areas of labour migration has attracted considerable attention across the country and has led several civil society organizations (CSOs) and labour activists to draw upon its experiences. The onset of Covid-19 and the resultant hardship faced by migrant communities has brought unprecedented attention to the organization's work, which seeks to ensure that migrant and informal workers who make enormous contributions to our economy can 'live and work with dignity everywhere'.

What Has Success Meant to Us?

Impact at scale: We have drawn satisfaction from the positive impact we have had on large numbers of vulnerable workers and families. Helping migrants acquire valid identity and visibility in cities, skilling and assisting young people to help them move ahead and enhance their earning capacity, providing legal aid and mediation to help workers recover large sums of unpaid wages, ensuring that thousands of excluded families are able to access their due entitlements—all these gains have been central to our ongoing journey. It has been extremely important for us to know that the outcome of our work is real and not abstract, and that it has been empowering in nature. Most of our big-ticket interventions began as small pilots which have then grown to substantial scale—both in terms of geographies and the populations that they impact. Beyond the numbers, there are hundreds of stories of real change and shifts at the individual, household and community levels that have inspired us to keep innovating and doing more.

Building robust community institutions: The community institutions we have promoted—workers' collectives, unions, volunteer cadres and *ujala samoohs*—have provided a robust foundation to our practice. Collectively, they drive our efforts to amplifying impact—first through enabling the understanding of issues among those affected and, progressively, by helping people raise their own voices on numerous platforms. Several collectives that we enabled are spearheaded by leaders who not only promote a vision for a labour-just world, they also inspire a vast cadre of workers to stand up for their rights and demand fairness and equity from the state and their employers. The effort of promoting community institutions and leadership has been a painstaking one—it has taken time and attention and has been fraught with many setbacks. Yet, at this time, it is on this foundation that Aajeevika Bureau's many programmes rest.

A distinct philosophy on labour migration: Aajeevika Bureau began its work with a distinct philosophy and vision of transforming labour migration into more promising opportunities for millions of rural poor who suffer hardships in the world of work. Concurrently we have sought to deepen our understanding of the socio-political processes driving migration, including rural distress, informality and exclusion. Through research and reflection on our own programmes, we are gaining a better appreciation of the complexities of the changing paradigm of work. We have sought to better understand both the challenges facing migrants and the trade-offs they must consider on a daily basis. Though our primary experience relates to one part of the country, we are also learning from other migration streams, and have been able to contribute to the new vocabulary on labour migration processes and experiences across the country.

Propelling labour migration to a practice and policy landscape: At the time we began work, there seemed to be scant recognition of the adversities faced by migrants as a sub-segment of India's vast informal labour force. The labour movement understood informality and exploitation; however, migration was not part of the larger imagination of development interventions in the CSO space. Through our work and a recognition of the issues faced by migrant workers, we were able to nuance the existing understanding of informal work with the realities of labour migration.

Understanding and Unpacking Success

The progress which Aajeevika Bureau has achieved since its inception in 2005 has been due to an array of factors, some of which we can claim at least partial responsibility for, while others are exogenous and relate to changing conditions in the economy and society.

Part of our success is definitely related to being in the right place at the right time, but also having the staff and financial resources to selectively pursue opportunities. Thus, the internal factors include our own human capital and the importance we placed on understanding the situations we chose as our primary focus. We also gave priority to securing funding which was critical to our institutional growth and the continuity of our efforts. Prominent among the external factors was a growing awareness of the importance of seasonal labour migration to the economy as a whole. That awareness extended to both an appreciation of adversities which migrants face as well as the potential benefits to society of investing in improving their skills, and their living and working conditions. This section expands on the internal and external factors that have shaped our evolution.

Our core capital: We have been very fortunate to have retained a core leadership group that has remained stable for over a decade. The growth of this leadership group has been deeply entwined with the expansion of Aajeevika Bureau's mandate which pushed everyone to expand the boundaries of their knowledge and skills. At present, all the organizational teams (STEP Academy, LEAD, FEP, CMLS Finance, the regional teams, and so on) are led by experienced people who combine strategic ability with strong implementation experience. Some of our units are in fact well-poised to becoming independent entities, as their work is growing beyond the mandate of Aajeevika Bureau's operational areas. The LEAD cell and CMLS are both good examples of this—fuelled not just by compelling external opportunities but also by the preparedness of their leaders to take on more independent responsibilities.

We have been almost stubbornly insistent on projecting and celebrating collective effort and shared leadership, and believe this has stood us well. The external world finds it easier to celebrate individuals for their vision, articulation and perceived 'sacrifice' but in such a narrative, the enormous contributions of many others tend to remain unsung. We have been deeply conscious of not letting Aajeevika Bureau be represented by one or two people. Our approach has generated a high level of outside confidence in the relatively large group of people in Aajeevika Bureau who lead their domains and foster independent networks and contacts, which in turn has helped them deepen their work.

In 2015, we began the onerous task of developing a human resource and personnel systems policy in order to rationalize the ad-hocism that had started to creep into the process of recruitment, assigning designations and levels and salary determination, and employment rules such as leave, benefits, travel allowances, etc. The outcome of this year-long consultative process was a 120-page document, prepared by a team led by an experienced organizational development advisor (Deepankar Roy), which immediately set in motion several positive outcomes. It signalled to the wider team that the organization was deeply invested in providing a stable work environment for all its staff. It also reinforced the importance of the values of equality and parity within the organization, while at the same time laying out rules for good processes and conduct so that the organization would be run as a value-driven collective.

Learnability: We conceptualized Aajeevika Bureau based on fairly simple premises: 'There is large-scale migration on account of poor opportunity in rural areas. Lack of documentation and identity in cities is a major challenge which migrants ought to overcome. Their livelihood will improve with quality skilling and through effective job placement in the market.' As our interactions with migrant workers grew and we became more familiar with the realities of the informal economy, it became evident that to be effective, we needed to do much more. We did not enter the world of labour migration with extensive expertise. However, we did possess the confidence of field practice, understood how inequities worked, and respected the value of rigorous research and deep immersion in pointing us to the future. Working at the grassroots in migration source communities gave us an understanding of the issues and also a degree of confidence and credibility that was essential to moving forward. This process and approach continues even today.

Within two years of starting work, we began to notice cases of wage fraud and outright exploitation of migrant workers, while registering for and being issued ID cards. We began tentatively to intervene in some instances, but it was only after a comprehensive study on wage theft among migrant workers that we came to realize that nothing less than a bold intervention through mediation, legal aid and litigation would work. This was the foundation of our legal education, which helped us in our mediation and aid work for informal, migrant workers.

We have understood that the scale and complexity of the problems we are addressing require grounded research which informs practice. We undertook considerable research to profile and examine occupational streams and spaces of migrant workers—characterizing their experiences and systems in the construction, textiles, brick, hospitality, agriculture and manufacturing domains. Beyond the more descriptive cataloguing of migration streams, we expanded to an examination of the more structural issues underlying informality, precariousness, work hazard and risk. Considerable research and writing has also been done on the feminization of work, impacts of male migration on women's work and agency, and the double burden borne by women in providing household care while engaging in sometimes highly precarious forms of waged work in cities. All these studies have not just directly shaped our perspective, they have laid the foundation of new themes, interventions and programmes.

Research is often the preserve of a few; it does not automatically become a shared resource. The methodology, pace and language of research can often be alienating to many who work in an action-oriented setting. It could also be viewed as merely an elite pursuit of interest to a few. Mindful of these possibilities, we have tried to the extent possible to democratize research within the organization. This has meant that field teams are directly involved in spelling out the research topics and in determining the research methodologies. They have also been central to data collection and analysis, which has in turn led to their determining shared agendas and future plans. Our researchers and writers are extremely sensitive to the possible chasm between knowledge production and field practice and, to their credit, they have walked that extra, more difficult, mile to research and write while taking everyone along. They have made learning more enjoyable and oriented to application and activism.

Timely and value-aligned funding: For a young organization trying to put down roots, finding timely and adequate financial resources to fuel its plans is immensely critical. Aajeevika Bureau's early years were sparingly funded, but the resources were sufficient to convert its ideas into action on the ground. This gave us the opportunity to demonstrate early successes to other larger donors who then felt more confident in stepping in with more substantial funding.

The infusion of external funding has remained steady in Aajeevika Bureau. Funding grew incrementally year on year; and our demand in turn has not spiked abruptly or dramatically as we scaled up. We believe this has created a level of confidence in our longer-term donors who have understood that our requirements are based not just on aspirations to grow and innovate, but have remained firmly aligned with our ability to absorb funds and spend judiciously. Long-term funding to us came from the Tata Trusts from 2007 till 2016, followed by the Human Dignity Foundation, IKEA Foundation, Bajaj CSR and finally the Azim Premji Philanthropic Initiative. There are two unusual funding partnerships which merit mention in this discussion for the unique value they have brought to our work.

Firstly, the EdelGive Foundation which provided a small but valuable fund annually to support our key human resource requirements. Spanning a period of six years the Foundation's funds helped plug-in salary gaps for senior management and under-funded personnel, and provided for ongoing human capital training and capacity building, and for small innovations which enabled us to test new ideas—thus contributing significantly to building our strategic core.

The second was our unique partnership with the Human Dignity Foundation (HDF)—an Irish charity that awarded us a multi-year unrestricted grant, rather than a budget tied to programme deliverables. We had the flexibility of working with a dynamic budget which was revised every six months. Our HDF years saw a spectacular expansion of our work, both geographically and thematically. We opened new frontiers in Gujarat, set up Labour Line for workers in distress, established the foundation of our work with migration-affected women, and managed to plug funding gaps for our non-profit finance company Shram Sarathi. Most importantly, we were able to use the funds to incubate Basic HealthCare Services—now an eminent primary healthcare organization which is housed in, and whose activities are convergent with, Aajeevika Bureau.

Unrestricted funding is a rare phenomenon in the world of giving and we are a testimony to its power to impact innovation and scale: it can change the framework and focus from programme outputs to enhancing institutional stability and value. While such flexible funding has been a rarity since our partnership with HDF concluded, the funding that we have received more recently through Dasra has given us a similar range of flexibility, enabling us to plug critical deficits and make small forays into new frontiers through pilots and innovations.

Targeted partnering at all levels through diverse approaches: If we were to depend mainly on our own resources and capacities, our efforts would at best make a modest dent. We have had reasonable success in identifying and sustaining partnerships with others, especially in areas we needed them most. This was because we adopted different formats to enable a context-specific 'replication' of our practices and methodologies.

With donors, we contributed to building a long-term agenda around funding work on labour migration, and played the technical support role in seeding our 'model' across high-density sending and receiving regions. In collaboration with reputed academic institutes, we designed and delivered several rounds of a certificate course aimed at building perspectives on labour migration among grassroots activists. We partnered with the Ministry of Rural Development in designing a comprehensive framework for migration support as part of the Deen Dayal Upadhyay Grameen Kaushal Yojana, their flagship skills training programme.

Through a strategic policy partnership with the International Labour Organization's Decent Work Team[2], we organized a series of policy roundtables with state governments to advocate for greater inclusion of migrants in state policies—two such consultations in Kerala contributed to the setting up of migrant support centres by the Kerala State Labour Department, along with dedicated budget allocations for these.

We have also extended more direct support to like-minded initiatives such as Gurgaon-based Safe in India, to help incubate their work on addressing the risks of injury among migrants in the automobile sector. Most recently, we are partnering with several industry players through a unique initiative called the Social Compact, where we are enabling more dignified and equitable practices across the supply chains of large industries. In collaboration with the Working Peoples' Charter, we are scaling up Labour Line, a high-impact, phone-based model of providing legal aid and mediation to workers in distress across several major urban areas.

Such strategic partnerships have been key in extending our experiences to newer regions and migration contexts, so that thousands of vulnerable migrant communities now have access to the promise of greater dignity, equity and security.

This plurality of approaches is of course not uncommon among public service organizations at all. An openness to diverse ideological and organizational strands and an alignment based on the value proposition of our vision and mission have served us substantially.

Staying on: Much of our success rests on a foundation of work built over many years. This has implied staying on in the same geographies and communities over a significant period, rather than moving on or out in the face of slow turnaround or progress. The frustration of stagnation has been fought by generating new ideas and programmes in the same areas and communities—we have several instances where success took several years or cycles of testing and piloting.

Some issues in our areas of work are probably intractable: such as our efforts to help tribal sharecroppers from Kotda block who labour on farms in north Gujarat for paltry sums; or our work on the shelter and safety crisis among migrants in an ultra-dense and dangerous industrial cluster in Mumbai. There are no quick turnarounds possible for these issues, and success often means making smaller gains on facets of the larger problem rather than substantially solving it. To our advantage we were able to make longer-term investments in some regions, despite the vagaries of funding or of human resources.

Attending to an issue of national relevance and recognition by the state: Aajeevika Bureau is addressing a reality faced by millions of Indians. Migration for work is an enduring feature of rural India and an essential ingredient of the country's urban and industrial prosperity. Without skill enhancement, adequate legislation, regulation or public provisioning, the contributions which migrants could make to their communities and the national economy will be far below potential.

When it started work, Aajeevika Bureau filled a void: state machineries largely left labour migration to the devices of the market: civil society organizations did not fully grasp or respond to the problems of a massive population on the rural–urban continuum: and trade unions failed to organize and represent the issues of the informal, migrant workforce within their traditional frameworks of constituency-building and collective bargaining. The unfettered availability of a massive reserve of rural workers, driven by distress, was a boon for business and industry as they sought to keep costs low and competitive in a highly contested global marketplace.

On the one hand, our familiarity and presence in rural south Rajasthan, which is among the densest out-migration regions of the state, gave us a first-hand experience of the steady decline in the rural economy and the resultant flight of rural youth to urban areas. On the other, our decision to be available and present in the major destinations of our migrant communities, i.e., industrial pockets of Gujarat and Maharashtra, afforded us the opportunity to understand the challenges facing migrants and ways to improve their well-being and conditions of service. Our presence on this spectrum of rural-to-urban/source-to-destination gave us a conceptual and moral platform for urgent action.

Our dedicated attention to this issue has garnered us important recognition from the state. Early authentication of the Aajeevika Bureau-issued migrant identity cards by the Rajasthan Labour Department helped to establish state acknowledgement of the phenomenon of labour out-migration. More recently, our partnership with the state has also translated into a strong endorsement, including consistent financial support for Labour Line that has helped recover Rs 30 crore to workers, who otherwise had no hope of recovering this money owing to wage thefts and other labour rights violations.

Finding champions: Our work has been greatly supported by several people in academic, corporate organizations, NGOs and government, with expertise and experience, whose voices are heard on many significant platforms. Ongoing engagement through the sharing of early experiences, dialogue, and writing has continued to clarify both the conceptual foundations and the practical relevance of Aajeevika Bureau's work to various voices of influence.

Much can be said about the importance of direct interaction and exposure to ground realities—data usually does not have the emotive power of experience, and by creating opportunity to visit and engage directly with communities we have brought many people closer to our issues. We have been fortunate to have the benefit of our work being amplified through several influencers' in diverse quarters—state, industry, the labour movement, academia and the media.

Though Aajeevika Bureau's founders found their feet and gained their early experience in more sombre times, Aajeevika Bureau was born in the age of new and visible philanthropy. Awards, recognitions, and media coverage have become integral to the mainstreaming, even public legitimizing, of social purpose and innovation. Since our early years, our selection to the India Development Marketplace, an initiative to promote innovative development ideas through a competitive process for seed funding, organized by the World Bank and Federation of Indian Chambers of Commerce and Industry, enrolment in the prestigious Ashoka Fellowship community, winning of the India Social Entrepreneurship award by the World Economic Forum, coverage on Outlook Ideas That Will Change the World, and several significant media outings, including a more recent appearance in Kaun Banega Crorepati, which took our ideas and work to crores of viewers, have all cumulatively contributed to a wider understanding and appreciation of Aajeevika Bureau's work, as well as the broader issues confronting migrant workers in the country.

Gaining visibility: Our extensive practice converging with the rigour of research has given our ideas and arguments a solid foundation of credibility. Aajeevika Bureau's research and policy team, at the CMLS, has been regularly called upon to contribute to conferences, seminars, workshops, edited volumes, journals, magazines and presentations. There is considerable appetite for fresh data and analysis in the labour rights ecosystem, especially from the quarters of labour agenda practice and activism. These invitations and the willingness of those in academia and policy circles to engage have helped lend wide visibility to many of Aajeevika Bureau's propositions.

We have consistently undertaken knowledge-building, writing and critiquing, and through this we have positioned labour migration as a distinct agenda on the development policy landscape. We have demonstrated that interventions to improve migration experiences are not only significant from the perspective of addressing deficits in developmental outcomes or enabling access to justice, they are also an imperative for building a robust workforce that can contribute to sustainable economic growth.

The vast scale of migration in the country and the many vulnerabilities of migrant workers was brought forcefully to the nation's notice during the Covid-19 lockdowns. It shook the conscience of a nation that had been indifferent about the issue until then. Many began to think about a longer-term, sustainable future for migrant workers. Judicial intervention has played a crucial role in this, as has a growing interest in industry circles to bring about more fundamental changes in their relationship with the migrant workforce.

Several individuals and institutions sought out Aajeevika Bureau for collaboration, and many offered their expertise to help amplify the organization's work and concerns. We were regularly invited to contribute to various webinars and consultations as well as to state committees and forums deliberating on migrant issues. The organization's partnership with the Working People's Charter kept it continuously engaged in critiquing state responses to distressed migrants during the lockdowns, but also beyond as long-term agendas became articulated.[3]

What Can Others Learn?

There are several positive lessons and cautionary tales one can take from a review of Aajeevika Bureau's story. The pandemic has been a learning experience and a dramatic illustration of both the challenges that migrant workers face and their resilience. What possibly stands out most is the importance of nourishing value-driven human capital in an organization intending to take on large, complex problems with no known solutions. This must manifest not just in a positive organizational environment, but in recruitment and compensation systems that help nurture stability and a leadership culture that genuinely respects collective processes and success.

Working on issues of current national and global relevance such as labour migration makes it possible for many diverse actors to engage as participants, partners or supporters. An issue of significance also binds the team with a spirit of service and change.

We are very convinced that funding will follow strong and relevant work. It is risky to radically modify our core focus to attract funding and we have experienced that disparate funding obligations can dilute the organizational focus. Partnering with other organizations can certainly be an effective way to expand the scope of interventions and enhance their impacts. However, partnering can consume considerable resources so it is important to be strategic and selective in developing partnerships. It does not serve our cause well to reject organizations and individuals of different ideological persuasion and a common ground and common cause must be attempted. Visibility can be critical, especially for a new organization, and communication can be a cost-effective way to enhance public perception. It has been important to describe the work in simple, de-jargonized terms, which helps one to reach a wide audience waiting to participate.

Finally, periodic reflection on goals, approaches and progress can be a valuable practice, especially when it is a team experience. Writing this chapter has been part of that process for us.

23

Janaagraha: Transforming the Quality of Life in India's Cities

SRIKANTH VISWANATHAN

INDIA'S SOCIO-ECONOMIC FUTURE CRITICALLY DEPENDS on our ability to transform the quality of life in our cities. There are over 40 crore people living in India's cities today. By 2050, that number is expected to rise to 80 crore, or over half the country's population. For the first time in its modern history, more Indians will be living in cities than in villages.

Fixing India's cities is crucial from three inter-related perspectives. First, cities need to be able to provide a basic quality of life to all citizens. This by itself is a significant policy agenda, because we would need to clear the prevalent deficit in services, and then provide for the exponential growth in population over the next three decades. Second, cities will continue to drive economic growth and job creation in India both directly and indirectly. India's ability to provide reasonable wage jobs and create pathways to prosperity for its population will depend on ensuring that our cities provide an enabling environment for creative and productive endeavours in trade and business. Third, the quality of democracy in India's cities will determine the quality of democracy in India itself. With one out of every two citizens expected to live in cities, they will exercise at least 50 per cent influence on democracy (and citizenship), if not more given their agglomeration effects.

India's urbanization and how we surmount its challenges and fully realize its possibilities will thus be among the most significant human development endeavours in the twenty-first century. Thus far, the development discourse in India has been dominated by union and state governments, and by sectoral development agendas. Twenty-first century challenges such as equity (including gender equality), environment sustainability, public health (including water and sanitation), migration, jobs and livelihoods, are global challenges that require local action in substantive measure. They all require a focus on people and places. Local governments and communities need to therefore be recognized as being at the heart of the solution. Places where citizens live, work and play are where these challenges converge and manifest in real ways in citizens' lives. Local governments are the 'first-mile' governments in these places, and the first touchpoint of political responsiveness and accountability for citizens.

The salience of India's cities has risen significantly since Janaagraha's [1] founding twenty years ago, and our mission of transforming the quality of life in India's cities remains ever more relevant. At Janaagraha, we define quality of life as comprising two inter-related but distinct aspects, quality of citizenship and quality of infrastructure and services. The quality of citizenship is the nature and extent of citizen participation in governance. We work with citizens, councillors and ward-level officials to catalyse participatory governance in city neighbourhoods, and with local, state and union governments to facilitate reforms to 'city systems'. 'City-systems' are root causes underlying most, if not all, aspects of the quality of life in our cities. We are striving to fix the system, rather than fix the problem directly, because we believe irreversible, sustainable transformation in the quality of life in our cities can only happen when we have robust city-systems.

In order to accomplish our mission, we pursue the two outcomes of trust and engagement between citizens and governments at the neighbourhood level, and robust 'city-systems'.

We seek to achieve trust and engagement between citizens and governments by catalysing formal platforms (like ward committees and area sabhas) for citizen participation, and by facilitating the participation of councillors and citizens in such platforms. In order to achieve this, we advocate with governments for such formal platforms, create tools for citizens and councillors (and ward-level municipal officials) to be informed and to participate, and also mobilize them.

We pursue four robust city-systems. These are: urban planning and design (spatial planning, land and design of public spaces); urban capacities and resources (finance, staffing, performance management, and digitalization in city governments); empowered and legitimate political representation (empowered and accountable mayors and councils); and transparency, accountability and participation (citizen participation in neighbourhood-level governance). We engage with specific stakeholders to impress upon them the significance of city-systems for better quality of infrastructure and services, and enlist champions among them to adopt city-systems reforms.

Therefore, on the one hand, we strengthen participatory governance by creating platforms and tools for citizens, councillors and ward-level officials to mobilize and engage with each other at a neighbourhood level. On the other hand, we work with governments to strengthen state capacities to deliver infrastructure and services, not by directly working on sectors such as water supply, waste management or roads, but by working on 'city-systems', across laws and policies, institutions and institutional processes, implementation capacities and accountability framework.

Janaagraha was founded in 2001 by Swati and Ramesh Ramanathan who were early pioneers in citizen participation and urban governance reforms in India's cities. Their contrasting experiences as citizens in Indian and global cities inspired them in their early thirties to devote their lives to fixing India's cities. Their approach was to build diverse institutions, with customized legal and funding structures, best suited to meet their respective social objectives. Janaagraha is therefore now part of a larger group of institutions incubated by Swati and Ramesh, comprising: Jana Urban Space Foundation (Jana USP), a professional services social enterprise, working on urban planning, design and architecture; Jana Urban Services for Transformation, a municipal consulting company; Janaadhar, an affordable housing company; and Jana Small Finance Bank, a small finance bank. The co-founders do not earn any monetary benefits from these organizations, thus preserving the social core. Janaagraha benefits from a broad horizon of thinking and institutional interventions spanning financial inclusion, affordable housing, land titling, master planning of cities, and integrated road and utilities design.

Significant Breakthroughs

We could reflect on our accomplishments so far, by thinking of our journey in four phases—the launch phase, systems phase, consolidation phase and the scale phase.

The launch phase

During the launch phase (2001–04), we pioneered hyperlocal citizen participation in India. Our founding was as a platform for citizen participation. This phase was therefore characterized by mobilizing citizens for collective action with a sharp focus on transparency in city budgets and works. These early campaigns went on to inspire participatory budgeting in Bengaluru and Pune, the Public Disclosure Law (PDL) for radical transparency in finances and operations in cities, and the Nagara Raj law (also known as the Community Participation Law or CPL) for formal polling booth-level citizen participation. Both of these were mandatory reforms under the Jawaharlal Nehru National Urban Renewal Mission (JnNURM), and formed the foundation for our subsequent work on civic technology. One of our earliest programs was Bala Janaagraha, a civic learning programme for school students.

The systems phase

The systems phase (2004–09) was the outcome of our realization and learning on the need for policy reforms to institutionalize citizen participation. More broadly, it led to 'whole of systems' thinking, that recognized the need to work with both citizens and governments, and across citizen participation and policy reforms. During this phase, we contributed to the conception and shaping of the JnNURM, India's largest urban mission till then, with a signature twin-track approach of projects-plus-reforms which has remained its lasting legacy. There were also seminal contributions to the second Administrative Reforms Commission, and the Thirteenth Finance Commission. The Jaago Re! campaign in partnership with Tata Tea on voter enrolment achieved pan-India scale and brought together both citizen mobilization and advocacy for systems reforms in voter list management in India's cities.

The consolidation phase

The next phase was consolidation of the work done across both citizen participation and policy reforms. This happened between 2010 and 2016. The unprecedented experience in citizen participation informed the organization's pioneering civic technology platforms, and its work with JnNURM and other nationally significant policy initiatives crystallized into the city-systems framework.[2] During this phase, the cofounders nurtured a second line of leadership, creating a roadmap for institutional continuity.

The hopeful phase—of wider scale and deeper impact

Since 2016, we have been striving to complete our toolbox for urban transformation in terms of products and programmes, building relationships with communities and governments for wider scale and deeper impact, and investing in leaders. Our ability to journey well further depends on finding, nurturing and growing leaders. It is they who will scale the organization and its programmes, stitch together partnerships and alliances, and deliver deeper impact.

The following are some of the major milestones in Janaagraha's journey so far:
- Mainstreaming the vocabulary and syntax of participatory democracy in India's cities including among school students;
- Conceiving and successfully advocating for JnNURM with the twin-track approach of projects plus reforms;
- Introducing the concept of area sabhas at a polling-booth-level as the lowest unit of participation in India's cities;
- Conceiving and implementing arguably India's largest civic technology platform, thus laying the groundwork for the future of participatory democracy in India's cities; and

- Ushering in radical transparency and accountability in municipal finances through www.cityfinance.in and the Fifteenth Finance Commission's recommendation on the mandatory publication of audited annual accounts for all municipalities.

Yet, what stands out is the culture of leadership and empowerment that we are building in the institution. Transforming India's cities like many other complex human development agendas is a relay race, and a marathon at that, and not an individual sprint. We need to find and nurture the right leaders to take on the baton and run with it.

Janaagraha's Impact in Numbers

- 16 lakh citizens in 2,900 urban poor settlements in Odisha were covered under participatory governance systems;
- Rs 120 crore (Rs 60 lakh per ward committee) was allocated in the municipal budget of Bengaluru through 'MyCityMyBudget', a first-of-its-kind participatory budgeting campaign;
- 'Swachhata' mobile app reached over 3,500 municipalities in India and was used by over 2 crore citizens, with over 5 crore interactions recorded over five years;
- About 4,00,000 students were covered under the civic learning initiative across 600 schools in thirty cities with over 20,000 civic learning projects undertaken;
- JnNURM was conceived and implemented with a national footprint and an outlay of Rs 1,20,000 crore;
- Twenty-five states enacted PDL and eleven states enacted CPL, infusing new energy and thinking into transparency and citizen participation in cities; and
- Rs 1,20,000 crore extended to municipalities under the Fifteenth Finance Commission grants, covered under a pioneering financial transparency and accountability platform.

Five Principles That Have Guided Us

On reflection, there are five principles that have served us well over the last twenty years.

Systems practice

Fixing India's cities is a systems problem. India's cities do not have a hundred different problems, they have the same problems repeated a hundred different times, over time and place. We need a 'whole of society' approach to fixing India's cities. This is about solving for all our cities as physical spaces, and solving for quality of life of all our citizens living in them, but by addressing root causes and engaging diverse stakeholders.

An endeavour of this proportion requires significant investment in evolving a theory of change, constantly reflecting on past practical experiences, and through practice re-informing that theory of change. At Janaagraha, we have hugely benefited from investing substantive time and mindspace in our theory of change. Secondly, there is need for continuous reflection to stay on course in the systems practice path. The systems practice path is an equal marriage of conviction and context. The dominance of conviction over context leads to a hasty retreat into an ivory tower, as we lose sight of what works in the real world. The dominance of context over conviction on the other hand, leads to co-option into the prevalent status quo. The joy and accomplishment of systems practice comes from this equal marriage, with all the communication, accommodation and reflection that goes into making it work. The dedication to systems practice has ensured we remain free from attachments to particular programmes and projects, and helped us put certain programmes into cold storage, add new programmes and change tracks in others, all through collaborative decision-making. A deliberative, collaborative approach with the theory of change serving as a compass, also helped unshackle ourselves from the burden of hierarchy, by empowering programme managers and further strengthening their ownership over their programmes and their impact.

A great example of systems practice is the Tender S.U.R.E. (Specifications for Urban Road Execution) roads of Jana USP, which continues to inspire and inform Janaagraha's own systems practice journey. It began with Swati Ramanathan identifying street design (including organizing underground utilities) as a catalytic reform with multiple benefits. Ducting of eight utilities (storm water drains, water supply lines, power lines, sewerage lines, optical-fibre cables, piped gas, street lighting and traffic surveillance) under footpaths (rather than roads) with inspection chambers, continuous, even and wide footpaths, joint tenders between water and power utilities and the municipality (to avoid road-cutting), junction redesign, safe crossings, uniform travel lanes, and street-side parking had the potential to raise public spaces in India's cities to a significantly higher trajectory of inclusion and service delivery, besides saving costs. Tender S.U.R.E. design is accompanied by a model tender document and detailed material specifications, thus facilitating improved project management and accountability for quality.

The seven phases in the journey of Tender S.U.R.E. over a dozen years and counting is instructive. It began with the conception of a systems solution, which addressed root causes and through it multiple symptoms (first step). It was followed by co-opting a collective of opinion leaders in the city drawn from business and civil society who spoke for Tender S.U.R.E. and co-owned it (second step). Then came a demonstration road on Tender S.U.R.E. design standards that served as a lighthouse or 'show and tell' (third step). This enabled enlisting champions within the government who advocated for it within government (fourth step). Adoption of the idea and project execution was made possible when the journey passed the important milestone of budget allocation in the state government's budget (fifth step). But the project would find acceptance only if it succeeded. So close project monitoring (including daily site inspections) to ensure success of the first roll out was critical (sixth step).

Finally, ensuring that the project survives beyond the pilot phase and is fully owned by the government needed a scale-up through the smart cities project (70 km of roads on Tender S.U.R.E standards; seventh step). The Tender S.U.R.E journey serves as a north star in systems practice for Janaagraha, including few lessons on doing it better going forward and not repeating the same mistakes.

Urgent patience

Human development challenges could span decades (think India's freedom movement), centuries (think the issue of race) or even millennia (think gender issues), and evolve across time and place. We need to be humble in acknowledging that often they will outlast and outlive us, and often our efforts will bear fruit, if they do, after our time. Yet, during our time we need to strive to surmount them. Urgency in our efforts laced with infinite patience for results is an imperative for systems practice. The long journey of human development cannot be abridged into neat three-year cycles with outcome measures. We need to work with longer time horizons of five to ten years, and invest in the inputs and processes. Outcomes need to be measured, but they are finally consequences and not actions. 'Urgent patience' is a modern rendering of sorts of karma yoga, of doing what we have to, irrespective of the outcomes. Our choice is between picking the salient problems of our times to work on, irrespective of whether we will solve them or not or the time horizon for it, or picking superficial problems because we are certain of solving them within a short time period.

At Janaagraha, we have resolutely picked 'city-systems', the root causes underlying quality of life in cities, as the problems we wish to work on, irrespective of whether we solve for them in our lifetimes or not. This choice has not always been easy to live with, as donors and even communities and governments oftentimes espouse a strong preference for and better understanding of quick wins and measurable, even physical impact. One of the greatest dangers confronting human development is the temptation to sacrifice urgent patience at the altar of ephemeral, superficial results. We will surmount this danger only if each of us as individuals place the pursuit of human development, including self-development, over personal attainment.

An example of urgent patience is our work on financial transparency and accountability of municipalities. Our work with the Fifteenth Finance Commission contributed to the mandate for publication of audited annual accounts by all 4,700 and more municipalities in India to access any of their grants. This is an unprecedented development and will, over the next three years, result in a large majority of municipalities publishing their audited accounts on a timely basis. This is an important milestone in a journey that commenced even before Janaagraha's founding twenty years ago, when Ramesh Ramanathan was engaged in fixing the Bengaluru municipality's accounting system and identified publication of audited annual accounts as a crucial reform agenda. Through lean years, when there was no purchase with governments and donors, we built our muscles and sharpened our tools, taking advantage of the smaller reform opportunities that came our way, yet keeping an eye out for the right time for the big thrust.

Constructive engagement

No single individual or organization can solve any human development challenge by themselves, not even governments. Governments, civil society, business, academia and media will need to partner to solve for twenty-first century challenges. We have chosen the mid-path between aggressive confrontation and toothless collaboration, and we call it constructive engagement. We have applied this in large measure to our work with governments, but the innate spirit would apply to other partnerships too. The searing impact of poor human development on individual lives can legitimately impel us to confront governments and exact accountability, but may not always make progress on solving the challenge particularly in resource-constrained settings. On the other hand, serving as a vendor to the government too can pass off as collaboration or partnership, but the inherent power dynamic almost always inhibits an equal relationship. Where governments have intent but lack capacities, it is the obligation of civil society to support them, not merely as vendors who execute the government's mandate, but as equal partners who bring the value of independence, aspiration and innovation. This has been an article of faith for us at Janaagraha and our work over the years with constitutional bodies, and union, state and local governments has tried to hold on to this line. A consistent non-ideological position, and open and honest communication around the same, has stood us in good stead. Further, there needs to be a fearlessness or openness to surmounting conflicts. Our co-founders led by example with the credo that the absence of conflict is not necessarily harmony.

A recent example is our engagement with the Bruhat Bengaluru Mahanagara Palike (BBMP) on a participatory budgeting campaign called

MyCityMyBudget, as part of which the BBMP allocated Rs 120 crores for ward committees to choose neighbourhood projects. Even as we work very closely with the senior leadership of the BBMP on this important agenda, we were engaged in a critical review of the new BBMP Act 2020 and continue to be vocal in the media about advocacy agendas for the city.

Body of an institution, soul of a movement

Our work at Janaagraha is all about fixing democracy and citizenship in India's cities. Janaagraha was in fact founded as a movement for citizen participation. That is our soul. However, to protect and nurture it, it needs to find a home in a strong institutional body which is well governed and sustainable. While on the one hand we need to preserve and nurture the passion, creative impulse, and responsiveness that are emblematic of movements, we need a strong institution that is able to sustain the movement over long periods of time. We have therefore systematically invested in building a strong institution particularly in recent years. The vision, genius and entrepreneurial impulse of our co-founders cannot be institutionalized, but institutional memory can be created and nurtured, the founding ideals retained as a foundation of organization culture, and operational excellence institutionalized. Corporate governance, human resources culture and practices, fund-raising, strategic communications, and performance management are all limbs of a strong institutional body. From the constitution of a governing board to creating an executive leadership team to succeed the co-founders, from executing a phased succession plan from cofounders to the executive leadership team to a CEO, to overhauling HR policies to create an engaged workplace (with particular emphasis on gender), we have passed few important milestones, but with a lot more work to be done.

Civic leadership

Human development cannot be gained through hierarchical leadership. The complexity of human development, most of all, the context of place and people, makes it imperative for leaders to co-own the mission and co-travel the pathway to the solution. At Janaagraha, we have embarked on a distributed leadership model not as a stated intent but as a way of working. This involves collaborative planning and decision-making based on mutual trust and understanding of roles and responsibilities, and circumscribed by accountability for performance and delivery. Hierarchy is leveraged for external engagements, and for covering operation risks, but responsibilities (including decision rights) are handled based on skills, capabilities and performance, and not on years of work experience.

For a civic organization, civic leadership within the organization may be key to inter-generational growth. As we complete twenty years of our founding, we need to create a culture of civic leadership within the organization, even as we strive to catalyze such a culture outside of it. Civic leadership is about living the value of active citizenship. When you live the value of active citizenship, you co-own the mission of Janaagraha, and do not just work for it. An environment that is able to nurture distributed and civic leadership will give to the world around it, missionaries for the cause, and not merely take from it, employees for the organization.

Gathering Tailwinds of Urban Transformation

Fixing quality of life in cities has finally become a political agenda in India in recent years. There is significantly higher funding for urban infrastructure and services, and political leaders who were generally loathe to be seen as pro-city, are now eager to be seen as action-oriented leaders with a sharp focus on project delivery and fast learning a new urban vocabulary. These tailwinds are certainly hastening the number, frequency and pace of our engagements with governments. The step-up in activity levels in urban infrastructure, services and governance when confronted by weak state capacities, has forced governments to engage to a far greater degree than before with business, academia and civil society. There is a reluctant yet gradual acknowledgement of the shift in power dynamics horizontally from governments to outside of them, as far as urban transformation is concerned.

Looking ahead we see even greater momentum in business, academia, civil society and government working collectively to alter the status quo. This optimism needs to however be moderated by the recognition that with few exceptions, strong political executives through their chosen executive teams (and partners from outside governments) are focusing on delivering better quality of infrastructure and services, and not necessarily better governance overall, with greater voice and agency for city councils and citizens. Janaagraha is responding to the increasing number of opportunities to build state capacities, but is also digging in its heels on empowering and enabling city councils and citizens.

What Could We Do Better Going Forward?

There are five areas where we would like to improve on our performance in the past. First, we would like to engage a lot more with political leaders, both elected and unelected. We need to better understand their views on our reform agendas, to both influence them and be informed by them, particularly on the boundary constraints within which they work, the incentives and disincentives for reforms, and trigger points for their decisions. Second, we would need to invest more in urban policy research, at the intersection of our work on participatory governance and city-systems on the one hand, and with gender, climate change, water and sanitation, and migration and jobs on the other. Third, we need to invest in partnerships and alliances. Scarce resources and bandwidth in civil society need to be aggregated and sharply focused, and not dissipated. While there is growing recognition and intent, not much ground has been covered. Fourth, we need to communicate our work in simpler and more impactful ways for different target stakeholder groups. We will need to become a lot more approachable and accessible to the rest of the ecosystem. Lastly, we need to systematically evolve further as a nursery for civic leadership. Ultimately, our success critically hinges on our ability to host, engage with and empower civic leaders. When passionate citizens with the requisite skills set their hearts and minds to a cause, then it is not whether they will achieve their mission, but when.

Holding on to the Rhythm amidst the Noise

In the last few years, there has been a surge of philanthropic and civil society action in India. Much of it comes from a deeply felt desire for change, and a desire to actively contribute to such change. It needs to be welcomed. Yet, this surge of action is also creating a lot of noise in the sector that may distract us from our rhythm. In the Indian context, it would serve us well to remember that we are a young democracy that is in several ways a work in progress.

Our democratic and participatory systems, and state capacities, are evolving, and there are no shortcuts to solving for this. They are the foundation for India's and its cities' human development. As civil society, we should err on the side of doing more serious and substantive work to strengthen them, rather than chase the mirage of short-term impact.

Politicians have five-year electoral time horizons and, in India, bureaucrats have even shorter ones. It is civil society that provides continuity in long-term human development agendas. We need to resist the temptation of getting co-opted into headlines without engaging with the details. Our experience suggests it is possible to strike the balance of engaging with communities and governments on their near-term priorities, yet pursue substantive long-term agendas. This requires systems practice, urgent patience and constructive engagement all rooted in moral courage.

24

Mitanin in Chattisgarh: Community Health Work as a Social Movement

SAMIR GARG

MITANIN[1] IS A COMMUNITY HEALTH worker (CHW) programme in Chhattisgarh established in 2002 as a collaboration between civil society and the state government. What sets this initiative apart is that it is a government-owned programme that has the character of a social movement. It has an all-women cadre of 72,000 CHWs—known as 'Mitanins'—working across 20,000 villages and 4,000 urban slums, serving nearly 2.5 crore people. The word 'Mitanin' is from the Chhattisgarhi dialect and means 'friend'.

Chhattisgarh is one of the newest states of India, carved out of Madhya Pradesh in 2000. It is also among the poorest states, with around a third of its population from the Scheduled Tribes (ST). The Mitanin CHWs are selected by the communities for whom they work. Each Mitanin looks after a habitation in a tribal area, which may have around twenty households, or an urban slum with about 200 families. They have three roles in the community: a health educator and primary healthcare provider; a link to the formal healthcare services of the government, promoting and facilitating access to them; and an activist and social organizer promoting intersectoral action on health and its social determinants and demanding better services and entitlements from the government.

Mitanins are trained, supervized and supported by a network of around 4,000 trainers and coordinators. A group of twenty Mitanins is led by a Mitanin trainer (MT). In an average block, there are about 400 Mitanins and twenty MTs. At the block level, leadership is provided by three block coordinators. This support structure is stewarded by the State Health Resource Centre (SHRC), an autonomous body tasked with managing the Mitanin programme on behalf of the state government. The SHRC works in close collaboration with the state's Department of Health.

Achievements

The Mitanin programme is a rare example of a model born from civil society's work[2] that has been replicated at scale by the government. For a long time, it was one of the largest programmes of women CHWs globally, and became the model for a nationwide programme on CHWs in India. This programme is known as Accredited Social Health Activist (ASHA) and now has over 10 lakh CHWs across the country. The Mitanin programme has been very successful across wide-ranging aspects of health and its social determinants.

Health education and behavioural change

Mitanins maintain close contact with pregnant women in their habitations, giving them advice on their diet and rest, and accompanying them on antenatal check-ups. They visit the family after a birth and remind them to ensure timely initiation of breastfeeding, to keep the baby warm and only handling him or her with clean hands. In these activities, Mitanins have been able to achieve coverage rates rarely seen in CHW programmes globally. For example, an evaluation in 2020 found that 96.4 per cent of families with newborns were visited by Mitanins and 75 per cent of these families were visited six or more times in the first six weeks after birth.

According to the National Family Health Survey of 2019, 84 per cent of new mothers received a postnatal visit by a health worker in Chhattisgarh, comparing favourably to the national average of 78 per cent. The proportion of newborns breastfed within twenty-four hours of birth improved from 30 per cent in 1998 to 90.3 per cent in 2015; further, the proportion of children exclusively breastfed till six months of age was 80.3 per cent in Chhattisgarh in 2005, while the national average was 46.4 per cent.

Rather than blame people for their beliefs and practices, Mitanins worked through constructive and reasoned dialogue. Based on their training—which stated that 'no mother wants her child to be sick or undernourished'—they established supportive relationships with mothers. This ensured that their advice was not seen as being condescending and enabled them to win the trust of the women as well as their families and communities.

Early childhood development was another area that was included in the Mitanin's ambit with the aim of building a holistic approach to childcare by bringing together the elements of health, nutrition and psychosocial development. As Chhattisgarh had serious issues with child malnutrition, Mitanins advised mothers on the care of their young children, with particular focus given to the practical steps they can take to prevent undernutrition. These efforts led to Chhattisgarh becoming the top-performing Indian state in reducing child malnutrition. Its stunting rate among children under the age of three came down from 60.8 per cent in 1998 to 34.6 per cent in 2019. A big improvement has also been seen in women's nutrition levels: in 1998, 48.1 per cent of the state's women citizens had a body mass index below 18.5; this came down to 23.1 per cent in 2019.

The rural infant mortality rate (IMR) of Chhattisgarh fell from 88 per 1,000 live births in 2001 to 61 per 1,000 in 2004, a decline of 27 per cent within the first three years of the Mitanin programme; the corresponding change at the national level was just 8 per cent. This decline in the IMR in Chhattisgarh equates to 17,000 newborn lives being saved every year. Chhattisgarh's achievements in health are even more significant considering it is home to one of the poorest populations in the country. Despite its poverty, poorly educated population and weak health infrastructure, the state was remarkably able to surpass the national averages in many indicators of health. Mitanins also advise families and communities on staying safe from waterborne diseases and give tips on treating diarrhoea and preventing malaria. In 2021, 77 per cent of the population of Bastar—the region with the highest number of malaria cases in Chhattisgarh—was found to be using bed nets.

In the urban slums, Mitanins work to prevent dengue and viral hepatitis. After Chhattisgarh underwent an epidemiological transition, non-communicable diseases and their prevention became important. The key problems identified were the extremely high use of tobacco, injuries from road accidents and mental health issues. Mitanins are now working on combating these newly recognized challenges and changing people's understanding of these issues and their causes and treatments.

Direct healthcare services

Mitanins realized the importance of treating many illnesses at the village level. Thus, apart from working on prevention, they began to provide direct healthcare in the community by identifying and treating communicable diseases and some common ailments. One of their first medical interventions was the provision of oral rehydration solution (ORS) for diarrhoea. They also taught families how to prepare ORS at home. The proportion of children receiving ORS for diarrhoea increased from 29.7 per cent in 1998 to 67.9 per cent in 2015. The national average in 2015 was only 50.6 per cent.

Over the years, the Mitanins' training has grown to encompass other health issues. In 2005, they were equipped with a drug kit that had twelve kinds of medicines. In 2015, they received point-of-care tests for malaria, enabling them to confirm the presence of malaria in communities more efficiently than they could before. By the following year, Mitanins were detecting and treating around two-thirds of all malaria cases in the state. The impact of this work was reflected in the dramatic fall in mortality due to diarrhoea and malaria in Chhattisgarh.

Mitanins also identified sick newborns and were able to treat them when a referral was not feasible. In 2017, they became equipped to identify and treat pneumonia in children. Other treatments provided by Mitanins are for simple skin infections, small injuries and aches and pains. Training in the treatment of reproductive tract infections in women was of great value because women were comfortable talking to Mitanins about their problems.

Considering the importance of regular follow-up in cases of hypertension, in 2020 around 11,700 Mitanins in the urban and peri-urban areas were trained to measure blood pressure. A study in 2019 found that Mitanins contributed to 17 per cent of all cases treated for acute illnesses in the state. Their proximity to people helped them provide timely care for their patients, thereby saving lives and costs.

Linking with formal health services

Mitanins also worked on convincing people to use the government's health services and helped them to access these services. In their role as a link between the government and the people, Mitanins promoted government schemes for the immunization of infants. The proportion of children fully immunized in Chhattisgarh jumped to 48.7 per cent in 2005 from 21.8 per cent in 1998, while it remained stagnant over the same period in the rest of the country. By 2015, 76.4 per cent of Chhattisgarh's children were fully immunized, ahead of the national average of 62 per cent.

Mitanins helped pregnant women access timely antenatal check-ups and institutional deliveries, resulting in the proportion of pregnant women receiving at least four antenatal check-ups in Chhattisgarh jumping from 19.4 per cent in 1998 to 54.2 per cent in 2005. The national average only improved marginally from 29.5 per cent to 37 per cent in the same period. In 1998, just 7.6 per cent of all deliveries in Chhattisgarh took place in government institutions. This, increased to 70 per cent in 2019.

The CHWs played an active role in improving people's access to a variety of contraceptive methods. By 2019, the total fertility rate of Chhattisgarh was 1.8, better than the national average of 2. Mitanins worked on identifying people exhibiting signs of tuberculosis or leprosy and took them to health centres for testing and diagnosis. As a result, the number of people being examined for tuberculosis more than doubled between 2012 and 2016. While most states under-reported cases of leprosy, Chhattisgarh continued to identify new cases due to the active role being played by Mitanins.

From 2018, Mitanins began helping health centres identify cases of chronic diseases such as hypertension, diabetes and sickle cell disease as well as mental illnesses. They conduct follow-up visits to ensure that those exhibiting symptoms undergo regular check-ups and take their medicines.

Activism

For Mitanins, good health is not just the absence of physical illness but also the presence of mental and social wellbeing. They understand that people's health will not improve unless they have access to nutrition, water and social security and that their social and economic situation will improve only with gender justice and social equality. An important element of the Mitanin programme is activism that goes beyond healthcare. This has been an inspiration for CHW programmes worldwide.

A crucial area of the Mitanins' activism is food security. They keep people informed of their entitlements under the government's food security programmes and check for wrongdoings in fair-price shops and public worksites. One of their demands is for better quality meals in anganwadi centres and schools. Where they find a problem, they encourage people to complain to the panchayat or block officials. They are aided by the Village Health Sanitation Nutrition Committee, which includes elected representatives of the panchayats. Chhattisgarh has emerged as one of the few states where such committees are vibrant, and the credit for this goes to the efforts of Mitanins. Keeping such community-based committees active places a burden on the Mitanin programme, but greatly strengthens their efforts towards social accountability.

In urban slums, Mitanins enlisted the support of other women in their neighbourhood to build active Mahila Arogaya Samitis (women's health committees). Another platform that has evolved to facilitate their push for accountability is the annual 'public dialogue' event, which takes place in each block in the state. Mitanins use these occasions to highlight problems that are unresolved at the local level to government officials and senior public representatives. They also discuss larger issues related to the socioeconomic rights of the communities.

The strength of the Mitanin programme has been based on women's agency, and consequently, a significant area of their activism concerns gender justice. Mitanins have conducted several campaigns to oppose domestic and social violence against women, using street theatre to question gender inequality at the root of gender-based violence. They have mobilized communities, panchayats and the police to act on such incidents.

A national survey showed that the proportion of women facing spousal violence in Chhattisgarh fell from 36.8 per cent in 2015 to 20.2 per cent in 2019, whereas the national average in the same period remained stagnant at around 30 per cent. Their efforts to promote girls' education and prevent underage marriage has led to the proportion of marriages in Chhattisgarh involving girls below eighteen years of age falling sharply from 44.3 per cent in 1998 to 12.1 per cent in 2019.

Mitanins have also fought for environmental justice in forested areas inhabited by tribal communities. In Koriya district—where Mitanins are highly organized and have access to legal support—they waged a successful struggle against state-sponsored deforestation. This brought them into direct conflict with the authorities and some of them had to face harassment in the form of court cases and even imprisonment.

Another tough domain where Mitanins have fought for peoples' rights is healthcare services. They identified villages rarely visited by formal health workers and were able to demand regular immunization and ante-natal care sessions for the villagers. A greater challenge is the poor and unresponsive service in local hospitals. For instance, when they accompany a pregnant woman to a public hospital for childbirth, they have to negotiate hard to ensure she receives satisfactory service. Mitanins have fought against corruption and the poor behaviour of health staff, and voiced their demand for better supply of essential medicines in government health facilities.

Documenting the deaths in their locality along with the likely causes has been another strategy used by Mitanins to exert pressure for improved health services. They rejected the privatized model of healthcare promoted by the government through insurance schemes promising free care in private hospitals. In their experience, patients have become bankrupt due to high private hospitals fees, even when they are covered under such schemes. In their annual public dialogues, they have demanded government action against wrongdoings by private hospitals. The popularity of Mitanins as leaders has become evident from their participation in panchayat elections. In every election since 2006, over 2,500 Mitanins and MTs have been elected into the panchayats. Some serve as presidents of the district or block panchayats.

The Mitanin programme has been externally evaluated several times. The first external evaluation was a couple of years after the programme began. It predicted the programme would fail in a year or two. However, the programme kept growing in strength, and subsequent evaluations have shown that it has had significant successes and that improvements in health and nutrition in Chhattisgarh can be attributed to its work. There have also been internal evaluations, which have provided useful suggestions for improvements in the programme. These could also offer lessons for the evaluation of many large community-based programmes.

What Made the Mitanin Programme Possible?

The government of the newly formed state of Chhattisgarh was free of the baggage of past failures and saw a political window of opportunity for introducing new initiatives. The civil society's view was that community participation is a must for any meaningful change in people's health status. Discussions with the state government led to the conclusion that a CHW programme could be essential to address the huge gaps in healthcare services and the severe shortages of qualified health personnel. The population was predominantly rural and required a health system capable of ensuring the services reach these rural areas. Civil society proposed the Mitanin programme as an innovative solution.[3]

The design of the Mitanin programme was based on lessons drawn from successful CHW models developed by NGOs, as well as from unsuccessful government-run CHW programmes. The NGO programmes were excellent in quality but limited in scale. They often had fewer than a hundred CHWs, nearly all of whom were women. There had also been several large-scale but unsuccessful CHW programmes initiated by the central or state governments, mostly with male CHWs. The government programmes largely focused on curative care, whereas the NGO programmes were more holistic, emphasizing prevention.

The process of selecting Mitanins was a significant contributor to their later success. Each rural habitation was asked to select its own Mitanin, who did not require any minimum educational qualification. The number of families in each hamlet was also small enough for a Mitanin to maintain close personal contact with each. The selection process was facilitated by motivators selected from the local areas and trained by the SHRC, but the community had a substantial say in it. Currently, 37 per cent of the Mitanins belong to the ST category and 14 per cent to the Scheduled Castes (SC), which is slightly above their overall proportion in the rural Chhattisgarh population. The rural elite were not interested in applying for the position as it did not promise any payment. The programme was also able to select Mitanins in conflict-affected areas.

Based on lessons from successful NGO programmes, a modular design was adopted for training the Mitanin CHWs. The large numbers to be trained necessitated a training cascade. The SHRC provided the leadership for this. Many sceptics predicted a large dropout rate due to the voluntary nature of the work, but the initial period saw only 5 per cent of the trainees dropping out. The annual dropout rate was eventually only 2 per cent.

Mitanins drew their motivation from being presented with an opportunity to participate as leaders in a social domain. The social recognition they received for their work was another big source of motivation. It gave them a sense of achievement when they saw their communities receiving good health services. The women enjoyed learning new skills they could apply in their neighbourhoods, which also helped increase confidence in their own abilities.

The support structure of the Mitanin programme is often seen as key to its success. The MTs who trained and supervised Mitanins were former Mitanins themselves. This created a career pathway for the CHWs, as the next level in the programme pyramid was accessible to them. The MTs were taught to be more supportive than supervisory. The differences between Mitanins and ASHA workers can be attributed to the role played by the SHRC. It had the character of a civil society organization, but with the goal of working closely with the government. The government had realized that its department structure would not be able to guide and develop a community-based programme like Mitanin, so it formed the SHRC to serve as a bridge between the communities and the government as well as between research and action and policy and implementation.

Apart from designing and facilitating the Mitanin programme, the SHRC provided technical support to the Department of Health to strengthen its supply-side systems. But its most important role was to ensure the survival and growth of the Mitanin programme by continuously negotiating with the government. It provided bipartisan support for the programme that helped provide continuity when the state's ruling political party changed. The SHRC's strategy of quickly expanding the programme was not welcomed by many experts, but having scale gave it substantial protection from attempts to change its basic nature.

The SHRC learned the lesson that social programmes need to keep growing to survive. The replication of Mitanin on a national level as ASHA has ensured its survival. Its inclusion in the National Health Mission (NHM) also solved the problem of finding sustained and secure funding. Another key contribution by the SHRC is its movement-building approach to the Mitanin programme. The ideas drawn from the literacy movement and the people's science movement were important in the initial stages of the SHRC and the Mitanin programme. It encouraged the interaction of Mitanin with other social movements involved in people's socioeconomic rights. The Mitanin programme could build a substantial role in activism because the SHRC's leadership believed in promoting rights-based collective action by communities.

The SHRC can be innovative because it is an autonomous institution. Its governing board consists mainly of civil society representatives, with the government being a minor stakeholder. Most importantly, the head of the institution is selected by the board and not the government. Its independence is a source of constant tension with the government, but this never reaches a breaking point. Instead, this tension plays a creative role as it keeps the SHRC on its toes while making the government realize the usefulness of the SHRC's autonomy.

The National Health Systems Resource Centre was set up at the national level with learning from the SHRC's role in Chhattisgarh. All state governments were encouraged to establish bodies similar to the SHRC in their own states to facilitate the ASHA programme and act as knowledge management hubs for strengthening the health system. However, none of them allowed an independent institution to emerge in this role. As a result, they could not build organizations as vibrant as the SHRC, and the ASHA programme remained underdeveloped in these states.

Debates and Some Unresolved Questions

Worldwide, there has been a debate about whether CHWs are 'lackeys' or 'liberators'—in other words, whether they are agents of the state or activists working to empower the people. In the case of Mitanins, there is no doubt that they act as activists on behalf of their communities. But does such work make the government feel threatened? Why has there been no attempt by the government to take over the Mitanin programme and the SHRC? Perhaps it is because of how Mitanins perceive the state. They see it not as an oppressor but as a source of welfare.

The actions of Mitanins demanding accountability for government welfare programmes often ruffle feathers at the local level but do not challenge the authority of the government; on the contrary, they increase the legitimacy of the state. Improvements in the entitlements reaching people due to Mitanins' activism reduce the disenchantment political leaders would otherwise face. It is true that the Mitanins' activism has often threatened large-scale corruption or the truly anti-poor actions of the government. And when it has—for example, during the anti-deforestation struggle—it was not a regular feature of a state programme.

While being conscious of their limitations, Mitanins have kept pushing the boundaries and gaining respect as socio-political activists. The size of the Mitanin network has protected them from any backlash from vested interests. Within five years of its inception, the programme was recognized as successful. It was an innovation that the Chhattisgarh government could be proud of. The sustained quality of Mitanins' work has also protected them as their huge credibility in the community made it very costly for politicians to antagonize them. Mitanins as a collective reaped the benefits of political support without aligning with any particular party, and this support protected them from bureaucratic overreach.

Another debate regarding the CHWs is whether their curative-care work takes away from their role as activists. The experience of the Mitanin programme shows that these different roles are mutually supportive. The stature of CHWs grew in the community when they could detect and treat a common illness at people's homes, and gaining confidence in one role helped them better perform their other roles, including activism. In fact, CHW programmes do not reach their full potential when governments are reluctant to equip them with skills and limit their roles to merely being links to the communities.

The Mitanin programme benefited from starting with a purely voluntary approach. This allowed the less-powerful sections of society an entry into the programme. But can the same approach be recommended for other community volunteer programmes? There is clearly a problem in relying on unpaid work for a sustained period. One view is that CHWs should be paid well, at par with skilled government workers; the opposing view is that payment will cost them their autonomy and hence their potential for activism. In the experience of the Mitanin programme, being volunteers empowered the workers.

Cash incentives were introduced for Mitanins when the ASHA programme was rolled out under the NHM. There were several positive outcomes of this policy, such as an increase in the effective population coverage by a Mitanin. The workers could dedicate more time to their jobs and felt more empowered within their families as they contributed to the family income. However, the introduction of a cash incentive did not reduce their activism in any manner. How could they continue questioning the government while receiving their money? It is because Mitanins still do not see themselves as government employees. They view the payment as a form of social recognition of their work by the government.

This does not stop the government from trying to leverage the payments to extract greater obedience from Mitanins. However, they continue to assert their autonomy. The SHRC also works as an ally for Mitanins' continued autonomy. While the Mitanin example offers some lessons, the appropriate nature of compensation for CHWs continues to be an unresolved question. How can the government better support CHWs like Mitanins?

CHWs should be equipped with skills and a regular supply of tests and medicines and should have a supportive network of trainers and community representatives. Mitanins rely on government services to get people the necessary care. They have been helped by the NHM in expanding its services. Governments need to keep increasing and strengthening their services so that the people can reap the full benefits of a programme like Mitanin.

25

JEEViKA: Fostering Pathways for the Transformation of Rural Bihar

ARVIND KUMAR CHAUDHARY AND
MAHUA ROY CHOUDHURY

THE BIHAR RURAL LIVELIHOODS PROMOTION Society, colloquially known as JEEViKA,[1] is a flagship programme for poverty alleviation in Bihar. It aims at improving livelihoods of poor rural households by developing institutions for women—such as self-help groups (SHGs) and their federations—to enable them to access better services and credit for creating self-employment opportunities. From its advent as a small-scale project in eighteen blocks in 2006, JEEViKA has transformed into a state-wide movement. It had impacted the lives of over 1.27 crore families by November 2021.

JEEViKA was set up as a state initiative to expedite poverty-alleviation interventions in the state. It implements the National Rural Livelihoods Mission and the World Bank-funded Bihar Transformative Development Project and is a platform for the targeted delivery of government policies and entitlement programmes. At the time of its initiation in 2006, the state's rural poverty was at 44.3 per cent—the second-highest in the country after Odisha—with 3.6 crore of the total state population of 8.2 crore living in poverty.[2]

The state was characterized by poor service delivery, complex political and social fluxes, a low level of inclusion of poor in institutions, limited economic opportunities and insubstantial development infrastructure.

JEEViKA was introduced in the districts of Gaya, Nalanda, Muzaffarpur, Purnea, Khagaria and Madhubani to provide rural households with innovative, scalable and sustainable models that would help improve their livelihood opportunities.

Over the past fifteen years, JEEViKA has mobilized rural women to form over 10 lakh strong and sustainable self-help groups (SHGs). These collectives have served as ideal platforms for building the village women's capacity to engage in largescale financial intermediation, leverage resources from formal financial institutions, access productivity enhancement services in agriculture and livestock through a community-based extension system, engage with markets on fair terms through scale economies and improve their access to government schemes and entitlements by facilitating awareness and participation.

JEEViKA believes in the innate capacity of rural women, so it has systematically nurtured and engaged them as community resource persons (CRPs) on a large scale. It has developed producer groups and SHGs simultaneously rather than sequentially. Most importantly, JEEViKA has deeply influenced rural and social development policies of the state, wherein the organization of poor rural women into strong community institutions is now a central strategy in tackling Bihar's rural poverty.

Social Inclusion

JEEViKA presently operates in 35,093 villages across 534 blocks and thirty-eight districts of Bihar. The state has the highest number of SHGs nationally with 10,52,289 groups; these have been further federated into 67,029 village organizations (VOs) and 1,326 cluster-level federations (CLFs) that reach 1.27 crore rural households and cover nearly 70 per cent of rural Bihar. The programme focuses on the most disadvantaged people, initiating social mobilization from the poorest hamlets in villages, ensuring their adequate representation among group and federation leaders, implementing specialized financial products around food and health security to reduce vulnerability and linking eligible households to key government schemes for accessing benefits and entitlements.

It has been able to reach 72 per cent of the Scheduled Caste (SC) and Scheduled Tribe (ST) population in the state; 29 per cent of SHG members and one-third of their office bearers are from these categories and 23 per cent of the CRPs are from vulnerable groups.

Sabina Khatun: Leading the Silent Revolution of Societal Norm Change in Bihar

Sabina Khatun belongs to a remote village in the Rajgir block of Nalanda district in Bihar. Married to a tailor, she is the mother of three children. When she was thrown out of her in-laws' house, she could barely manage financially. She joined an SHG, where her fellow group members would conduct SHG meetings in hideouts, as their husbands were strictly against these. When Sabina was selected as a community mobilizer, she attended her training in a burkha. Her husband threatened her with talaq if she continued her training and she had to ask a senior SHG member to help convince him to allow her to continue. After a fortnight, she bought a sewing machine from her resource fee of Rs 6,000, and persuaded her husband to set up his own tailoring shop instead of working in other shops. She also did away with the burkha as it hampered her in the course of her training. People threatened to ostracize her, but for Sabina, there was no looking back.

She motivated others and started mobilizing women into forming SHGs. She later went to Uttar Pradesh as an external CRP, earning over Rs 1 lakh as a resource fee. She bought a piece of land in her name, and also decided to complete her matriculation at the age of forty. She is currently pursuing her graduate studies along with her daughter. Her husband is proud of her and acknowledges her grit. Sabina is not alone—millions of JEEViKA didis are flagbearers of the silent revolution in Bihar.

Financial Inclusion

JEEViKA has adopted the approach of SHG-based financial access to enable banks to expand their client base by servicing smaller sets of community institutions. The programme provides catalytic funding in the form of a community investment fund (CIF) to initially stimulate financial intermediation, instil the habit of on-time repayment and build credit histories for its members. Articulate SHG members with a proven track record of adhering to on-time loan repayments are identified as community mobilizers who facilitate the SHG meetings and maintain records of their financial transactions.

With a proven credit history and a small corpus generated through savings and interest, the SHGs have been able to leverage larger credit amounts from banks. Most of the project funds are consolidated from the SHGs at the VO level and then redistributed based on members' needs. This fuels a virtuous cycle of ongoing reinvestment into income-generating activities, thereby enhancing incomes at the household level.

The CLFs act as largescale financial intermediation platforms addressing a wide variety of community financial needs. CLFs monitor the overall financial health of member institutions and act as vital points of contact for banks. SHG–bank linkages in Bihar have undergone an inspiring transformation over the last decade. Under the programme, community institutions have been successful in leveraging large amounts of credit against low investments. For example, against a direct project investment of Rs 4,250 crores in the form of CIF, they have leveraged Rs 14,500 crores in bank credit while generating a further Rs 1,232 crores in community savings. This puts the leveraging ratio of the project at 1: 3.4, indicating that for every Re 1 invested in it, community institutions have been able to generate an additional investment of Rs 3.4.

Furthermore, project investment along with community savings form a significant corpus fund for community institutions, enabling them to leverage more formal credit. These institutions have emerged as vital stakeholders for banks, leveraging Rs 4,500 crores in 2020–21 alone.

Ensuring Security of Livelihoods

Realizing the importance of agriculture in Bihar's economy, JEEViKA has implemented several large-scale farm-based interventions—such as promoting the system of crop intensification, encouraging 'nutrition gardening' among small farmers and landless people and developing FPOs. Farmer producer companies run by JEEViKA's SHGs have emerged as strong market forces leading to improved trading practices in local markets.

Similarly, large-scale programmes around livestock—including backyard poultry and goat-rearing—have been implemented in more than 1,00,000 households, leading to improved incomes and nutrition. More than 50,000 rural youths have been identified and supported for skill development, which was followed by placement in formal jobs or self-employment enterprises.

Farm productivity enhancement

The enhancement of agricultural income can significantly lower poverty levels and improve food security in the state. The set of practices JEEViKA promotes are not high-cost technology-intensive solutions but a mix of scientifically proven methods, indigenous knowledge and better management of soil, water, plants and nutrients.

Its single-window system for small and marginal farmers provides all the services at their homes. The key elements of this system are:
- Lowering input prices through bulk procurement of materials by VOs and the establishment of village tool banks and custom-hiring centres for farm mechanization;
- Access to credit through bank linkages;
- Providing customized extension services through engaging trained community-cadre agri-entrepreneurs; and
- Providing weather forecasting, agro-advisory services and climate mapping with the help of an automatic weather station and rain gauge.

Livestock-based interventions

JEEViKA has collaborated with the Bihar State Milk Co-Operative Federation Ltd (COMFED) and National Dairy Development Board's Dairy Services to promote dairy-based livelihoods in the state. The installation of automated milk collection units in the dairy cooperative societies has increased daily milk production. Forward-market linkages in dairy intervention have been supplemented with backend support services such as animal health and awareness camps and community-managed dairy extension support.

The backyard poultry intervention has converged with the state government's Department of Animal Husbandry and Fisheries Resources to expand the viable livelihood options for poor and marginalized communities. It is a significant source of a secondary income for households and has also helped to improve their nutrition.

JEEViKA caters to landless, small and marginal farmers by enhancing their capacities for goat-rearing by reducing the occurrence and spread of disease through preventive healthcare such as vaccinations and deworming. It has ensured sustainability by setting up a cadre of community-based health workers providing fee-based preventive health services and helping with identifying good breeding bucks from among the existing herds. Facilitating farmers' access to more remunerative markets through collective sales and exploring community-based insurance models have also been important factors.

Non-farm-based microenterprise promotion

JEEViKA has promoted 6,15,068 microenterprises engaged in non-farm activities such as production of incense sticks, beekeeping, painting and artworks, food and beverages, rural grocery shops, metalworks, stitching units and rural transportation along with several rural start-ups aimed at increasing the market share of SHG members involved in these activities. The project roped in leading private companies to provide technical assistance and purchase finished products.

It also helps artisans market their products through participation in craft fairs across the country. Starting an e-portal for product sales has increased the production and quality of their goods, improved market linkages, skills and designs and helped develop a market-oriented product line for artisans. The project also subsidises inputs for beekeepers in convergence with the State Horticulture Mission. These activities have improved the overall resilience and skill-levels of producer groups in non-farm activities.

The service provided by the JEEViKA-promoted canteens—colloquially called '*didi ki rasoi*' and run by SHG members—in public hospitals during the Covid-19 pandemic was greatly appreciated by the state government, which decided to start these canteens in all public hospitals in the state. The SHG members also produced over 11 crore two-layer cotton masks during the pandemic, which were procured by different government departments.

Skill development and placement

To increase employability of the rural youth, JEEViKA provides skill training and placement facilities through programmes like Deen Dayal Upadhyaya Grameen Kaushalya Yojana—the national flagship scheme for skill development—and RSETIs. The project undertakes a two-pronged strategy under its skill-based interventions: direct placement and placement through training.

Community institutions play a vital role in mobilizing youth looking for jobs in the formal sector. JEEViKA has partnered with skill-development agencies to work on enhancing their skills. The project has set up a Migration Resource Centre in Delhi NCR to help migrant workers employed in the region.

Value chain interventions

JEEViKA has promoted twenty-six farmer producer companies in dairy, poultry and art and crafts. It supports these companies by deploying subject matter specialists and through diversifying the commodity portfolio by increasing the focus on value addition. Retail sales are done through physical stores and websites, creating a multi-buyer ecosystem and linkages with agri-input licenses. It also explores opportunities for price-hedging and risk management. The impact of the successful outcomes of JEEViKA's productivity enhancement interventions resulted in the state government incorporating these interventions for paddy and wheat as part of its agriculture roadmap in 2011 for implementation across Bihar.

Social Development Initiatives

JEEViKA's social and behavioural change approach uses communication to change behaviours and promote social change by influencing knowledge, attitudes and social norms through capitalizing on the vast network of community institutional platforms. This includes the demand for services and the consistent long-term maintenance of behaviour. Social and behavioural change for community institutions includes review, reinforcement and recognition at the institutional level, review at the cluster level, household-level counselling and community-level events for creating an enabling environment.

JEEViKA's social and behaviour change strategy on health and nutrition integration has had a significant positive impact on key health and nutrition indicators. The CARE HH survey[3] has shown more than two-fold increase (from 12.8 per cent to 26.1 per cent) in the minimum dietary diversity among SHG members of the health and nutrition interventions blocks. A similar increase (from 9.8 per cent to 19.9 per cent) was seen in the minimum acceptable diet of children aged nine to eleven months in the same blocks. An independent evaluation by the Population Council shows a significant improvement in the indicators in the intervention areas against the control areas.

The SHG women formed wider collectives to create pressure on the government to impose prohibition of alcohol sales in the state in 2016. The VOs and SHGs played a critical role in protecting poor households engaged in the liquor business while at the same time helping enforce the alcohol ban. The activities of the VOs and SHGs moved from prevention and campaign-oriented work to vigilance and reporting on legal violations. The CLFs submitted the list of affected households to the local police and district administrations and SHGs helped addicted persons receive hospitalization or admission into rehabilitation centres.

JEEViKA collaborates with various government departments to ensure the rights and entitlements of SHG members. The network of community institutions and the trained pool of CRPs have engaged in key tasks such as social audits. They have also run cluster facilitation teams for Mahatma Gandhi National Rural Employment Guarantee Act (MGNREGA) and public distribution system (PDS) shops besides generating awareness about Systematic Voters' Education and Electoral Participation. SHG members are seen as professionals capable of mobilizing and delivering specialized services at scale to poorer rural women.

JEEViKA groups play a vital role in sanitation by facilitating finance and materials for toilet construction and ensuring sustainability through the participatory monitoring of toilet usage and maintenance. SHGs have emerged as a potent force for social change, functioning as a vigilant citizens' platform supporting local institutions such as schools and anganwadi centres while also actively participating in campaigns against alcohol prohibition, dowry and child marriage.

Despite progress made by JEEViKA in social inclusion of the poor, a share of poor households has either remained excluded or dropped out of SHGs. JEEViKA realized that effectively addressing the needs of the poorest households would require more nuanced and targeted approaches. In August 2018, the state government approved a budgetary outlay of approximately Rs 840 crores for a new programme called the Satat Jeevikoparjan Yojana (SJY) with the target of extending JEEViKA's economic inclusion effort to one lakh of its poorest constituents.

SJY participants choose a productive asset package depending on their local context and needs and then receive asset-specific skills training and weekly coaching at their homes. The asset packages include various types of livestock, sewing machines, farm equipment, inventories for small shops or other productive assets. Participants also receive a subsistence allowance called the 'livelihood gap assistance' of Rs 1,000 per month for seven months. A total of 1,25,000 families have been endorsed under the SJY and 93,000 families have received livelihood gap assistance for integrated asset creation.

Lessons Learnt

JEEViKA has evolved new approaches based upon learnings gained through its programme interventions. It realized that specialized human resources and a defined organization structure is key for any complex poverty alleviation programme. The human resources systems must evolve to enable efficient expansion. The programme emphasized well-designed human resources for the community institutions and the project management units at the block, district and state levels. The human resources system is characterized by strong accountability mechanisms and internal capacity building processes.

JEEViKA invested in putting in place efficient support procedures, building local technical support capacity and gradually devolving responsibility to block-level staff and communities. Young professionals from leading management institutions were recruited to provide daily analytical support and create a leadership talent pool. It involved political decision-makers and senior state government officers in its design process. The CEO of JEEViKA was assured a stable tenure because consistent leadership was critical to manage a large and complex programme.

Rigour and transparency in the organizational and fiduciary systems at all levels enables rapid expansion. Capacity needs to be built for financial management and procurement systems at all levels, including enhancing community engagement, capacity and trust to handle large funds, expand responsibilities and make efficient use of project investments.

Social mobilization and building community institutions are fundamental for community institutions to develop social networks of their own within the communities and beyond. This gives them social capital and leads to economically and socially disadvantaged women gaining access to a well-defined network across caste and religious boundaries within and outside the village. They can also take on new leadership roles and work with new knowledge systems. By initiating the formation of SHGs in hamlets with SC/ST inhabitants, JEEViKA could target very poor communities, including landless labour, small and marginal farmers, rural artisans and the self-employed in urban informal sectors.

It was also important to evolve institutional mechanisms for social inclusion, such as the transfer of responsibility to VOs through subcommittees, giving monetary incentives to CRPs for the inclusion of SC/ST households and adding social inclusion as one of the quality indicators for VOs. JEEViKA depends on VOs to implement SJY at the household level. They perform functions such as targeting and endorsing selected households, initial asset procurement and routing funds to households. The implementation of the programme is largely done by CRPs who handle functions such as targeting for SJY through intensive community-level drives.

To build the capacity of community-based organizations so that they can address societal issues, there needs to be a gradual delegation of authority for project implementation that increases policymakers' trust in community institutions. The state government has asked the VOs to endorse residential proof of those eligible for ration cards under the PDS—a task that was earlier done by a circle officer—resulting in an expedition of the process. The federations have generated important opportunities to meet their members' needs, including for links to markets, employment, nutrition and sanitation. This further stimulates member inclusion and a demand for services and increases interest in monitoring service delivery and the needs of marginal communities.

Building community capacity and ownership requires respecting and nurturing the collective voice and creating a culture of trust. Regular reviews help to refocus the programme strategy on its core elements and to strike a balance between poverty targeting and value-chain support. Strong financial discipline in community institutions is fundamental and a simplification of procedures is essential.

JEEViKA has worked on addressing key constraints of both supply and demand through building local capacities by developing strong community-led facilitation with locally identified community mobilizers and book-keepers to provide accounting services to community institutions. It also introduced simplified, uniform records for financial transactions so that the project could standardize performance measurement systems and instituted largescale annual audits of the federations to further strengthen and maintain financial management within the community institutions.

SHG members in banks acted as interfaces to facilitate transactions between the two institutions. These informal helpers who were not employees of the bank could help the community from within. Based on an analysis of the credit consumption patterns of SHG members, the programme introduced specialized financial products at the VO level. A food security fund was introduced to finance collective procurement of food grains and a health risk fund ensured members could borrow at low rates for health-related emergencies. JEEViKA agreed formal MoUs with financial organizations such as National Bank for Agriculture and Rural Development (NABARD) and Reserve Bank of India as well as state-level banking committees to facilitate timely bank support to SHGs. This helped to enhance the minimum amount of loans for SHGs from Rs 8,000 to Rs 1,50,000.

JEEViKA launched the Bihar Innovation Forum to help identify private and non-profit organizations with new ideas and potentially high social impact but which are unable to expand operations due to either a lack of resources or poor access to public institutions. The idea behind the forum is the understanding that innovation, entrepreneurship and partnerships are increasingly important for addressing challenges related to poverty, inclusion and sustainability. The forum brings together various stakeholders to form partnerships for customized support to inclusive innovations that enable the development of viable, scalable business models for maximum impact on livelihoods.

JEEViKA also partners with over 5,000 branches of commercial and rural banks and collaborates with other organizations to obtain technical support for domain-specific inputs in programme implementation. It adopts both financial and non-financial modes of association. JEEViKA facilitated community institutions to establish strong convergence with government departments to ensure that the benefits of government programmes reach SHGs. Some examples include the CLFs that are operating 137 custom-hiring centres in collaboration with the state government's agricultural department, making transactions of Rs 1.55 crore and netting a profit of Rs 61.2 lakh. Then there are the Kaushiki women milk producers, who have 570 milk collection centres and 28,445 members selling their produce. The average daily milk collection is 37,380 litres and total transactions amount to Rs 74.4 crore.

The agricultural department has also helped 4,145 SHG members engage in beekeeping, which has resulted in sales worth Rs 24.42 crore, with a net profit of Rs 7.23 crore. Collaboration with COMFED has led to the promotion of 854 dairy cooperative societies, while SHG members have set up canteens in forty-seven hospitals and ten residential schools for SCs and STs, generating a cumulative turnover of Rs 6.3 crore. Under the Jal Jeevan Hariyali Mission, with the Department of Forest, Environment and Climate Change, SHG members have established 519 nurseries and 133 public ponds have been allocated to CBOs to nurture fisheries.

Project expansion requires adaptive management, strong monitoring and evaluation and strategic communication. JEEViKA has a robust management information system and digital platforms are being used for effective programme implementation. The programme has promoted adaptive learning through innovation support at all levels, reinforced by strong monitoring and evaluation, with responsive process monitoring. Designed pilots were undertaken across thematic areas to reduce risks while the inherent replicability ensures that the project develops standardized protocols to enable efficient expansion.

A knowledge management and communication strategy helps JEEViKA to establish itself as a global community knowledge hub by using digital technology. It uses mass media and social media platforms extensively to reach out to a wider external domain for effective policy advocacy. Its strategy has always been to participate in strategic and relevant government events and present themselves as brand ambassadors of development and empowerment.

Today, it is common to see JEEViKA women grouped together in a rural neighbourhood, discussing and resolving their social and economic issues without external assistance. JEEViKA continues to work towards empowering and enabling rural households to have greater social and financial freedom and improved access to nutrition, sanitation and other important public services. The journey of the programme until now demonstrates that this mammoth outreach programme is poised to generate massive transformation in rural Bihar.

Acknowledgements

THIS BOOK IS THE RESULT of the advice, effort and support of a large number of people. It is not easy to convey our appreciation and gratitude to all of them adequately.

We owe our greatest debt of gratitude to the twenty-four contributing authors. They are the protagonists of this story of independent India. We are indebted to them for taking the time to write their stories and for the patience with which they responded to our requests for additions and modifications. We are grateful for the candour and honesty that they brought to their writing. We are privileged to have had them as our partners.

We sought the advice of 'elders' in the space of grassroots interventions even as we were developing the concept and framework for this book. We tested our thoughts against their greater experience and knowledge, and were inspired by their encouragement. We take full responsibility for the structure and shape of the product, but if credit is accorded, a large part must be shared with these elders. We would like to thank in particular, Vijay Mahajan, who, from the time this book was a seed in our mind, set aside time to provide guidance on the steps required to bring it to fruition. We are also deeply grateful to Ashoke Chatterjee, N.C. Saxena, Rajesh Dahiya, Rashmi Sharma, Sanjiv Mehta, Shankar Venkateswaran and Vineet Nayar for their support.

Center for Social and Economic Progress (CSEP) does not have a revenue model. All of its activities need to be funded from external sources. This book would not have been possible without the financial support provided by the HCL Foundation, Axis Bank Foundation and Bajaj Foundation. Aside from the money for which we are most grateful, we appreciate the respect that the donors have shown towards CSEP's core values of integrity, independence and impact. At no time did they look to influence the editors.

The book benefited greatly from the diligence of two interns that joined CSEP as summer interns and were assigned to this project. Rhea Sethi spent three months on the project and then moved into another role within CSEP. Nathan Glover extended his internship even as he returned to the London School of Economics to continue his master's degree. Both did the initial work of researching Civil Society Organizations (CSOs); summarizing their activities; helping in the task of CSO selection and keeping detailed records of all internal and external conversations. In this context, special mention must be made of Nathan, who—despite the pressure of classes, exams and differing time zones—stayed on the project till the very end. He was an integral and invaluable member of the team. His intellectual insights and comments won him our fulsome respect. We would also like to thank Anuradha Bhasin for her editorial support and for helping us prepare the submissions for publication.

CSEP provided us institutional support. The project gained traction because of the encouragement of the president, Rakesh Mohan and the administrative help of the chief operating officer, Shishir Gupta, and his team. We thank the institution, and are proud to be part of it.

Finally, we owe much to Swati Chopra, the executive editor of Harper Collins. She was unhesitatingly supportive. She provided sharp but constructive suggestions and spurred us to bring the project to completion ahead of the seventy-fifth year of India's independence. We were fortunate to have had her as our point of contact. We also want to thank Hina Khajuria of Harper Collins for her meticulous and sharp editing. She detected errors that had slipped past the three of us.

It goes without saying that the responsibility for the contents of this volume vests with the authors whose byline appears under their respective chapters.

About the Authors

MYRADA

Aloysius Prakash Fernandez was executive director of MYRADA from 1982 till 2009. He pioneered the concept of self-help affinity groups in the mid-80s. In 1995, he founded Sangamithra, a not-for-profit microfinance company. He also led efforts to empower sex workers and devadasis through group action and livelihood support. Later he worked with the Canadian International Development Agency and the World Bank. He was awarded the Padma Shri in 2000.

Seva Mandir

Neelima Khetan is a corporate social responsibility and social sector expert. She has nearly four decades of experience in this space, having worked with leading for-profit and non-profit organizations in the country. Her current affiliations include Visiting Fellow, Centre for Social and Economic Progress and partner, Nous Consultants. Neelima worked with Seva Mandir for twenty-five years, during which she worked as its chief executive from 1999 to 2011.

The Jamkhed Model

Aparna Thomas is a professor of politics and gender, sexuality, and women's studies, at Cornell College, Iowa. She leads courses in gender and development in Comprehensive Rural Health Project (CRHP), Jamkhed, and is a faculty fellow for the CRHP summer practicum, a course in sustainable development.

Shobha Arole, co-director and trustee of CRHP, Jamkhed. She has over forty years of experience as a medical doctor, surgeon and faculty member of CRHP's community-based international health and development centre. As an evaluator of international projects, she has a wide perspective on issues related to health and development.

Ravi Arole, director of CRHP, Jamkhed, is a medical doctor, with degrees in computer science as well as an MBA. After over twenty years working as a senior consultant with various corporations, Ravi returned to India to live and work among the rural poor. He has implemented sustainable development programs in South Asia and Africa.

Eklavya

Hriday Kant Dewan (fondly known as Hardy) has been working in teacher development and elementary education for the last thirty-five years and continues to devote his energies for systemic improvement in public education. Hardy currently leads the Translations Initiative, Azim Premji University, Bengaluru. He is a founder member of Eklavya Foundation and worked there for over twenty years.

Tultul Biswas works with the teacher education, outreach and advocacy programme of Eklavya Foundation and is engaged in designing learning opportunities, workshops and short-term courses for teachers and grassroots-level education activists to bring about change in classroom practices. With a master's degree in chemistry and sociology, Tultul has been with Eklavya for almost three decades.

Beyond Cerebral Palsy

Rajul Padmanabhan is on the governing bodies of Vidya Sagar (formerly the Spastics Society of India) in Chennai, and Worth Trust in Vellore, which work on disability issues. She was director of Vidya Sagar between 2006 to 2017. With over thirty-five years' experience in the disability sector, she has been instrumental in the development of indigenous technology, in augmentative and alternative communication in partnership with technical institutions.

Gram Vikas

Liby T. Johnson is a development management specialist with over twenty-five years of experience in design, implementation and support to large-scale, impactful poverty alleviation efforts. His multi-sectoral experience spans water, sanitation, livelihoods, disaster management and community institutions. Liby regularly contributes to policymaking at the national and state levels. Liby worked with Gram Vikas from 1998 to 2005 and returned as the executive director in 2017.

Dastkar

Laila Tyabji is a social worker, designer, writer and craft activist. In 2012, Tyabji was honoured with the Padma Shri for her contribution to India's crafts sector, augmenting artisans' skills and creating links between artisans and buyers. She is the co-founder and now the chairperson of Dastkar—a society for crafts and craftspeople, which has worked to use craft skills as a means of earning and empowerment.

Meals That Educated Generations

Chandra Mohan B, is a medical doctor and a member of the Indian Administrative Service (IAS). He writes on health, nutrition and urban development issues. In over twenty-five years as an IAS officer, he served as commissioner, Greater Chennai Corporation; managing director, Chennai Metro Water and principal secretary to government departments of Tourism, Culture and Religious endowments, Revenue, Transport, Energy, and Information Technology.

A. R. Meyyammai is an independent journalist with experience in print and digital media. She writes on social issues that affect the disadvantaged in society and is the recipient of many awards. She is also engaged in content creation and teaching.

PRADAN

Narendranath Damodaran is former executive director of PRADAN. Over thirty-two years, he has contributed to evolving ideas and programmes around rural livelihoods and women's empowerment. He has actively participated in research and documentation efforts to build knowledge from practice. Naren set up the National Resource Centre for Livelihoods in PRADAN which influences development policies and initiatives of Government of India.

Smita Mohanty is a senior HR professional who helped set up systems and processes for PRADAN's human resource function including the flagship development apprenticeship programme. She was an active member of the Steering Group of 'Making PRADAN a better place to work for Women' and is a life member of the Institute for Group Facilitation.

Wealth Creation through Community-owned Enterprise

Anish Kumar is co-lead at Transforming Rural India Foundation, which focuses on transforming life opportunities in the poorest villages of India. His areas of expertise include creating business organizations run by poor communities and facilitating participation of smallholder farmers in modern value chains. He lived and worked for several years in Kesla, where he contributed to developing the women-led smallholder poultry model including NSPDT, where he is currently the chairperson.

Development Support Centre

Sachin Oza was executive director of DSC from 2001 to 2016 and is currently the executive director of DSC Foundation, which focuses on capacity building, research, documentation and policy advocacy. He has over thirty-two years of experience as a development professional. He has co-authored six books and several papers on participatory management of natural resources and has been a member of policy forums at the state and national level.

Mohan Sharma, the executive director at DSC, Ahmedabad, has twenty-three years of experience in the field of participatory natural resource management. He has designed and implemented award-winning collaborative projects on participatory land, water and farming system development in western India that feed into training, research and policy changes. He has served as a director in the Indian Network of PIM, DSC Foundation and Gujpro Agri-Business Consortium.

ANANDI

Srilatha Batliwala is a feminist activist, researcher, scholar and trainer. She is senior advisor, Knowledge Building at Creating Resources for Empowerment in Action (CREA); senior associate, Gender at Work and honorary professor of Practice at School of Oriental and African Studies (SOAS), University of London. She has forty-five years of experience in grassroots movement building with marginalized women in India, research, grant-making, building knowledge from practice, and capacity building to advance feminist movement leadership.

Sejal Dand and Neeta Hardikar are feminist activists engaged with organizing rural women from marginalized communities over the past thirty years and are founder members of ANANDI holding executive leadership positions in the organization. They have been lead trainers and technical advisors for engendering development programmes for several civil society organizations, Government and UN Women in India. Together they have been active in state and national campaigns for Right to Food and Work, Jan Swasthya Abhiyan, Mahila Kisan Adhikar Manch, advocating for gender-just laws and policies.

SELCO

H. Harish Hande is recognized as a pioneer of rural energy service across the globe. He co-founded SELCO India and SELCO Foundation, which demonstrated that decentralized energy solutions can be truly sustainable when combined with appropriate technology, financing and ownership models suited to the contexts of the poor. For these pioneering efforts,

SELCO has received The Skoll Award for Social Entrepreneurship (2018) and Asia's prestigious Ramon Magsaysay Award (2011).

Surabhi Rajagopal has been with SELCO Foundation since 2011, focusing on aspects of ecosystem building for energy access including financing, skill development and policy, from a practitioner perspective. Her work includes bottom-up planning, programme design and policy engagement to integrate sustainable energy solutions for livelihoods and healthcare, including in humanitarian settings.

Basix Social Enterprise Group

Vijay Mahajan co-founded PRADAN, which has promoted livelihoods of over a million poor households since 1983, and the Basix Social Enterprise Group, which has supported livelihoods of fifty lakh poor households since 1996. He has served on Indian and international policy forums and on the boards of NGOs and social enterprises. He was selected among 60 Outstanding Social Entrepreneurs at the World Economic Forum, Davos. Since 2018, he is CEO of the Rajiv Gandhi Foundation.

Kudumbashree

S.M. Vijayanand is a former secretary, Ministry of Panchayati Raj, Government of India, and former chief secretary, Government of Kerala. Considered one of the architects of Kerala's decentralization, he headed its local self-government department through the years of decentralization and the People's Plan Campaign. He was a member of the task force that recommended the state-wide implementation of Kudumbashree as Kerala's Poverty Eradication Mission and has contributed significantly to the design of National Rural Livelihoods Mission (NRLM).

Sajith Sukumaran is chief operating officer, Kudumbashree, leading its work as a National Resource Organization under NRLM supporting State Rural Livelihood Missions in enabling convergence between self-help groups and panchayati raj institutions, and promoting enterprises among rural poor. He worked as project coordinator of Information Kerala Mission, which computerized the local governments in the context of decentralization and the People's Plan Campaign during 1997–2004.

Goonj

Anshu Gupta, popularly known as the Clothing Man, founded Goonj with the objective of highlighting neglected issues and people missing from the development agenda. He was a freelance journalist before initiating Goonj in 1999. He has received wide recognition for his work on human dignity and disruptive innovation with the world's surplus as a new currency. An Ashoka and Schwab Fellow for Social Entrepreneurship, he is a recipient of 2015 Magsaysay award.

Society for Elimination of Rural Poverty

K. Raju joined IAS in 1981 and served as Collector, Nellore and Kurnool districts of Andhra Pradesh, National Program Coordinator—UNDP's South Asia Poverty Alleviation Program, CEO of SERP and principal secretary, Rural Development Department, Government of Andhra Pradesh. Part of the National Advisory Council from 2010–13, he contributed to the formulation of a number of rights-based and pro-poor policies and legislations.

ITC e-Choupal

Sivakumar Surampudi is a member of the corporate management committee of ITC Limited, a multi-business conglomerate with interests in consumer goods, hotels, agri business paperboards, packaging, and information technology. Sivakumar oversees the company's agri and IT businesses, as also the company's social investments. Topper of the class of 1983 from the Institute of Rural Management, Anand (IRMA), Sivakumar served a farmers' cooperative for six years before joining ITC in 1989.

the ant

Sunil Kaul, medical doctor, left the Army Medical Corps in 1994 to work in rural India. He co-founded the ant in 2000. He has served on the board of Public Health Foundation of India and Jan Swasthya Sahyog. An Aga Khan Scholar and an Eisenhower Fellow, Sunil was State Representative (Education) for the National Commission for Protection of Child Rights and the state advisor to the Supreme Court Commissioners in the Right to Food campaign.

Jennifer Liang, a trained social worker, moved to Assam in 1996 and co-founded the ant with her husband, Sunil in 2000. A Chevening Gurukul Fellow, Jenny works with the Institute of Development Action, within the ant to lead the capacity building team and conducts research. She also works part-time with the Paul Hamlyn Foundation and serves on the board of OXFAM India.

The Brewing of Araku Coffee

Manoj Kumar began his career in development banking and microfinance before becoming the founding CEO of Naandi Foundation in 2000. Naandi's successful regenerative agriculture philosophy implemented in Araku and replicated elsewhere under the aegis of 'Arakunomics' was recently awarded the Food System Vision Prize by the Rockefeller Foundation. A Robert McNamara Fellow of the World Bank, Manoj is the moderator and Fellow of Aspen Institute, USA.

Seeding and Shaping the Labour Migration Agenda

Rajiv Khandelwal is co-founder and executive director of Aajeevika Bureau, which has pioneered innovative solutions and services catering to India's vast and vulnerable migrant, informal workforce through legal aid, skilling, social security and collective action. Over three decades, Rajiv has held leadership roles in development organizations, implementing programmes, conducting research and providing advice and guidance. Rajiv was named an Ashoka Fellow (2005) and India Social Entrepreneur of the Year (2010).

Divya Varma is a director of the Centre for Migration and Labour Solutions, anchoring knowledge and policy work within Aajeevika Bureau. Learning through establishing and managing Aajeevika's Migrant Resource Centres, Divya has over seventeen years of experience in policy analysis, advocacy and research, non-profit strategy, management and fund-raising. Divya is a Fulbright Scholar, holding a degree in public administration from the Harvard Kennedy School of Government.

Janaagraha

Srikanth Viswanathan is chief executive officer of Janaagraha Centre for Citizenship and Democracy, which works to transform the quality of life in India's cities. A leading practitioner of city governance reforms, particularly on the application of systems thinking to governing cities, he works closely with governments and constitutional bodies to implement long-term reforms. He worked in banking and audit for close to a decade before joining Janaagraha in 2011.

Mitanin in Chhatisgarh

Samir Garg works as executive director of the State Health Resource Centre in Chhattisgarh, India. He has a PhD in health systems management. He has experience of more than two decades as a practitioner, policy advocate and researcher. His area of interest is the management of public services including public health, nutrition and food security. His work focuses on strengthening community engagement and primary health care.

Jeevika

Arvind Kumar Chaudhary, an IAS officer, with over twenty-seven years of experience, is presently the principal secretary, Labour Resources Department and Environment Forest and Climate Change Department of the Government of Bihar. He was part of designing national and state level programmes including NRLM, and Jal Jeevan Hariyali Abhiyan. He was CEO of JEEViKA from April 2007 to June 2014. He was instrumental in organizing Bihar Innovation Forum and establishing Development Management Institute, Patna.

Mahua Roy Choudhury, is programme coordinator, governance and knowledge management, JEEViKA, and focuses upon enhancing organization capacity in strategic planning. With over twenty years of experience, she has worked with Government of Bihar, Council for Advancement of People's Action and Rural Technology, UNDP, PRADAN and Basix. She is a Chevening Clore Leadership Fellow and also a NUFFiC fellow.

Notes

1. T. S. Eliot, 'Burnt Norton' in Four Quartets (New York: Harcourt, Brace and Co., 1943).

1. Synthesis: Towards a Framework for Grassroots Interventions

1. Jawaharlal Nehru, 'Tryst with Destiny', transcript of speech delivered to the Constituent Assembly of India, New Delhi, 14 August 1947, in *Penguin Book of Twentieth Century Speeches*, ed. Brian McArthur (London: Penguin Viking, 1992), pp. 234–237.
2. Bhimrao Ramji Ambedkar, 'Concluding Remarks on the Draft Constitution', transcript of speech delivered to the Constituent Assembly of India, New Delhi, 25 November 1949, Lok Sabha Debates, http://164.100.47.194/Loksabha/Debates/Result_Nw_15.aspx?dbsl=503&ser=&smode=#M65*14.
3. Melissa Leach, 'Introduction: States, Markets and Society – Looking Back to Look Forward', IDS Bulletin, Vol. 47, No. 2A (2016), https://bulletin.ids.ac.uk/index.php/idsbo/article/view/2805/ONLINE%20ARTICLE
4. Please see Chapter 23, Srikanth Viswanathan, 'Janaagraha: Transforming the Quality of Life in India's Cities' in this volume.
5. Dipankar Gupta, *From 'People' to 'Citizen': Democracy's Must Take Road*, (London: Routledge, 2017).
6. Thomas Humphrey Marshall, *Citizenship and Social Class and Other Essays*, (Cambridge: Cambridge University Press, 1950).

7. Dipankar Gupta, 'We the Citizens of India: The Constitution lights the path from passions to fraternity, enmity to respect,' *The Times of India*, 28 March 2016, https://timesofindia.indiatimes.com/blogs/toi-edit-page/we-the-citizens-of-india-the-constitution-lights-the-path-from-passions-to-fraternity-enmity-to-respect/.

2. MYRADA and the Emergence of Self-Help Groups in India

1. https://myrada.org/
2. Letter sanctioning Rs 10 lakh by NABARD to MYRADA to support credit management groups, dated 24 October 1987. Ref No. NB.EAPD/1434/R&D/Proj.56/97-98.
3. Guidelines related to a bulk loan to the group and loans to unregistered groups were given in NABARD's circular of 26 February 1992 (No. NB DPD.FS/4631/92-A/91-92), signed by Y.C. Nanda.

3. Seva Mandir: Exploring the intersections of *Seva*, *Sadhna*, and *Kranti*

1. With inputs from Ajay Singh Mehta (trustee) and Ronak Shah (chief executive) of Seva Mandir.
2. Mohan Singh Mehta was born on 20 April 1895 in Bhilwara, Rajasthan. He did his graduation from Agra College, postgraduation from Allahabad University, and in 1928, received a PhD in history from the London School of Economics. From 1923 till 1947, he was an administrator in the princely states of Mewar and Banswara. He served as education minister and revenue minister in Mewar and as the dewan of Banswara on two separate occasions. He was also appointed to the Constituent Assembly, which framed India's Constitution. In 1949, he was appointed as India's first ambassador to the Netherlands. Subsequently, he served as the Indian high commissioner to Pakistan from 1951 to 1955, and as ambassador to Switzerland and the Vatican from 1955 to 1958. He was then vice chancellor of Rajasthan University from (1960 to 1966). From 1967 till his death in 1985, he worked for Seva Mandir as its life president. He was awarded the Padma Vibhushan in 1969.
3. Letter from Raj Desai, dated 13 November 2018, Seva Mandir archives.
4. www.sevamandir.org.
5. *Young India*, 1921, p. 170.

4. The Jamkhed Model: Sowing the Seeds of Community-based Primary Healthcare

1. www.crhpindia.org.

5. Eklavya's Journey of Adaptation and Evolution in Public School Education

1. www.eklavya.in

6. Beyond Cerebral Palsy: The Growth of Spastics Societies and Their Contribution to the Disability Movement

1. Mithu Alur, *A Birth that Changed a Nation* (New Delhi: Sage, 2017), p. 1.
2. Malini Chib, *One Little Finger* (New Delhi: Sage, 2011). The film *Margarita with a Straw* starring Kalki Koechlin was released in 2014.
3. Historically, the word 'spastic' referred to the condition of cerebral palsy. But the term, like many other descriptions of identity, took on a derogatory character and began to be used as a term of general abuse. Keeping in mind the sensitivities of those with cerebral palsy and those working in this area, the term went into disuse. One fallout of this was that many institutions changed their names, removing the word spastic or spastics from them. However, some disability activists want these names restored as they feel it both defines and strengthens their identity.
4. 'How 1950s parents were forced to fight for children with cerebral palsy's right to education', The Conversation, 22 February 2018, https/theconversation.com/how-1950s-parents-were-forced-to-fight-for-children-with-cerebral-palsys-right-to-education-73779.
5. United Cerebral Palsy, https://ucp.org/our-history/.
6. Personal interview with the author.
7. Reena Sen, Juliet Goldbart and Sudha Kaul, 'Growth of an NGO: The Indian Institute of Cerebral Palsy from 1974 to 2006' in *Journal of Policy and Practice in Intellectual Disabilities*, Vol. 5, Issue 2 (2008).
8. Pramila Balasundaram, 'The Journey Towards Inclusive Education In India', Paper presented at Seisa University, Ashibetsu Shi, Hokkaido, Japan, 2005.

7. Gram Vikas and the MANTRA for Inclusive Community Development

1. www.gramvikas.org
2. Esther Duflo, Michael Greenstone, Raymond Guiteras and Thomas Clasen, 'Toilets Can Work: Short and Medium Run Health Impacts of Addressing Complementarities and Externalities in Water and Sanitation', National Bureau of Economic Research, NBER working paper series, September 2015, DOI 10.3386/w21521, https://www.nber.org/papers/w21521.
3. Heather Reese, et. al., 'Assessing longer-term effectiveness of a combined household-level piped water and sanitation intervention on child diarrhoea, acute respiratory infection, soil-transmitted helminth infection and nutritional status: a matched cohort study in rural Odisha, India', in *International Journal of Epidemiology*, Volume 48, Issue 6 (December 2019), DOI 10.1093/ije/dyz157, https://pubmed.ncbi.nlm.nih.gov/31363748/.
4. 'Scaling up community ownership and management in piped water', November 2019, supplyhttp://www.indiaenvironmentportal.org.in/files/file/scaling-up-community-ownership-and-management-in-piped-water-supply.pdf
5. Rashmi Verma, 'A clean bonanza', *DownToEarth*, 15 February 2017, https://www.downtoearth.org.in/news/health/a-clean-bonanza-56963

8. Dastkar: A Crafted Route to Development

1. https://www.dastkar.org/.
2. Laila Tyabji, 'The Problem', in *India Seminar: Celebrating Craft*, March 2003, https://www.india-seminar.com/2003/523/523%20the%20problem.htm.
3. 'Crafts Bazaar', in *Craft Traditions of India Past, Present and Future* (New Delhi: NCERT, 2011), p. 89–100, https://ncert.nic.in/ncerts/l/lehc107.pdf.

9. Meals That Educated Generations: Lessons from Tamil Nadu

1. N. John Benhar, J. Lidiya Priscilla and I. Joe Sanjay, "The Unseeables" the Struggle of Puthirai Vannan Community', IOSR *Journal of Humanities and Social Science* (IOSR–JHSS), Volume 24, Issue 4, Ser. 6 (April. 2019) p. 1–9, www.iosrjournals.org.

2. D. S. Rajabhushanam, Annual Statistical Abstract for the Madras State for 1954–55 and 1955–56, Madras, Controller of Stationery and Printing (1982).
3. Policy Note 2021–22, Social Welfare and Women Empowerment Department.
4. The UNICEF/WHO/WB Joint Child Malnutrition Estimates (JME) group released new data for 2021 (6 May 2021); https://www.who.int/news/item/06-05-2021-the-unicef-who-wb-joint-child-malnutrition-estimates-group-released-new-data-for-2021

10. PRADAN and the Idea of a Development Professional

1. Excerpt from the review report at the end of Tata Trust's third Human Resource grant to PRADAN.
2. https://www.pradan.net/.
3. Currently Godda district is in Jharkhand; however, at the time the pilot project started, it was in Bihar. Santhal Pargana is spread across Bihar and Jharkhand states.

11. Wealth Creation through Community-owned Enterprise: NSPDT's Model of Cooperative Smallholder Poultry

1. www.nspdt.org.
2. An index that captures all the key productivity indicators into a comparable score which when linked to producer payments. It discriminates between good and poor efficiency and thereby incentivizes better productivity, ensuring high overall production efficiency.
3. Rob Walker, 'The Guts of a New Machine', *The New York Times Magazine*, 30 November 2003, https://www.nytimes.com/2003/11/30/magazine/the-guts-of-a-new-machine.html.

12. Development Support Centre: Mainstreaming the Idea of Water Users' Associations

1. www.dscindia.org.

13. ANANDI: The Long Road to Gender Just Development

1. Short films on these sangathans can be seen at https://www.youtube.com/c/ANANDIIndia/playlists.
2. https://www.justassociates.org/en/feminist-popular-education
3. Sejal Dand and Georgina Aboud, 'Right to Food in Gujarat: Local Organising Contributing to National Change', *Bridge*, 2015, http://www.wocan.org/sites/default/files/Gender%20and%20FS%20In%20Brief.pdf. This is a case study of ANANDI and Devgadh Mahila Sanghatan.
4. We use these terms in their original sense as articulated by Maxine Molyneux in her benchmark paper, 'Mobilization without Emancipation – Women's Interests, the State and Revolution in Nicaragua', *Feminist Studies*, Vol. 11, No. 2 (Summer, 1985), pp. 227–254, viz., *practical needs* are the day-to-day material needs for survival (income/employment, food, water, healthcare, education, training, credit, etc.), and *strategic interests* in terms of challenging their location within societal power structures, their subordination, seeking their rights and equality.

14. SELCO: Building Inclusive, Sustainable and Climate-Resilient Solutions

1. The World Bank Data, 'Access to electricity, rural (% of rural population) – India', https://data.worldbank.org/indicator/EG.ELC.ACCS.RU.ZS?locations=IN
2. www.selcofoundation.org
3. Sub-centres, health and wellness centres and primary health centres represent the primary level of public healthcare and the first point of contact for last-mile communities.

15. Basix Social Enterprise Group: Innovations in Microfinance to Promote Livelihoods for the Poor

1. www.basixindia.com

16. Kudumbashree: Where Women Climb the Ladder of Empowerment

1. https://www.kudumbashree.org/
2. The Kudumbashree Story, http://thekudumbashreestory.info/landing/index.html

17. Goonj: Reviving the Barter Economy and Changing the Lens with Dignity at the Centre

1. https://goonj.org/.

18. Society for Elimination of Rural Poverty: A Paradigm Shift in How Government Tackles Poverty

1. https://www.serp.ap.gov.in/SHGAP/.
2. https://www.serp.telangana.gov.in/SHGTG/.
3. Mandal is the second-tier local body institution covering about twenty gram panchayats, equivalent to a block in other states, but smaller in size.

19. ITC e-Choupal: A Lighthouse for Truly Inclusive Value Chains

1. https://www.itcportal.com/businesses/agri-business/e-choupal.aspx.

20. the ant: Stepping Away from the Trees to Notice the Forest

1. www.theant.org.

21. The Brewing of Araku Coffee: Regenerating the Economy and Ecology

1. As told to the author by a tribal farmer from Araku
2. www.naandi.org.
3. www.arakucoffee.in.

22. Seeding and Shaping the Labour Migration Agenda: Aajeevika Bureau's Journey

1. https://www.aajeevika.org/.

2. 'Road Map for Development of Policy Framework for the Inclusion of Internal Migrant Workers in India', (Switzerland: International Labour Organization, December 2020), https://www.ilo.org/newdelhi/whatwedo/publications/WCMS_763352/lang--en/index.htm
3. 'Unlocking the Urban: Reimagining Migrant Lives in Cities, Post-Covid-19' (Rajasthan: Aajeevika Bureau, April 2020), https://www.aajeevika.org/assets/pdfs/Unlocking%20the%20Urban.pdf.

23. Janaagraha: Transforming the Quality of Life in India's Cities

1. www.janaagraha.org.
2. Annual Survey of India's City-Systems (ASICS) 2017: Janaagraha Centre for Citizenship and Democracy (https://janaagraha.org/asics/report/ASICS-report-2017-fin.pdf)

24. Mitanin in Chattisgarh: Community Health Work as a Social Movement

1. www.shsrc.org.
2. Sulakshana Nandi and Helen Schneider, 'Addressing the social determinants of health: A case study from the Mitanin (community health worker) Programme in India' in *Health Policy and Planning*, Vol. 29 (2014), pp. 71–81, https://www.ncbi.nlm.nih.gov/pmc/articles/PMC4202921/.
3. Devaki Nambiar and Kabir Sheikh, 'How a technical agency helped scale up a community health worker program: An exploratory study in Chhattisgarh State, India' in *Health Systems & Reform*, Vol. 2 (2016), pp. 123–134. Available at https://www.tandfonline.com/doi/full/10.1080/23288604.2016.1148802

25. JEEViKA: Fostering Pathways for the Transformation of Rural Bihar

1. http://brlps.in/.
2. Central Statistical Organization, 2004
3. CARE India conducts a rigorous RMNCH+N focused Household Survey every year since 2016 to evaluate block-level program performance, state and

district level point estimates and change in estimates for all RMNCH+A indicators. The data collection process primarily starts in the month of September every year. The primary data collection takes place in all 534 blocks across all thirty-eight districts of Bihar. And approximately, 78,435 respondents are covered every year. The respondents covered in data collection are mothers of children aged (0–2 months), (3–5 months), (6–8 months), (9–11 months) and (12–23 months). Each age group has 15,687 participants every year, and has group specific questionnaire. Multi-stage sampling methodology has been used where Anganwadi centres are selected proportionate to the population size. At the first level, Anganwaadi centre is selected from each block, and from each select AWC, they select one participant for each age group. Data quality assurance is done through Logic Check, Spot Check and Back Check and audio verification (physical file and metadata) by the supervisors as well. The data is digitally captured using CAPI.

About the Editors

Vikram Singh Mehta is chairman and Distinguished Fellow of the Center for Social and Economic Progress (CSEP). He is an independent director of several companies including Larsen and Toubro Ltd and Mahindra and Mahindra Ltd. He received Asia House's 'Businessman of the Year' award for 2010 and 'Best Independent Director in India' award for 2016 from Asia Centre for Corporate Governance and Sustainability. He is the editor of *The Next Stop: Natural Gas and India's Journey to a Clean Energy Future* (2021).

Neelima Khetan is a Visiting Fellow with CSEP. She also does consulting work on development issues, especially strategy, governance, design and impact. She has worked extensively with civil society organizations and corporate social responsibility groups, and currently serves on the boards of several foundations and non-profits. Other than family and friends, books and plants bring her abiding joy.

Jayapadma R V has keen interest and engagement in sustainable social development. For close to three decades, she has journeyed through, learnt from and contributed to the work of community-based organizations, bilateral aid and corporate social responsibility organizations, as well as academic institutions. A connector and catalyst is how she imagines her work to be. Travel, writing and music are some things she holds space for. Jaya is an alumnus of the Institute of Rural Management Anand (IRMA) and a Chevening Scholar.